Contents

Unit 1 Religion and life

Unit 8 Religion and society

endorsed by
edexcel

GCSE
Religious
Studies
for Edexcel

for
UNITS
1 & 8

Religion and Life (Unit 1) and
Religion and Society (Unit 8)

Christianity and Islam

Diane Kolka

HODDER
EDUCATION
AN HACHETTE UK COMPANY

With many thanks to my family, friends and students who have knowingly or unknowingly helped me with this book.

Much love to Richard, Hannah, Laura, Ben and Rachel.

This material has been endorsed by Edexcel and offers high quality support for the delivery of Edexcel qualifications. Edexcel endorsement does not mean that this material is essential to achieve any Edexcel qualification, nor does it mean that this is the only suitable material available to support any Edexcel qualification. No endorsed material will be used verbatim in setting any Edexcel examination and any resource lists produced by Edexcel shall include this and other appropriate texts. While this material has been through an Edexcel quality assurance process, all responsibility for the content remains with the publisher. Copies of official specifications for all Edexcel qualifications may be found on the Edexcel website www.edexcel.com.

The Author and Publishers would like to thank the Chair of the Education Committee of the Muslim Council of Britain, Sheikh Dr Hojjat Ramzy for advising them on the content of this book.

For acknowledgements and photo credits, please see page 236.

Every effort has been made to trace all copyright holders, but if any have been inadvertently overlooked the Publishers will be pleased to make the necessary arrangements at the first opportunity.

Although every effort has been made to ensure that website addresses are correct at time of going to press, Hodder Education cannot be held responsible for the content of any website mentioned in this book. It is sometimes possible to find a relocated web page by typing in the address of the home page for a website in the URL window of your browser.

Hachette UK's policy is to use papers that are natural, renewable and recyclable products and made from wood grown in sustainable forests. The logging and manufacturing processes are expected to conform to the environmental regulations of the country of origin.

Orders: please contact Bookpoint Ltd, 130 Milton Park, Abingdon, Oxon OX14 4SB. Telephone: (44) 01235 827720. Fax: (44) 01235 400454. Lines are open 9.00–5.00, Monday to Saturday, with a 24-hour message answering service. Visit our website at www.hoddereducation.co.uk

© Diane Kolka 2012
First published in 2012 by
Hodder Education,
An Hachette UK Company
338 Euston Road
London NW1 3BH

Impression number   5   4
Year   2016 2015 2014

Cover photo: © NLshop–Fotolia
Typeset in 11.5/14pt Rockwell Light and produced by Gray Publishing, Tunbridge Wells, Kent
Printed in Dubai

A catalogue record for this title is available from the British Library

ISBN: 978 1444 16445 9

Religion and life

Section 1: Believing in God

1.1 Religious upbringing

● The main features of a Christian upbringing

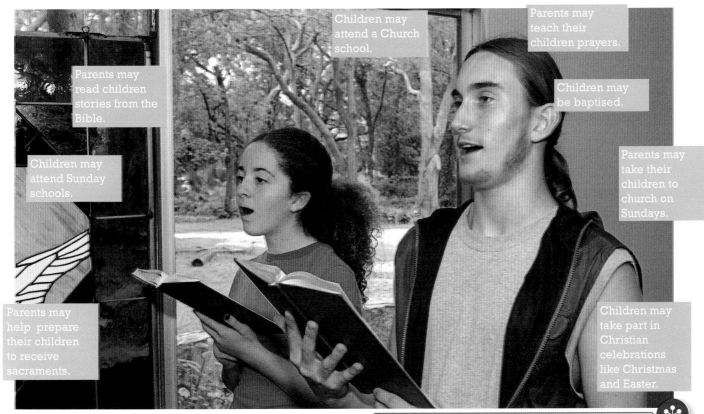

Children may attend a Church school.

Parents may teach their children prayers.

Parents may read children stories from the Bible.

Children may be baptised.

Children may attend Sunday schools.

Parents may take their children to church on Sundays.

Parents may help prepare their children to receive sacraments.

Children may take part in Christian celebrations like Christmas and Easter.

A Christian upbringing is the way a child is raised or treated by their parents so that they grow up believing in Christianity. Christian parents teach their children their faith and set a Christian example. Some Christians:

- want to give their children what they believe is the right faith
- want their children to believe and hold important the same things they do
- promise to raise any children they have as Christians when they get married.

Knowledge check ❋

1 What is a Christian upbringing?
2 List three things a parent may do to encourage their child to believe in the Christian faith.
3 Which celebrations teach a child about Christianity?
4 What type of schools might Christian parents send their children to?
5 Make a list of at least three reasons why you think Christian parents bring their children up as Christians.

● How a Christian upbringing leads to belief

I believe because my parents told me about my faith and I trust them to tell the truth.

I believe because prayer makes me feel closer to God.

I believe because the sacraments I have received make me feel God loves me.

I believe because I meet all my friends in church and we all believe the same.

I believe because Sunday school explained that what I see around me comes from God.

I believe because what I have been taught in school gave me evidence that God exists.

A01

Imagine you are a priest or vicar of a local parish church. Write a leaflet for parents. The leaflet should explain how parents should bring up their children so that they become Christians.
   Include in your leaflet:

✓ why parents should raise their children as Christians
✓ the main things parents are expected to do
✓ why these activities will help their children become Christians.

A02

Prepare for a class debate on: 'Christian parents should always give their child a Christian upbringing'.

1 Write the debate title as a heading and then draw a table listing reasons to support the statement and reasons to argue against the statement.
2 Hold the debate. Ensure there is a chairperson and at least two people to speak on the issue. Ask questions of the speakers before taking a class vote.

These are photographs I have from my childhood. Until I looked at them recently, I did not realise how many of them are linked to my Christian upbringing.

Do you think my upbringing affected whether I believe in God or not?

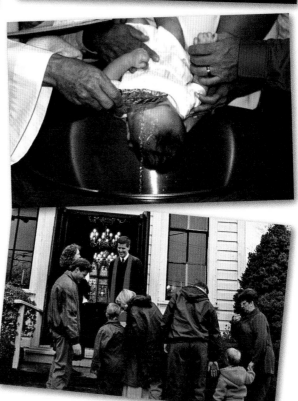

exam practice b

Do you think religious parents should raise their children to believe in God? Give **two** reasons for your point of view.

Examiner's hint: Make sure you start your answer with 'I think ...'. (AO2)

exam practice c

Explain why a religious upbringing may lead to belief in God.

Examiner's hint: Write four reasons. Start each of the reasons on a new line. (AO1)

exam practice d

'All children should have a religious upbringing.'
In your answer you should refer to at least one religion.
i) Do you agree? Give reasons for your answer.
ii) Give reasons why some people may disagree with you.

Examiner's hint: Make sure all reasons in i) are for your opinion and all the reasons in ii) are opposite to your opinion. Do not muddle up the opinions. (AO2)

1.2 Religious experience

● How religious experience may lead to belief in God

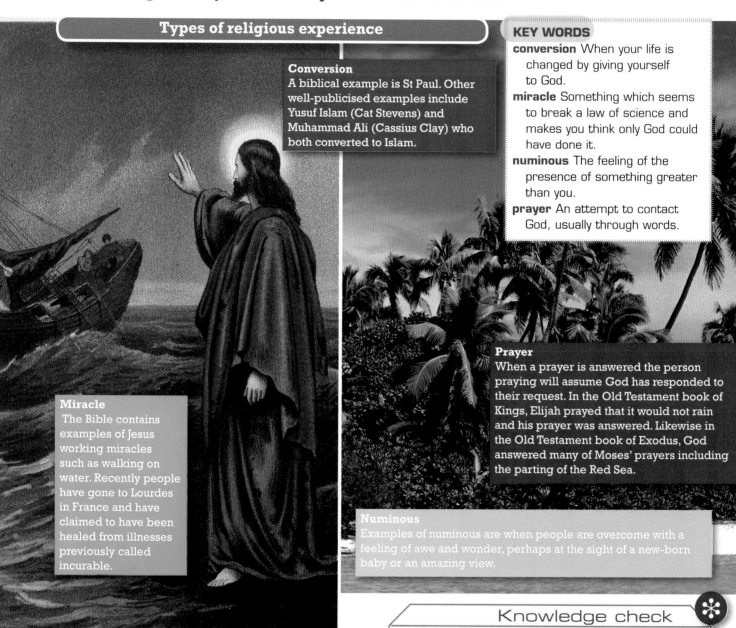

Types of religious experience

Conversion
A biblical example is St Paul. Other well-publicised examples include Yusuf Islam (Cat Stevens) and Muhammad Ali (Cassius Clay) who both converted to Islam.

Miracle
The Bible contains examples of Jesus working miracles such as walking on water. Recently people have gone to Lourdes in France and have claimed to have been healed from illnesses previously called incurable.

Prayer
When a prayer is answered the person praying will assume God has responded to their request. In the Old Testament book of Kings, Elijah prayed that it would not rain and his prayer was answered. Likewise in the Old Testament book of Exodus, God answered many of Moses' prayers including the parting of the Red Sea.

Numinous
Examples of numinous are when people are overcome with a feeling of awe and wonder, perhaps at the sight of a new-born baby or an amazing view.

KEY WORDS

conversion When your life is changed by giving yourself to God.

miracle Something which seems to break a law of science and makes you think only God could have done it.

numinous The feeling of the presence of something greater than you.

prayer An attempt to contact God, usually through words.

Knowledge check ✳

1 What is a religious experience?
2 List four types of religious experience.
3 Name two experiences a person might describe as numinous.
4 Name two people who have had a conversion experience.
5 Give two examples of miracles.
6 Give two examples of answered prayers.

A religious experience is something that makes a person think that in some way they have come into contact with God. Miracle, numinous, conversion and prayer are four such experiences. When they happen to a person they usually lead to a new or increased belief in God.

● How religious experience may lead to belief in God

French nun healed after praying to Pope

Sister Marie Simon-Pierre suffered from Parkinson's disease, a condition which affects the nervous system. Sister Marie says she prayed to Pope John Paul II and the disease that she had suffered from for four years has now completely disappeared.

Sister Marie Simon-Pierre explained that two months after the Pope died, in June 2005, she had woken to find she was cured from the disease.

In a news conference she said: 'When I woke up, I felt I was not the same … There was no more heaviness in my muscles, I could move normally. For me it was a new birth, a second birth.'

Pope Benedict XVI, who succeeded Pope John Paul II, confirmed the miracle and it was part of the case for the beatification of Pope John Paul II which took place on 1 May 2011.

Why might this example of a miracle lead to belief for the person it happened to? Do you think it might affect the faith of people who read about it in the newspaper? Why?

Why religious experience might lead to belief in God	Why religious experience might not lead to belief in God
It proves that God exists	People might be lying about it
It changes people's lives	People might be ill or under the influence of drugs and hallucinating
There must be a reason why such events occur – people believe this must be God	People might be capable of these things and we are not yet aware of it
It makes people aware of the presence of God, and that he is real	Science can explain, or will be able to explain, why some things happen

A01

1 In small groups discuss the different kinds of religious experiences.
2 Some surveys show that more than half of people have had a religious experience. Discuss religious experiences the group have heard about or look up the conversion of St Paul in Acts, Chapter 9, and discuss it and the experience of Sister Marie in the article above.
3 Draw a poster to describe religious experiences. Include the different types and examples of the different experiences.

A02

Prepare to answer questions about religious experience in a hot-seat situation as if you have had a religious experience.

1 Decide which experience you will answer questions on and think about the effect it would have on a person.
2 Copy the table above listing reasons why the experience might or might not support belief in God. Try to add at least two more reasons to each column.
3 Take part in the hot-seat discussion either as the person in the hot seat being questioned or as the questioner.
4 At the end of the activity try to add more reasons to your table.

exam practice b

Do you think religious experiences lead to a belief in God? Give **two** reasons for your point of view.

Examiner's hint: Make sure you give two reasons in your answer. (AO2)

exam practice c

Explain why an answered prayer may lead to a belief in God.

Examiner's hint: If you cannot think of four reasons why then write two reasons and develop each one with an example. (AO1)

exam practice d

'Religious experiences do not prove the existence of God.'
In your answer you should refer to at least one religion.
i) Do you agree? Give reasons for your answer.
ii) Give reasons why some people may disagree with you.

Examiner's hint: Make sure you include reference to a religion in your answer. (AO2)

1.3 The argument from design

● How the design argument may lead to a belief in God

The argument from design is an argument to prove that God exists based on the evidence from the world around us. It is also called the teleological argument; teleological comes from the word *telos* in Greek, which means 'purpose'. The argument relies on the idea that things that are complex and seem to have a purpose should have a designer who designed them to be this way.

The universe and the things in it are complex and seem to have a purpose, so the argument from design says they must have been designed. This leads to the conclusion that God must be the designer of the universe, because only God is powerful and intelligent enough to have designed the world. And if God is the designer of the world, God must exist.

Could a car's engine have appeared without someone designing it? Why?

Do you think a flower could appear without it being designed? Why?

Knowledge check

1 What is the design argument?
2 What is another name for the design argument?
3 What kind of things need to have a designer?
4 Why does the universe need to have a designer?
5 Why does the design argument say that God must be the designer of the universe?
6 a) Give an example of a manufactured item, such as a computer, and give two reasons why it must have been designed.
   b) Do these two reasons apply to a natural item such as a flower? Why?

If you found a watch when walking through a field you might wonder how it came to exist. You would assume that at some time someone must have had a reason or purpose to design it and all its complex parts. The universe appears to have been designed as everything seems to have a purpose and is extremely complex; these need an intelligent creator, God.

Adapted from *Natural Theology* by William Paley (1802)

A01

1 In pairs, draw a flowchart to show the main parts of the design argument. Try to add pictures to illustrate the ideas.
2 Join up with another pair and use your chart to explain the argument to them.

● Arguments used against the argument from design

The world is not very well designed; it contains natural things which do not benefit humans in any way. Even if you accept it is designed, it does not have to be designed by God or it could be designed by many Gods.

The world might not be designed, it might be human beings who think it is designed but it actually could happen by chance. A person could also ask: if there is a God, who designed God?

A02

Draw and complete a table to list reasons why people might believe the argument from design proves the existence of God and reasons why they might disagree with this opinion. Use the information above to help you.

exam practice b

Do you think the world is designed? Give **two** reasons for your point of view.

Examiner's hint: The easiest way to develop a reason is to give an example. (A02)

exam practice c

Explain why the argument from design may lead to belief in God.

Examiner's hint: Start each of the reasons on a new line. (A01)

exam practice d

'The design argument proves the existence of God.'
In your answer you should refer to at least one religion.
i) Do you agree? Give reasons for your answer.
ii) Give reasons why some people may disagree with you.

Examiner's hint: Make sure you start your answer to i) with 'I think …'. (A02)

1.4 The argument from causation

The argument from causation is an argument to prove God exists, much like the design argument. It is based on the evidence from the world around us. It is also called the cosmological argument, from the word *cosmos* or universe.

The causation argument looks at the world and says that everything that is in the world was caused by something else. Nothing can come into existence on its own so it must be caused by something else.

Living organisms such as people, animals and plants were caused by their parents reproducing. Items which are not alive, like chairs and clothes, are caused by a mixture of designers and manufacturers.

Everything has a cause, for example hunger is caused by not eating, and happiness can be caused by having a laugh with friends. Therefore, the universe itself must have a cause.

> The causation argument says that everything in the universe has a cause.

> The universe itself must have a cause.

> The first cause of the universe must be all-powerful (omnipotent) and eternal.

> The first cause of the universe must be God.

> Therefore God must exist.

● How the causation argument may lead to a belief in God

In the world we find there is an order of causes. There is no case known (neither is it, indeed possible) in which a thing is found to be the cause of itself. It is not possible for causes to go back forever (to infinity). Therefore it is necessary to admit a first cause, to which everyone gives the name of God.

Adapted from
Summa Theologica by
Thomas Aquinas (1265–74)

The argument from causation was set out by the philosopher Thomas Aquinas. He argued that everything needs a cause and nothing can cause itself. This means that there must be a cause right at the beginning of everything, which he calls the 'first cause'. Aquinas says the first cause is God.

A01

In pairs, produce a PowerPoint presentation to show the main parts of the causation argument. Add diagrams or pictures to illustrate the ideas. Present your explanation of the causation argument to the rest of the class.

A car does not come into existence on its own, something must cause it to be built. In the same way, the universe and everything in it was brought into existence by a first cause, this first cause must be God.

● Arguments used against the argument from causation

It is possible that some things might not need to be caused.

Mathematical ideas of infinity mean that there does not need to be a beginning.

Arguments against the argument from causation

Our understanding is limited, human beings should not assume anything without evidence.

The first cause does not have to be a God.

If everything needs a cause then surely God would need a cause.

A02

1 Draw and complete a table to list reasons why people might believe the argument from causation proves the existence of God and reasons why they might disagree with this opinion.
2 Use this information to participate in a 'decision alley'. This is when the class divides in two, one side thinks of reasons why the argument leads to belief and the other thinks of reasons why it does not. Each side then lines up shoulder to shoulder with an alley between. A member of the class then walks down the alley asking for advice from members on either side. When they get to the end they make a decision. At the end, the class can see what the majority view is.

exam practice b

Do you think the causation argument proves that God exists? Give **two** reasons for your point of view.

Examiner's hint: Each reason must be developed. (A02)

exam practice c

Explain the argument from causation.

Examiner's hint: Read the question carefully. Does the question need reasons or, as in this case, does it need description? (A01)

exam practice d

'The causation argument does not prove the existence of God.'
In your answer you should refer to at least one religion.
i) Do you agree? Give reasons for your answer.
ii) Give reasons why some people may disagree with you.

Examiner's hint: The easiest way to answer each part should be to write three brief reasons. (A02)

1.5 Scientific explanations of the world

There are many suggestions as to how the universe began (cosmology) based on scientific theories. Some of them have more evidence than others and are more acceptable than others. The one that is thought most likely is the Big Bang theory; however, some scientists support either the Oscillating Universe theory or the Steady State theory.

The Big Bang theory

This is the most accepted model of cosmology. The Big Bang theory has many forms; however, most scientists think that, almost 14 billion years ago, the universe came into existence in a rapid expansion called the Big Bang. From the Big Bang came everything that exists: atoms, planets, stars, galaxies and space.

There is evidence to prove that the Big Bang occurred; background radiation shows that the universe was once much hotter than it is today. Red light or red shift (expanding light waves make red light) shows that the universe is still expanding today.

Oscillating Universe theory

Some scientists believe that there is an oscillating universe: the universe expands rapidly (Big Bang) and then collapses (Big Crunch).

This cycle is sometimes called the Big Bounce and the argument is favoured by some scientists as it means that the universe does not have a beginning (or an end) and that the state of the universe just changes in form.

Some scientists do not like this as they say that it is more likely the universe will continue expanding until the Big Freeze and then the universe will end.

The Steady State theory

The Steady State theory was developed in 1948. It is based on the idea that the expansion of the universe is matched by the production of matter, meaning that the universe is steadily developing and remaining equally dense.

The idea has been generally dismissed since the evidence of background radiation has supported the Big Bang theory.

Knowledge check

1 What does cosmology mean?
2 List three theories for the cosmology of the universe.
3 Which theory has most evidence to support it?
4 Describe the Big Bang theory.
5 What two pieces of evidence support the Big Bang?
6 Describe the Oscillating Universe theory.
7 Why do some scientists think the Oscillating Universe theory is incorrect?
8 Describe the Steady State theory.
9 Why is the Steady State theory not accepted by most scientists today?

Which picture do you think of when a person describes the Big Bang theory to you?

The image of a balloon expanding slowly is regarded as a more scientifically accurate image of the Big Bang. Why is this the case?

A01

1 In small groups discuss the different scientific theories.
2 There are some excellent programmes about the Big Bang. Ask your science department at school and watch one.
3 Draw a Venn diagram with three circles and write into each circle a description of the theory (remember much of the Big Bang and Oscillating theories overlap) and add any evidence that you have found out for each theory.

A02

Draw a spider diagram to record information as to why some people would support the scientific theories and another one giving reasons why they would not support the scientific theories.

exam practice b

Do you think that the Big Bang theory explains how the universe was created? Give **two** reasons for your point of view.

Examiner's hint: The reasons you give in b) questions do not have to be religious. (A02)

exam practice c

Explain why the scientific explanation of the origin of the world may lead some people not to believe in God.

Examiner's hint: Many questions are based on the wording of the specification. Make sure you know what words the exam board uses. (A01)

exam practice d

'Scientific explanations for the creation of the universe have proved that God does not exist.'
In your answer you should refer to at least one religion.
i) Do you agree? Give reasons for your answer.
ii) Give reasons why some people may disagree with you.

Examiner's hint: Repeating the question at the beginning of your answer might help you remember what you agree or disagree with. (A02)

1.6 Christian responses to scientific explanations of the origin of the world

There are many different Christian responses to the scientific explanations of the origin of the world. The different opinions are based on the different views that Christians have towards the cosmology described in the Bible (biblical cosmology).

The biblical explanation of the origin of the world is found in the Old Testament book of Genesis. It says that God created the world out of nothing (*ex nihilo*) in six days and on the seventh day rested. It also says that everything he made he said was good and that humans were created last.

God creating the earth as illustrated in this ancient icon above from Greece. Can you see the representation of each day's creation?

> Then God said, 'Let us make mankind in our image, in our likeness, so that they may rule over the fish in the sea and the birds in the sky, over the livestock and all the wild animals, and over all the creatures that move along the ground.' So God created mankind in his own image, in the image of God he created them; male and female he created them.
>
> God blessed them and said to them, 'Be fruitful and increase in number; fill the earth and subdue it. Rule over the fish in the sea and the birds in the sky and over every living creature that moves on the ground.'
>
> Then God said, 'I give you every seed-bearing plant on the face of the whole earth and every tree that has fruit with seed in it. They will be yours for food. And to all the beasts of the earth and all the birds in the sky and all the creatures that move along the ground – everything that has the breath of life in it – I give every green plant for food.' And it was so.
>
> God saw all that he had made, and it was very good. And there was evening, and there was morning – the sixth day.
>
> Thus the heavens and the earth were completed in all their vast array.
>
> By the seventh day God had finished the work he had been doing; so on the seventh day he rested from all his work. Then God blessed the seventh day and made it holy, because on it he rested from all the work of creating that he had done.
>
> Genesis 1: 26–31, 2:1–3

exam practice c

Explain why some religious people agree with the scientific explanations of the origin of the world.

Examiner's hint: Underline key words in the question. This helps you understand what the question is asking. (AO1)

AO1

Write a newspaper article to explain the Christian responses to the scientific explanations of the origins of the world. The article should include a brief description of the responses.
   Your article must include:

✓ a brief description of biblical cosmology
✓ a brief description of scientific cosmology
✓ Christian responses to the scientific explanations of the cosmology
✓ at least one illustration or picture.

exam practice b

Do you think there should only be one religious response to the scientific explanations of the world? Give **two** reasons for your point of view.

Examiner's hint: Development must add more information to the answer to the question set; it must not be vague. (AO2)

God started the Big Bang.

Scientific theories, such as the Big Bang, Steady State and Oscillating Universe, are only ideas; they have not been proven.

Many scientists still believe God is responsible for the design of the world.

The seven days of the week in Genesis could be seven ages of time.

Christian responses to the scientific explanations of the origin of the world

Only God could have made sure that the world was made as beautiful as it is.

The biblical story is symbolic – it shows God was the creator and is not meant to be believed literally.

Some Christians accept the scientific theories and say they do not conflict with belief in God.

Some Christians say that the scientific explanations are wrong and the biblical one is correct.

Knowledge check

1 What is the biblical cosmology?
2 How does the biblical cosmology describe the creation of the world?
3 List the Christian responses which accept the scientific explanations.
4 List the Christian responses which reject the scientific explanations.

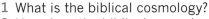

A02

Prepare to answer the d)-type question: 'All Christians should accept the scientific explanations for the origin of the world'.

1 In pairs, one person takes on the role of a Christian who believes only in the biblical explanations and the other person takes on the role of a Christian who believes only in the scientific explanations.
2 Each person has two minutes to convince the other person that they must accept their point of view. The other person cannot interrupt or ask questions.
3 After two minutes, each person can ask the other person two questions which the other person must answer.
4 At the end decide which argument was more convincing and why.

Write an answer for the d)-type question. In your answer you should refer to at least one religion.

i) Do you agree? Give reasons for your answer.
ii) Give reasons why some people may disagree with you.

exam practice d

'Religious responses to scientific cosmology prove God exists.'
In your answer you should refer to at least one religion.
i) Do you agree? Give reasons for your answer.
ii) Give reasons why some people may disagree with you.

Examiner's hint: Start each reason on a new line or with a new paragraph. (A02)

1.7 Unanswered prayers

● Why unanswered prayers may lead some people not to believe in God

A prayer is an attempt to contact God, usually through words. Prayers can be said publicly in worship or privately. They are an important feature of all religions. When a person prays they feel that they in some way contact God and build a relationship with God.

People pray for many reasons but some reasons given include: worshipping God, to give thanks, to become closer to God, to be comforted, and frequently prayer is used to ask for something from God.

The Bible says: *If you believe, you will receive whatever you ask for in prayer (Matthew 21:22)*.

This leads Christians to think that they will be given what they pray for.

In unanswered prayer, people pray but feel that they have not been in contact with God because they do not feel closer to God or comforted and they do not receive the things that they have asked for.

Believers can find unanswered prayer difficult to cope with, as most religions instruct their followers to pray, and teach that a good prayer life is an essential part of belief. If a person feels that their prayers are unanswered they may begin to think that there is no one listening to their prayers and then they may start to lose faith in God.

Believers who think that God is all-powerful (**omnipotent**) and knows everything (**omniscient**) will think God can do anything. So why doesn't he answer the prayers? Believers who think God created them will wonder why a God who created them would not look after them by answering their prayers, and believers who think God is good (**omni-benevolent**) will wonder why he does not answer their prayers to stop bad things happening. This may lead some Christians to begin to doubt whether God exists. When a person doubts whether God exists, they may be called 'agnostic' (**agnosticism**).

KEY WORDS

agnosticism Not being sure whether God exists.
omni-benevolent The belief that God is all-good.
omnipotent The belief that God is all-powerful.
omniscient The belief that God knows everything that has happened and everything that is going to happen.

Why unanswered prayers may lead some people not to believe in God
God cannot be all-good and ignore people's prayers
God would respond to the prayers of people who believe in him
God cannot be all-powerful and not be able to answer everybody's prayers
If people cannot feel the presence of God when they pray he cannot exist

Knowledge check

1 What is a prayer?
2 Why do people pray?
3 How might people feel when they do not think that their prayers have been answered?
4 Why might unanswered prayer cause difficulties for believers?

God should care for everyone. If he doesn't answer prayer it shows he does not care or probably doesn't exist.

Praying does not help me feel closer to God, it feels like I am talking to no one.

I thought God would heal my illness as so many people have prayed for me, but he hasn't so I don't think he exists.

The Bible says if a person prays they will receive. I haven't received, so prayer doesn't work.

If prayer worked I would believe in God but I haven't seen it work.

I can't see that prayer has done any good for anyone so they can't be communicating with anything, especially not a powerful God.

A01

1 In small groups discuss the different reasons why unanswered prayer might lead to people losing faith in God.
2 Make a list of four reasons why you think many people think that prayers are not answered.

A02

In small groups prepare a drama to show how a person might lose faith in God when their prayers are unanswered.

● Decide on a situation when a person might pray, how your group will act out the person praying and the results of the prayer being unanswered.
● Include in your drama:
  – the person praying
  – what the person would like to happen as a result of prayer
  – the prayer remaining unanswered
  – what happens to the person as a result of the unanswered prayer
  – what people surrounding the praying person say to them
  – how it affects the person's belief in God.

exam practice b

Do you think unanswered prayers lead people not to believe in God? Give **two** reasons for your point of view.

Examiner's hint: Read the question carefully. (A02)

exam practice c

Explain why an unanswered prayer may lead some people not to believe in God.

Examiner's hint: Develop your reasons by giving an example. (A01)

exam practice d

'Unanswered prayers are proof that God does not exist.'
In your answer you should refer to at least one religion.
i) Do you agree? Give reasons for your answer.
ii) Give reasons why some people may disagree with you.

Examiner's hint: It is easy to develop a reason by quoting from scriptures, for example a Bible reference. (A02)

1.8 Christian responses to unanswered prayers

There are many different Christian responses to the problem of unanswered prayers. Some of the responses are based on the reasons why people pray, some are based on the characteristics of God and some are based on Bible teaching. All of the reasons Christians give show that just because a prayer does not seem to be answered it does not mean that God does not exist.

> **KEY WORDS**
>
> **free will** The idea that human beings are free to make their own choices.

God gave human beings **free will**, he cannot control what they do by answering prayers.

God might answer prayers, just not in the way expected.

If God is like a loving Father, sometimes the answer to requests is no.

Prayer has to agree with what God wants for humanity, it cannot go against the will of God.

Christian responses to unanswered prayers

James 4:3
When you ask, you do not receive, because you ask with wrong motives, that you may spend what you get on your pleasures.

Sometimes prayer is selfish and God would not help a person act in selfish ways.

Human beings are not meant to understand what God wants for them, or how he answers their prayers.

1 Peter 3:12
For the eyes of the Lord are on the righteous

and his ears are attentive to their prayer,

but the face of the Lord is against those who do evil.

Life would be chaos if God gave everyone everything they asked for.

Believers have to have complete faith in God for prayers to be answered.

Matthew 21:22
If you believe, you will receive whatever you ask for in prayer.

Mark 9:23
' "If you can"?' said Jesus. 'Everything is possible for one who believes.'

A01

In small groups, create a poster advertising campaign to encourage people to continue praying even though prayers seem to be unanswered. The posters should be aimed at Christians who might be thinking of giving up praying and should include reasons why they might feel like stopping praying as well why they should not stop.

Knowledge check

1 What do the Christian responses to unanswered prayers try to show?
2 List reasons why God might choose not to answer prayers.
3 List reasons why God might answer prayers but human beings might not be aware that they have been answered.

> I remember a scene from my childhood. As my eleventh birthday approached I let my parents know by broad hints that I wanted a full-size bicycle. They thought it was too soon for that and therefore gave me a typewriter, which was in fact the best present and became the most treasured possession of my boyhood. Was not that good parenthood and a very positive answer to my request for a bicycle? God too allows himself to improve on our requests when what we ask for is not the best.
>
> *Knowing Christianity* by J. I. Packer (1973)

Before computers were in common use, people would use typewriters to enter their text on to a sheet of paper. How might this compare to using a modern computer?

A02

1 In pairs discuss the reasons given for unanswered prayers and decide which are the best reasons and which you feel are not so good.
2 Work on your own and write a list of the reasons in order starting with the best reason and finishing with the least good.
3 Draw a line across your list at the point at which you stop agreeing with the reasons.
4 Return to pair work and discuss why you have put your list in this order.

exam practice b

Do you think there are good reasons to explain why God does not seem to answer prayers? Give **two** reasons for your point of view.

Examiner's hint: A quote is a good way to develop a reason. (A02)

exam practice c

Explain how some religious people respond to the problem of unanswered prayers.

Examiner's hint: This question does not include the word 'why' but still needs reasons. Read questions very carefully. (A01)

exam practice d

'Unanswered prayers do not cause a problem for religious people.'
In your answer you should refer to at least one religion.
i) Do you agree? Give reasons for your answer.
ii) Give reasons why some people may disagree with you.

Examiner's hint: In Section 1 of Unit 1 candidates can use any religion to answer the question so the question will not say 'Christian', it will say 'religious'. (A02)

1.9 Evil and suffering

● The problem of evil and suffering

It is clear that some suffering is due to the action of other people, for example when people steal from or hurt other people – this is called **moral evil**. This is because humans have free will so they can choose to do evil instead of good.

Some suffering is not because of the action of others, but happens in the world because of things that happen naturally – this is called **natural evil**.

The problem of evil is connected to the characteristics of God. Natural evil causes a problem for people who believe in a God who knows everything (omniscient), is completely powerful (omnipotent) and wants only good things (omni-benevolent). The problem is:

- If God is all-knowing, he will know natural evils will cause suffering.
- If God is all-powerful, he is able to stop natural evil.
- If God is all-good, he would want to stop natural evil.
- But natural evils still happen.
- So God does not know evil is happening, does not have the power to stop the evil or he doesn't want to, in which case God does not exist.

This can lead some people to give up their faith and say that God does not exist – this is called **atheism**.

Some people would add that if God existed, only bad people would suffer, not innocent or religious people. Other people would say that if God allowed evil and suffering to help humans learn and become better people then only small amounts of suffering would be needed, not the huge numbers that suffered in the Holocaust or in the 2007 Boxing Day tsunami, or the 2011 Japanese earthquake and tsunami.

> **KEY WORDS**
>
> **moral evil** Actions done by humans which cause suffering.
>
> **natural evil** Things which cause suffering but have nothing to do with humans.
>
> **atheism** Believing that God does not exist.

Knowledge check

1 Look at the pictures on the right. What do you think caused the suffering in each situation?
2 What is moral evil?
3 What is natural evil?
4 Outline the problem of evil.

A01

Imagine you are one of the people in the pictures. Explain why you think that if there was a God he would be able to stop your suffering.

A02

In small groups produce a presentation to explain the problem of evil. Include explanations for all the specialist language that you use. You could include in your presentation:

● examples of moral and natural evil
● a PowerPoint presentation
● a short drama to illustrate the problem of evil.

exam practice b

Do you think evil and suffering mean that God does not exist? Give **two** reasons for your point of view.

Examiner's hint: Start each reason on a new line. (A02)

exam practice c

Explain why evil and suffering cause problems for people who believe in God.

Examiner's hint: A quote is a good way to develop a reason. (A01)

exam practice d

'Humans are the cause of all evil and suffering.'
In your answer you should refer to at least one religion.
i) Do you agree? Give reasons for your answer.
ii) Give reasons why some people may disagree with you.

Examiner's hint: Read the stimulus quote carefully before you decide what your opinion is going to be. (A02)

1.10 Christian responses to the problem of evil and suffering

God gave people free will. They choose to do wrong. Otherwise they would be like robots, not real people.

The Devil tempts people into doing wrong, like in the Garden of Eden when he tempted Eve to eat the apple.

Christians should work hard for justice, to make the world a better place to live in. They should copy the example of Jesus.

People can never know what God's reasons for allowing evil are. Humans are not as all-knowing and perfect as God.

Although humans think natural evil is bad it might have another effect that humans are not aware of, for example, forest fires allow new trees to grow.

Evil and suffering give people a chance to do good deeds so that people can become better.

A new-born child has to cry, for only in this way will his lungs expand. A doctor once told me of a child who could not breathe when it was born. In order to make it breathe the doctor gave it a slight blow. The mother must have thought the doctor cruel. But he was really doing the kindest thing possible. As with new-born children the lungs are contracted, so are our spiritual lungs. But through suffering God strikes us in love. Then our lungs expand and we can breathe and pray.

Sadhu Sundar Singh, an Indian Christian missionary

Knowledge check

1 Look at the different Christian responses to the problem of evil and suffering above. Read through them carefully. Which responses do you think are the best and which ones do you think are not so good?
2 Write the reasons briefly in order from the one you think is the best downwards.
3 Which reason is Sundar Singh supporting? Do you like the example he gives? Why?

In 2011, 7.2 million people in Somalia were in need of help because of drought and twenty years of conflict in the country.

A01

You are a journalist and your newspaper has asked you to write an article about the drought in Somalia to go with the picture above. You have to write about the way Christians should respond to the situation. Use the responses that the Christians have given in this section to help you.

A02

Imagine you have been employed by the Church to explain why people should believe in God even when there is evil and suffering. In groups, design either:
a) a poster campaign (a group of four posters that have a common theme); or
b) a text message campaign (a group of four texts that have a common theme); or
c) an internet pop-up campaign (a group of four pop-ups that have a common theme).
Explain your campaign to the rest of the class and decide which of the campaigns is the most effective.

exam practice b

Do you think natural evil proves that God does not exist? Give **two** reasons for your point of view.

Examiner's hint: Reasons can come from more than one section in this book (or from one bullet point in the exam specification). (A02)

exam practice c

Explain how Christians respond to the problem of evil and suffering.

Examiner's hint: When a c) question starts with the words 'Explain how ...' you need to give descriptions of the ways rather than reasons why. (A01)

exam practice d

'God should not allow evil and suffering to happen.'
In your answer you should refer to at least one religion.
i) Do you agree? Give reasons for your answer.
ii) Give reasons why some people may disagree with you.

Examiner's hint: If you can't think of three reasons then write two reasons and develop each one. (A02)

1.11 Two programmes about religion

● How two films about religion may affect a person's attitude to belief in God

There are many different programmes and films that include reference to religion that can be used to answer questions about this. You will need to watch the programme or film and work out reasons why it might affect a person's belief in God. You might find that some of issues looked at in this section will help you if they are also shown in the film. You will not need to describe the whole of the film or programme in answers, but you will need to give examples from the film.

Films and programmes might strengthen a person's belief in God if they give a positive view of God. Someone might want to get closer to God and if the films or programmes provide evidence for God it might strengthen a person's faith.

Films and programmes might weaken a person's belief in God if they give a negative view of God. Someone might decide not to worship a God like that and if they provide evidence to prove God does not exist it might take away a person's reasons for believing.

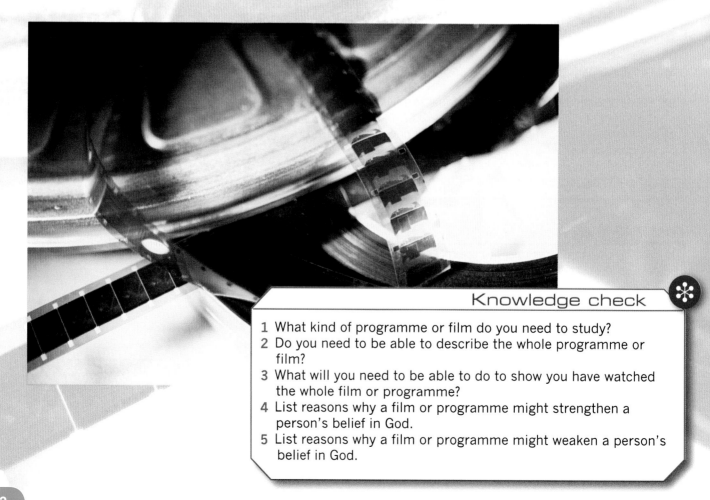

Knowledge check

1 What kind of programme or film do you need to study?
2 Do you need to be able to describe the whole programme or film?
3 What will you need to be able to do to show you have watched the whole film or programme?
4 List reasons why a film or programme might strengthen a person's belief in God.
5 List reasons why a film or programme might weaken a person's belief in God.

Bruce Almighty

Morgan Freeman plays God in the film *Bruce Almighty*, while Jim Carrey is the lead as Bruce, who gets God's powers.

Bruce is a man who is ambitious and when he loses his job blames God. God then gives Bruce his powers; while Bruce has God's powers he realises that he had to change the way he was living if he wanted to be happy.

Bruce Almighty is a film that could support a person's belief for many reasons, but if they saw it only as humorous fiction it might weaken a person's faith.

How the film *Bruce Almighty* might affect a person's belief in God

When Bruce has God's powers he cannot make Grace love him. It shows that God cannot interfere with free will.

When Bruce answers yes to all prayers there is chaos. It shows why God will not say yes to all prayers.

When Bruce walks on water. It shows God can work miracles.

At the end Bruce realises that using God's powers will not give him what he wants. He has to help others at the end. He gives blood and says 'be the miracle'. It shows that God wants humans to help one another.

The film makes many references to things that happen in the Bible, for example, the parting of the Red Sea, the Golden Calf, and turning water into wine. It shows that these were possible.

A02

1 Watch the film *Bruce Almighty*. Note down the parts of the film that might affect a person's belief in God, either to strengthen belief or to weaken it.
2 In pairs, use your notes and the information given above to produce a PowerPoint presentation to show the parts of the film that might affect belief.
3 Use your PowerPoint presentation to explain to the class how the film might affect a person's belief in God.

Wonders of the Universe

In this series Professor Brian Cox explains how the universe developed from a scientific point of view, including an explanation of the Big Bang theory.

You can watch a clip here:
www.bbc.co.uk/learningzone/
clips/12236.flv

'Science programmes might lead to a person questioning their faith.' Do you think this is true? Why?

How the programme *Wonders of the Universe* might affect a person's belief in God

Professor Cox does not refer to God at all. It shows that God is not needed for the creation of the earth.

It shows scientifically how the universe came into existence. This is nothing like the story in Genesis.

It shows that the creation of the earth took 13.7 billion years. This differs from the one-week creation story in the Bible.

It provides evidence that people do not have to turn to God to find out how the world was created. It does not refer to God.

A02

Draw two spider diagrams. One should record information as to why some programmes or films would support belief in God. The other should record information as to why some programmes or films would weaken belief in God.

exam practice b

Do you think films affect someone's faith in God? Give **two** reasons for your point of view.

Examiner's hint: An example from a film is a good way to develop a reason. (A02)

exam practice c

Explain how one programme or film may affect a person's attitude to belief in God.

Examiner's hint: In media questions make sure you name the programme or film you are using. (A01)

exam practice d

'Programmes and films cannot affect a person's belief in God.' In your answer you should refer to at least one religion.
i) Do you agree? Give reasons for your answer.
ii) Give reasons why some people may disagree with you.

Examiner's hint: Do not be tempted to write a lot of detail about what happens in specific programmes; it will not gain you many marks. (A02)

Examination practice

In Section 1 you will be assessed on your spelling, punctuation and grammar (SPaG). There are 4 marks available for this, so write clearly, check your spelling and try to use specialist words.

Below is guidance on how to answer the question b) from Section 1: Believing in God. As it is a b) question, it is worth 4 marks.

In every section there are two b) questions to choose from. Try question 1b) using the hints provided below. Then apply these steps to question 2b).

Sample question

1b) Do you think miracles lead to a belief in God? [4]

Sample question

2b) Do you think all religious experiences lead to a belief in God? [4]

How to answer

To get full marks on a b) question, you must give your opinion and support it with two reasons and develop each of the reasons.

Step 1

● Think of one reason why a miracle may lead to belief in God. Make sure you write down that it is your opinion at the beginning. It does not matter whether you agree or disagree with the statement.

I think that a miracle gives proof that God exists.

Step 2

● Think of a way to develop the reason. The easiest way to develop a reason is to give an example or a quote.

If a person asked God to help them pass a difficult exam and then they passed they would have proof that God exists.

Step 3

● Think of a second reason why a miracle may lead to belief in God. Write the second reason as a new paragraph.

Secondly, a miracle makes a person aware of God's presence leading to belief in God.

Step 4

● Develop your second reason. Ensure the development is about your reason and still answers the question.

For example, if a person had a vision of God they would know that God was with them and they would believe.

Examiner's comment

✓ **Maximum marks will be awarded for two reasons that have been developed as long as they answer the question.**

✓ **Development must link to the question set. It cannot be vague or include comments such as 'and all Christians believe in Jesus'.**

Below is guidance on how to answer the question c) from Section 1: Believing in God. As it is a c) question, it is worth 8 marks.

In every section there are two c) questions to choose from. Try question 1c) using the hints provided below. Then apply these steps to question 2c).

Sample question
1c) Explain why a religious upbringing may lead to a belief in God. [8]

Sample question
2c) Explain why Christian parents give their children a religious upbringing. [8]

How to answer
There are several ways to get full marks on a c) question. One way is to give four separate brief reasons.

Step 1
● Think of one reason why a religious upbringing may lead to belief in God.

A child may grow to believe in God if they have a religious upbringing because they believe what their parents say is true.

Step 2
● Think of a second reason. Write each new reason on a new line.

Also, if they have been to a religious school, they believe in God because all their friends will believe.

Step 3
● Think of a third reason why a religious upbringing may lead to belief in God. Make sure you are not repeating yourself.

In addition, a religious school will provide evidence in lessons for the existence of God.

Step 4
● Give a fourth reason. Ensure you are still answering the question.

Finally, they have been taught to pray which means they may have developed a close relationship with God.

Examiner's comment
✓ **Maximum marks will be awarded for four valid and different reasons.**
✓ **Make sure you write in good English and that your spelling is accurate.**

Religion and life

Section 2: Matters of life and death

2.1 Christian beliefs about life after death

● Why Christians believe in life after death

Christians believe that they will have life after death. Most Christians believe that if they have lived a good life then they will be rewarded in heaven and those who have not lived a good life will be punished in hell. Some believe that it is a person's soul that lives on (**immortality of the soul**) and some believe it is their body as well. Some people, for example Roman Catholics, believe that there is a place in between heaven and hell where people go to have sins forgiven (purgatory). Christians also believe in **resurrection**.

> **KEY WORDS**
>
> **immortality of the soul** The idea that the soul lives on after the death of the body.
>
> **resurrection** The belief that, after death, the body stays in the grave until the end of the world when it is raised.

Why Christians believe in life after death

Jesus rose from the dead. *For we believe that Jesus died and rose again (1 Thessalonians 4:14).*

Jesus taught that there would be life after death. *My Father's house has many rooms; if that were not so, would I have told you that I am going there to prepare a place for you? (John 14:2).*

It comforts people – it makes them feel better to know that one day they will be with God who is perfect.

The resurrection of Jesus is one of the teachings of the Church. It is found in letters from Church authorities and in the Catechism of the Catholic Church.

It means good people are rewarded with a good afterlife. Jesus teaches this in the Parable of the Sheep and the Goats. *The righteous [go] into eternal life (Matthew 25:46).*

… those who have done good will rise to live … (John 5:29).

It is in the creeds. *Jesus Christ … was crucified, dead, and buried: He descended into hell; The third day he rose again from the dead. (The Apostle's Creed).*

It is described in the Bible. *Not everyone … will enter the kingdom of heaven, only the one who does the will of my Father … (Matthew 7:21).*

Knowledge check ✳

1 Outline what Christians believe about life after death.
2 Give four reasons why Christians believe in life after death.
3 Write down two Bible references that show that there is life after death.

Jacob left Beersheba and set out for Harran. When he reached a certain place, he stopped for the night because the sun had set … He had a dream in which he saw a stairway resting on the earth, with its top reaching to heaven, and the angels of God were ascending and descending on it. There above it stood the Lord … When Jacob awoke from his sleep, he thought, 'Surely the Lord is in this place …' He was afraid and said, 'How awesome is this place! This is none other than the house of God; this is the gate of heaven.' (Genesis 28:10–19).

This is a painting called Jacob's Ladder by William Blake. The description of Jacob's ladder appears in the book of Genesis in the Old Testament.

● How beliefs about life after death affect the lives of Christians

All the letters in the New Testament showed the early Christians that living a good life will be rewarded by life in heaven so I try to live a good life by sharing with others, acting in a charitable way and avoiding behaving badly.

Jesus said 'I am the way, the truth and the life', so I believe my faith in Jesus will lead to everlasting life.

As a Christian, I believe in life after death. I have been taught in the Bible that God sent Jesus to earth to save us from our sins and give us eternal life. The Bible tells me that I will go to heaven if I follow the teachings of Jesus so I try to ensure that I look at his teachings before I make decisions.

The Church teaches that I will have life after death if I recognise the power of God in my life so I attend Church and pray every day.

A01

Imagine you are a priest or vicar of a local church. Write a leaflet for children to explain how they should live their lives if they want to have life after death.

Include in your leaflet:

✓ why Christians believe there is life after death
✓ the main things a Christian should do to achieve life after death
✓ why doing these things will help a Christian achieve life after death.

A02

Prepare for a class debate on: 'Christians will have life after death just because they have faith in Jesus'.

1 Write the debate title as a heading.
2 Draw a table. The first column should list reasons to support the statement, such as Bible references which indicate that faith in Jesus is important and that you cannot get to heaven unless you follow Jesus.
3 The second column should list reasons to disagree with the statement, such as Bible references which indicate that faith in Jesus is important, but action is essential, that in actions towards others a person shows love for Jesus and teachings like the commandment: Love your neighbour.
4 Hold the debate. Ensure there is a chairperson and at least two people to speak on the issue. Ask questions of the speakers before taking a class vote.

exam practice b

Do you think Christians should believe in life after death? Give **two** reasons for your point of view.

Examiner's hint: Make sure you answer the question with two reasons. Concentrate on providing reasons, with development, rather than discussing whether Christians should do anything. (A02)

exam practice c

Explain why belief in life after death may affect a Christian's life.

Examiner's hint: Try to use biblical references – they don't have to be the exact wording. (A01)

exam practice d

'Death is not the end.'
In your answer you should refer to Christianity.
i) Do you agree? Give reasons for your answer.
ii) Give reasons why some people may disagree with you.

Examiner's hint: This question requires a reference to Christianity in your answer. Read the line following the quote carefully. (A02)

2.2 Muslim beliefs about life after death

Muslims believe that they will have life after death (Akhirah). Muslims believe that after they are buried they wait until the end of the world. During this wait called Barzakh, the body and soul separate. At the end of the world a trumpet will blow and all people will die. The trumpet will be sounded again and all people will be resurrected from their graves to come in front of Allah. Allah will then judge everyone. People then pass on to the bridge (Siraat) over hell's fires. Those who can cross will enter paradise (Jannah) and those who do not will enter hell (Jahannum).

Those whose lives the angels take in state of purity, saying 'peace be on you; enter paradise for what you were doing' (Qur'an 16:32).

Did ye think that ye would enter Heaven without Allah testing those of you who fought hard (In His Cause) and remained steadfast? (Qur'an 3:142).

● Why Muslims believe in life after death

It is one of the six fundamental beliefs of Islam.

The hadith recorded by al-Bukhari reported Prophet Muhammad describing life after death.

Belief in paradise helps me face the tests that I face in life.

Al-Ghazali describes life after death in his commentaries on the hadith.

Knowledge check

1 Describe Muslim beliefs about life after death (Akhira).
2 List four reasons why Muslims believe in life after death.
3 Write down the two references from the Qur'an that show that there is life after death.
4 Explain what each of the references says about life after death.

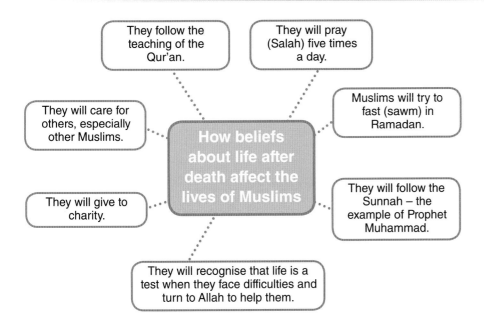

A01

1 In pairs study each reason in the spider diagram and discuss why a Muslim might do this. Is it because it is part of Muslim teaching? Is it one of the obligatory five pillars? Is it because it strengthens the Muslim community (ummah)?

2 Draw a table with two columns. In one column write 'The ways belief in life after death affects how a Muslim lives'. In the second column write 'The reasons why a Muslim would do this'.

A02

1 Imagine you were going to interview one of the Muslims on page 32.

2 Think of what questions you would ask them about how important it is to live life in a way that prepares you for life after death.

3 Compare your questions with another person and try to answer some of them.

exam practice b

Do you think giving to charity will help a person receive life after death? Give **two** reasons for your point of view.

Examiner's hint: Make sure you develop each of your reasons. (A02)

exam practice c

Explain how Muslims should live if they want to go to paradise.

Examiner's hint: A question that begins with 'Explain how ...' could be answered with four different descriptions. (A01)

exam practice d

'Life after death is not a good reason for behaving well in this life.'

In your answer you should refer to one religion other than Christianity.

i) Do you agree? Give reasons for your answer.

ii) Give reasons why some people may disagree with you.

Examiner's hint: Make sure you include reference to a religion other than Christianity if it says this in the question. (A02)

2.3 Non-religious reasons for belief in life after death

There are many people who are not religious, but still have beliefs in life after death. Many have had **paranormal** experiences. Here are some of their beliefs.

I believe there must be something other than this life – life must have some kind of bigger meaning.

I believe the evidence of mediums who say that they can contact the dead and speak with them.

It is important for me to believe that I will be rewarded for my good deeds in another life.

I believe in paranormal experiences like ghosts. I think they provide evidence that there must be something else after this life.

I know that I have lived before. I can remember previous lives. I believe in **reincarnation**.

I want to feel that there is somewhere for my friends and relatives to go so that I can still be with them after they die.

Believing in life after death stops me feeling scared of death.

I nearly died. I had a **near-death experience** where I saw a bright light. I have spoken to others who have said they have had visions. We all believe that this is evidence that there is another life to the one that we experience now.

Ghosts have been reported for centuries, so they must exist.

People have experienced the paranormal even when they did not believe in ghosts.

Mediums provide details about people's lives that they could not know unless they had contacted dead people.

Television has provided evidence for ghosts and mediums on programmes like *Most Haunted*.

KEY WORDS

near-death experience When someone about to die has an out of body experience.

paranormal Unexplained things which are thought to have spiritual causes, e.g. ghosts, mediums.

reincarnation The belief that, after death, souls are reborn in a new body.

Knowledge check

1 Why do people think that mediums provide evidence for life after death?
2 Which reasons provide evidence that there must be life after death?
3 Which reasons are to do with people's emotions about life and death?

My Grandma

I was painting the cupboards in my bedroom. For some reason, although the rest of the room was blue, I had chosen to paint them black. I suddenly had the strong feeling that my Grandma was with me. She was looking at the cupboards and laughing.

Later in the day I spoke to my mother and she explained that my Grandma had also painted cupboards black. I then knew that, although my Grandma had died several years previously, she was still with me.

A01

1 In pairs discuss whether you think mediums provide enough evidence to believe in life after death.
2 Write down a list of reasons why a person might think that mediums provide good evidence that there is life after death.

A02

1 Draw an advertisement to convince people that they should believe in life after death, without referring to religion in any way. This section requires non-religious reasons – this means you should not mention God or heaven.
2 Use the information above and on page 34 to help you. Make sure you include what the different reasons are and why people think these are good reasons.

exam practice b

Do you think that ghosts exist? Give **two** reasons for your point of view.

Examiner's hint: You can use examples from films and TV programmes to develop your reasons. (A02)

exam practice c

Explain why some non-religious people believe in life after death.

Examiner's hint: A key word in the question is non-religious so make sure you do not include reference to religious ideas such as heaven or paradise. (A01)

exam practice d

'Everyone should believe in life after death.'
In your answer you should refer to at least one religion.
i) Do you agree? Give reasons for your answer.
ii) Give reasons why some people may disagree with you.

Examiner's hint: If you can't think of a quote to develop a reason then use your own example. (A02)

2.4 Reasons for non-belief in life after death

Life after death is just a fantasy

From frightening monsters to sensitive romantics, vampires are portrayed in all shapes and sizes in films and on TV. Does this add to the belief that life after death is just a fantasy?

Films like *The Twilight Saga* and the TV programme *The Vampire Diaries* have all popularised the view of the evidence for life after death. In *New Moon*, vampire Edward refuses to make his girlfriend Bella into a vampire. He believes that although it will make her immortal like him, it will also take away her soul. He believes that having no soul makes him a monster.

New Moon is just one example where mass media use the paranormal as evidence for life after death. There is a reason why they do this – it is good fictional entertainment. However, it does not prove that there is life after death.

For years people have been trying to prove there is another life after this one. The reason they have not been able to find a valid or scientific evidence for life after death is that there is no life after death.

People might say, 'but what about the evidence of the paranormal, things like ghosts and mediums?' This evidence is all easily explained by people giving things away when they talk and by clever tricks.

Near-death experiences can be explained by scientists who say that the effects of drugs and lack of oxygen can cause the brain to have these experiences. They don't actually prove anything about life after death.

When people talk about remembered lives, it is possible that they heard, saw or read something which they then think they have remembered.

Knowledge check

1 According to the magazine article above why do the media like using the paranormal?
2 What does this article suggest as a reason for why no one can find scientific evidence for the existence of life after death?
3 What explanation is given in this article for paranormal experiences?
4 What do medical authorities say about near-death experiences?

You can also watch Richard Dawkins speaking on CNN in 2010: search for this on www. youtube.com

If you're an atheist, you know, you believe, this is the only life you're going to get. It's a precious life. It's a beautiful life. It's something we should live to the full, to the end of our days.

Where if you're religious and you believe in another life somehow, that means you don't live this life to the full because you think you're going to get another one. That's an awfully negative way to live a life.

Being an atheist frees you up to live this life properly, happily and fully. Being an atheist frees you up.

Richard Dawkins, scientist and author of *The God Delusion*, speaking on a TV news programme

exam practice b

Do you think belief in life after death is a fantasy? Give **two** reasons for your point of view.

Examiner's hint: Even if the question does not appear to be religious, you can use religious reasons to support your point of view. (A02)

exam practice c

Explain why some people do not believe in life after death.

Examiner's hint: Your own opinion is not required for c)-type questions. (A01)

A01

In pairs use the information given to produce a PowerPoint presentation to show the main reasons why people do not believe in life after death. Add diagrams or pictures to illustrate the ideas. Present your findings to the rest of the class.

exam practice d

'If you believe in another life somehow, that means you don't live this life to the full.'
In your answer you should refer to at least one religion.
i) Do you agree? Give reasons for your answer.
ii) Give reasons why some people may disagree with you.

Examiner's hint: Make sure that the reasons you give for d) ii) are for the opposite opinion to those given in d) i). (A02)

A02

1 Draw and complete a table to list reasons why people might believe in life after death and reasons why they might disagree with life after death.
2 Use this information to participate in a 'decision alley'. This is when the class divides in two, one side thinks of reasons why the argument leads to belief and the other thinks of reasons why it does not. Each side then lines up shoulder to shoulder with an alley between. A member of the class then walks down the alley asking for advice from members on either side. When they get to the end they make a decision. At the end, the class can see what the majority view is.

2.5 The nature of abortion

● British law on abortion

Abortion is more properly called artificial abortion and it is a medical action that ends a pregnancy before the foetus can live outside the womb.

The most recent law in Britain came into place in 1990 and is called The Human Fertilisation and Embryology Bill. This bill states that abortion can take place providing certain conditions are met. The conditions that need to be met in order for an abortion to take place are as follows:

- The abortion must take place before the pregnancy is 24 weeks (unless there are severe problems later in the pregnancy).
- Two doctors must agree.
- It must take place in a government-recognised medical facility.
- One of the following conditions must also be met:
  - The mother's life is in danger.
  - The mother's health (physical or mental) is at risk.
  - The health of existing children may be at risk.
  - The baby might be seriously ill.

Abortion is not allowed 'on demand' simply because a woman does not want a baby. For an abortion to take place the conditions listed above must be met. It cannot be simply because it is inconvenient or gets in the way of a woman's career. A woman who wants an abortion must show that there are good medical reasons for it.

The law is different in Northern Ireland where abortion is usually illegal unless it is to 'save the life of the mother' or prevent the pregnant woman becoming a 'physical or mental wreck'. This usually means that there can be exceptions.

> **KEY WORDS**
>
> **abortion** The removal of a foetus from the womb before it can survive.

Knowledge check

1 What is an abortion?
2 When was the most recent law on abortion?
3 What is the most recent abortion law called?
4 At least four conditions must be met for an abortion to be legal.
   a) Which three conditions must be met for all abortions?
   b) There are four additional conditions, one of which must also be met. What are the four other conditions?

A01

1 In small groups discuss the law on abortion; ensure that you understand the different parts of the law.
2 Design a poster or produce a PowerPoint presentation to explain the current law on abortion.

● Why abortion is a controversial issue

Some people think the present laws are good because they protect healthy pregnancies but allow abortions in situations where they are needed. However, abortion is a topic that lots of people argue about. Some people think the present laws make it too easy to get an abortion and some think the laws make it too difficult.

Abortion is a controversial issue which brings out strong feelings from people. The demonstrations against abortion (pro-life) and for abortion (pro-choice) in these photos both use a crucifix to make a point. What point do you think they are trying to make?

It is too difficult to get an abortion ...	It is too easy to get an abortion ...
A woman should have complete control over her own body. This is described as being pro-choice	Life starts at conception and should be protected. Pro-life supporters believe that the foetus must have the chance of life
The developing baby (foetus) is not a real baby	A baby can survive after being born before 24 weeks so the dates should be reduced
People will have illegal abortions if they cannot meet the legal conditions for an abortion	A developing baby should have the same rights as any other person
Abortion is a personal issue. The decision should be made by the woman, not doctors	Doctors should protect life, not end it

A02

1 Discuss the table above in small groups. Are there any other reasons you can think of?
2 Draw a spidergram to record information as to why some people would like abortion laws tightened or abortion made completely illegal.
3 Draw a spidergram giving reasons why some people would like the laws on abortion changed to make it easier to get an abortion.

exam practice b

Do you think the abortion law makes it too easy to get an abortion? Give **two** reasons for your point of view.

Examiner's hint: Make sure you are clear about the law on abortion before you begin to answer the question. (A02)

exam practice c

Explain why people argue about abortion.

Examiner's hint: Your explanation does not have to be religious. (A01)

exam practice d

'The law on abortion is wrong.'
In your answer you should refer to at least one religion.
i) Do you agree? Give reasons for your answer.
ii) Give reasons why some people may disagree with you.

Examiner's hint: This question could be answered: 'Yes it is wrong. It makes it too easy.' or 'Yes it is wrong. It is too difficult.' Make sure you are clear what your opinion is and stick to it. (A02)

2.6 Christian attitudes to abortion

There are different Christian attitudes to the topic of abortion. All Christians agree that abortion is not good because as God created life, it is holy. We call this the **sanctity of life**.

However, one Christian attitude says that all abortion is wrong and will only accept it in the extreme situation that the pregnancy threatens the life of the mother. Another Christian attitude states that abortion is not ideal but will accept that it is necessary in some situations.

KEY WORDS

sanctity of life The belief that life is holy and belongs to God.

Abortion should sometimes be allowed	Abortion is wrong
A woman should have complete control over her own body	Life starts at conception and should be protected
Life starts when the baby can survive independently	God started the life so only God has the right to end it
Christians are supposed to reduce suffering – an abortion could be to prevent suffering	Doctors should protect life, not end it
Life is taken in the Bible and according to God's will, so why not before birth?	Because life is holy (the sanctity of life), it should not be interfered with
Abortion is a personal issue – the decision should be made by the woman, not by doctors	One of the Ten Commandments says 'Do not murder'

Jeremiah 1:5
Before I formed you in the womb I knew you; before you were born I set you apart; I appointed you as a prophet to the nations.

1 Corinthians 3:16
Don't you know that you yourselves are God's temple and that God's Spirit dwells in your midst?

Genesis 1:26
Then God said, 'Let us make mankind in our image, in our likeness, …'

Galatians 1:15
But when God, who set me apart from my mother's womb and called me by his grace, was pleased …

Exodus 20:13
You shall not murder.

Knowledge check

1 What are the two main Christian attitudes to abortion?
2 List four reasons why some Christians think that abortion is wrong.
3 List four reasons why some Christians think abortion should sometimes be allowed.

A01

Write a leaflet or make a poster to explain why some Christians think that abortion is wrong. Your leaflet or poster must include:

✓ a brief description of the law on abortion
✓ Christian reasons why someone might think abortion is wrong
✓ at least two Bible references.

A02

Mrs X is a 35-year-old woman who is married with five children. She has just lost her job as a secretary. Two days ago, she found out that she is pregnant. She is now considering whether she can look after six children and afford to raise them financially.

Write an answer to Mrs X's problem. Make sure that your answer is balanced and includes a response from the viewpoint of Christians who think it is wrong to have an abortion and from the viewpoint of those that think that in some circumstances it is acceptable.

exam practice b

Do you think Christians should not accept abortion? Give **two** reasons for your point of view.

Examiner's hint: You could use Bible references to develop your reasons. (A02)

exam practice c

Explain why some Christians accept abortion and some do not.

Examiner's hint: Your answer must have reasons for Christians accepting abortion and reasons for Christians not accepting abortion. You would not get full marks if you gave a one-sided answer. (A01)

exam practice d

'All Christians should accept abortion.'
In your answer you should refer to Christianity.
i) Do you agree? Give reasons for your answer.
ii) Give reasons why some people may disagree with you.

Examiner's hint: Make sure you give your personal opinion in the d) i) part. (A02)

2.7 Muslim attitudes to abortion

There are different Muslim attitudes to the topic of abortion. All Muslims accept that as Allah is the creator and Muslim family life is important, then abortion is not good.

However, using quotes from the Qur'an there are two different Muslim attitudes to abortion. Some Muslims say that abortion is not allowed, and will only accept it in extreme situations. Another Muslim attitude states that abortion is not ideal but will accept it up until the point when the soul enters the body, which is usually regarded as 120 days.

● Muslim teachings on abortion

And do not kill the soul which Allah has forbidden, except by right (Qur'an 17:33).

Whoever kills a soul unless for a soul or for corruption [done] in the land – it is as if he had slain mankind entirely (Qur'an 5:32).

Do not kill your children out of poverty; We will provide for you (Qur'an 6:151).

Those will have lost who killed their children in foolishness without knowledge and prohibited what Allah had provided for them, inventing untruth about Allah. They have gone astray and were not [rightly] guided (Qur'an 6:140).

And do not kill your children for fear of poverty. We provide for them and for you. Indeed, their killing is ever a great sin (Qur'an 17:31).

Then We made the sperm-drop into a clinging clot, and We made the clot into a lump [of flesh], and We made [from] the lump, bones, and We covered the bones with flesh; then We developed him into another creation. So blessed is Allah, the best of creators (Qur'an 23:14).

Knowledge check

1 What do all Muslims think about abortion?
2 What are the two main Muslim attitudes?
3 Explain using two quotes why some Muslims think that abortion is wrong.
4 Explain using two quotes why some Muslims think abortion should sometimes be allowed.

Abortion should sometimes be allowed	Abortion is not allowed
Mother is very disabled and unable to look after a child	Allah is the creator of life. Only Allah has the right to end life
Life starts at 120 days (ensoulment)	The Qur'an says do not kill your child because of want
An abortion could be to prevent danger to the mother's life	Because of the sanctity of life (life is holy)
The mother has been raped	The Qur'an says that those who kill have gone astray
	Life begins at conception

A01

1 In small groups discuss the different Muslim attitudes to abortion.
2 Prepare a presentation using either posters or PowerPoint on the different Muslim attitudes to abortion. The presentations must include:
✓ Muslim reasons why someone might think abortion is wrong
✓ Muslim reasons why someone might think abortion is sometimes acceptable
✓ at least two references.

A02

Prepare to answer questions about Muslim attitudes towards abortion and the reasons for them in a hot-seat situation. You will have to choose to support one attitude and be against the other one.

1 Decide which attitude you will answer questions on and think about the effect it would have on a person.
2 Study reasons for the different Muslim attitudes toward abortion given. Try to add more reasons and explanations to these.
3 Take part in the hot-seat discussion either as the person in the hot seat being questioned or as the questioner.
4 At the end of the activity draw a table to include four reasons why Muslims might allow abortion and four reasons why they might not allow abortion.

exam practice b

Do you think Muslims should not accept abortion? Give **two** reasons for your point of view.

Examiner's hint: You could use references from the Qur'an to develop your answer. (A02)

exam practice c

Explain why some Muslims do not accept abortion.

Examiner's hint: This question only asks for reasons why some Muslims do not accept abortion. You would not get any marks for any reasons why some Muslims do accept abortion. (A01)

exam practice d

'All Muslims should accept abortion.'
In your answer you should refer to at least one religion.
i) Do you agree? Give reasons for your answer.
ii) Give reasons why some people may disagree with you.

Examiner's hint: If you start a new line for each reason you can make sure you give enough reasons to get full marks. (A02)

2.8 The nature of euthanasia

● The law on euthanasia

Euthanasia is the deliberate ending of a person's life when they are suffering from an illness that cannot be cured. There are several terms used in law to describe euthanasia:

- If the person who is suffering asks for euthanasia then it is called **voluntary euthanasia**.
- If the person suffering is unable to ask for euthanasia then it is called **non-voluntary euthanasia**.
- If the person suffering asks for help to kill themselves then it is called **assisted suicide**.

In the UK euthanasia is illegal. Euthanasia is regarded by the law as murder and can be punished as such. Assisted suicide is not punishable as murder since suicide is not illegal; however, assisted suicide is not legal and it can be punished by up to 14 years' imprisonment.

It is not illegal for medical authorities to switch off life-support machines. Providing terminal sedation is also legal. This is when the patient is given drugs which mean they are not conscious and do not feel pain, although it may also speed up a person's death.

KEY WORDS

assisted suicide Providing a seriously ill person with the means to commit suicide.

euthanasia The painless killing of a person dying from a painful disease.

non-voluntary euthanasia Ending someone's life painlessly when they are unable to ask, but you have good reason for thinking they would want you to do so.

voluntary euthanasia Ending life painlessly when someone in great pain asks for death.

Knowledge check

1 What is euthanasia?
2 What is the legal position for euthanasia in the UK?
3 How is euthanasia punishable? Why?
4 How is assisted suicide punishable? Why?
5 How is switching off a life-support machine or terminal sedation punishable? Why?

Sir Terry Pratchett calls for euthanasia tribunals

The author Sir Terry Pratchett is calling for euthanasia tribunals to give sufferers from incurable diseases the right to medical help to end their lives.

Pratchett, author of the bestselling *Discworld* fantasy novels, was diagnosed two years ago with a rare form of early onset Alzheimer's disease.

In his lecture, 'Shaking Hands With Death', the author will volunteer to be a test case before a euthanasia tribunal himself.

The tribunal panels would include a legal expert in family matters and a doctor with experience of serious long-term illness.

'If granny walks up to the tribunal and bangs her walking stick on the table and says "Look, I've really had enough, I hate this bloody disease, and I'd like to die thank you very much young man", I don't see why anyone should stand in her way.'

He said there was no evidence from countries where assisted dying is allowed of granny being coerced into dying so relatives could get their hands on her money.

'Choice is very important in this matter. But there will be some probably older, probably wiser GPs, who will understand. The tribunal would be acting for the good of society as well as that of the applicant – and ensure they are of sound and informed mind, firm in their purpose, suffering from a life-threatening and incurable disease and not under the influence of a third party.

'If I knew that I could die, I would live. My life, my death, my choice.'

www.guardian.co.uk

A01

1 In small groups discuss the article about the author Terry Pratchett and his view on euthanasia.
2 Write a list of five questions you would like to ask him about his view on euthanasia.
3 Swap your questions with another group in your class. Answer the other group's questions as if you were Terry Pratchett.

● Why euthanasia is a controversial issue

People argue about euthanasia because they hold different views about whether it is right to end a person's life because of the **quality of life** they have.

Some people think that euthanasia should remain illegal because:
● The law protects life.
● Some might not want to die but are forced into it.
● It is murder and all murder should be illegal.
● Doctors should save life, not end it.

Some people think that euthanasia should be made legal because:
● It gives a person choice; it allows them to practise their own free will.
● Some people want control over what happens in their medical care.
● If quality of life is very poor, life is not worth living.
● It will allow medical resources to be used to help people who can recover.

A02

1 In pairs discuss the reasons given for supporting euthanasia and decide which are the best reasons and which you feel are not so good.
2 On your own, make a list of the reasons in order, starting with the best reason and finishing with the least good.
3 Draw a line across your list at the point at which you stop agreeing with the reasons.
4 In pairs, discuss why you have put your list of reasons in this order.

exam practice b

Do you think euthanasia should be made legal? Give **two** reasons for your point of view.

Examiner's hint: Make sure you know what the words legal and illegal mean and that you do not confuse the two. (A02)

exam practice c

Explain why people might argue about euthanasia.

Examiner's hint: Read the question very carefully. This question needs reasons for and against euthanasia to explain why people argue. (A01)

exam practice d

'The law on euthanasia should not be changed.'
In your answer you should refer to at least one religion.
i) Do you agree? Give reasons for your answer.
ii) Give reasons why some people may disagree with you.

Examiner's hint: Make sure you state that euthanasia is illegal before you give your opinion. (A02)

2.9 Christian attitudes to euthanasia

All Christians agree that euthanasia is not acceptable because of the sanctity of life. God is the creator and the only true taker of life. Euthanasia is also illegal. The issue is complicated because of the different types of euthanasia.

One Christian attitude says that all euthanasia is wrong and will only accept the turning off of life-support machines if the medical authorities have said that the person is already dead (brain dead) and it is acceptable to refuse types of treatment that could be described as aggressive. This is because in these cases there is no quality of life. Another Christian attitude states that euthanasia is not allowed but turning off life-support machines, refusing treatment and terminal sedation are not wrong.

● Different Christian attitudes to euthanasia

Euthanasia in the form of turning off life-support machines, refusing treatment and terminal sedation should be allowed.	**Euthanasia, except in turning off the life-support machine of someone who is already brain dead, is wrong.**
• People have free will and should choose what medical care they have. • Christians are supposed to reduce suffering – this includes preventing suffering of the patient and their family. • These forms of euthanasia are allowed within the law so should be accepted. • It should be up to the individual to choose their treatment, not medical authorities. • Death is a natural process and humans should not interfere with it.	• Although the Ten Commandments say do not murder, the person is already dead so this is not murder. • God has already taken the person's life. Medicine is keeping the person alive artificially. • The person has no quality of life so the person's life should be ended. • Life-support machines cost lots of money and this money could be better used helping others. • Churches teach that this is acceptable.

A01

1 In pairs, one person writes out on five cards the reasons why some Christians think that certain forms of euthanasia are acceptable and the other person writes five reasons why some Christians think euthanasia, except for those people on life-support machines, is not acceptable.

2 Then organise the reasons into two lists, in order of what you both consider to be the best reasons. The best reason should be first.

Locked-in syndrome man seeks right to die

Tony Nicklinson, a former engineer and rugby fan, suffered a stroke in June 2005 which left him unable to speak. He is paralysed except for the ability to move his head and blink. This is a condition known as locked-in syndrome.

Mr Nicklinson, 56, has begun legal action to clarify the law on mercy killings. He wishes for his wife to be allowed to help him die, but does not want his wife to be prosecuted for murder.

His wife Jane says she is prepared to inject him with a lethal dose of drugs. However, doing this would mean that she would be prosecuted for murder, as the law does not consider motivation and circumstance in murder cases.

You can read more about this case on the following website:

http://news.bbc.co.uk/1/hi/programmes/hardtalk/9577291.stm

A02

1 Discuss the case of Tony Nicklinson (more information is available on the internet) in small groups. Do you think euthanasia should be allowed in his case?
2 Draw a spidergram to record reasons why a Christian would not accept euthanasia in this case.

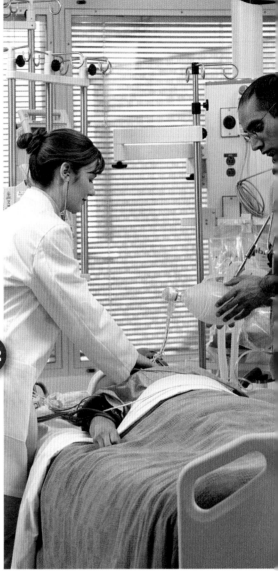

Are the circumstances ever right to end a life?

exam practice b

Do you think Christians should ever support euthanasia? Give **two** reasons for your point of view.

Examiner's hint: Make sure you clearly state whether you think euthanasia is or is not acceptable. This will be credited as development of your reasons. (A02)

exam practice c

Explain why some Christians will not accept any forms of euthanasia.

Examiner's hint: Ensure answers to this question refer to Christianity. (A01)

exam practice d

'Anyone who is sick should have the right to end their own life.'
In your answer you should refer to at least one religion.
i) Do you agree? Give reasons for your answer.
ii) Give reasons why some people may disagree with you.

Examiner's hint: Remember this question must refer to a religious view of euthanasia. (A02)

2.10   Muslim attitudes to euthanasia

The main Muslim attitude to euthanasia is that it is not acceptable. Muslims regard all life as sacred. Muslims believe that Allah has plans for all humans and they should not interfere with his plans. Muslims believe it is important to show care for family members when they are ill.

There are many teachings in the Qur'an and Hadith that support the idea that euthanasia is wrong and most modern Muslim medical scholars agree, so the use of euthanasia is not supported.

However, modern Muslim scholars do agree that once life has ended it is wrong to keep a person alive artificially. Therefore they allow life-support machines to be turned off if a person is brain dead. This is because the life that Allah planned for the person has ended. The Islamic Medical Association says: 'when the treatment becomes futile, it ceases to be mandatory ...'.

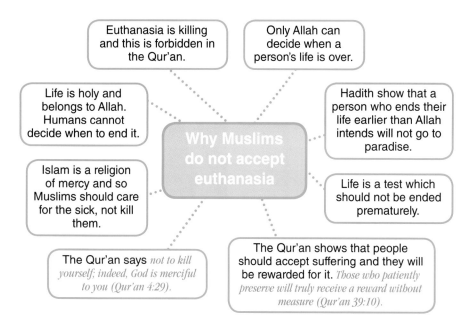

Euthanasia is killing and this is forbidden in the Qur'an.

Only Allah can decide when a person's life is over.

Life is holy and belongs to Allah. Humans cannot decide when to end it.

Hadith show that a person who ends their life earlier than Allah intends will not go to paradise.

Why Muslims do not accept euthanasia

Islam is a religion of mercy and so Muslims should care for the sick, not kill them.

Life is a test which should not be ended prematurely.

The Qur'an says *not to kill yourself; indeed, God is merciful to you (Qur'an 4:29)*.

The Qur'an shows that people should accept suffering and they will be rewarded for it. *Those who patiently preserve will truly receive a reward without measure (Qur'an 39:10).*

Knowledge check ✳

1 What are the Muslim attitudes to euthanasia?
2 List four reasons why most Muslims do not accept euthanasia.
  a) Describe the situation when some Muslims think that euthanasia might be acceptable.
  b) Explain why Muslims might accept euthanasia in this situation.
3 How do Muslims think that sick people should be treated?

When my grandmother was seriously ill she told me that I should place my trust in Allah. Allah gave us life and we should care for it as well as we can. My family and I helped my grandmother by giving her medicine and trying to make sure she was not in too much pain.

I realised it was in Allah's plans that when her term was finished he would reward her for her patience. It would have been wrong to interfere with Allah's plan for her so our family looked after her until she died.

Fairooza

A01

1 In small groups discuss Fairooza's comments about caring for her grandmother.
2 On an A3 sheet of paper, produce a mind map or poster to show Muslim attitudes to euthanasia. Ensure you include at least two references to the Qur'an.
3 Present your mind map or poster to the class.

A02

1 Play 'pass the buck' with an exam question.
2 Work in groups of four. Write on the top of a piece of paper the question 'Explain why some followers of one religion other than Christianity do not accept euthanasia'.
3 Each person has to write one reason on the paper and pass it to the next person who has to write a different reason.
4 When it gets back to the first person they have to change a reason to improve it and then pass it to the second who improves it again and so on.
5 When it gets back to the first person it should be a perfect answer which the entire group can write down.

exam practice b

Do you think that all religious people should allow the use of euthanasia? Give **two** reasons for your point of view.

Examiner's hint: The reasons you give in this b) question must refer to a religious point of view but you do have to agree with it. (A02)

exam practice c

Explain why some Muslims would allow the use of euthanasia.

Examiner's hint: This question does not have many reasons to support it so you would have to use references and examples to develop reasons in order to get full marks. (A01)

exam practice d

'All religious people should have the right to decide when their life should end.'
In your answer you should refer to at least one religion other than Christianity.
i) Do you agree? Give reasons for your answer.
ii) Give reasons why some people may disagree with you.

Examiner's hint: This question refers to religious people in the stimulus and 'one religion other than Christianity' in the question so you must discuss a religion other than Christianity to get full marks. (A02)

2.11 The media and matters of life and death

The media, which include television, film, newspapers and the internet, are highly influential. They provide information that educates people and helps them to form opinions.

There are people who say that the media should not criticise religious teachings about issues such as what happens after you die, abortion and euthanasia. Then there are other people who maintain that it is important that the media are allowed to criticise religious teachings.

● Arguments for and against the media being free to criticise what religions say about matters of life and death

The media need to explain what religions believe so that people are fully educated.	The opinions the media give can make religious people seem misguided and this encourages conflict.	The media may not give all the facts in a situation or may give inaccurate information about a religious view.
Religious groups use the media to explain their point of view, so it is only fair that the media criticise to give a balanced view.	Matters of life and death are very personal and the media could upset people very easily by criticising religious teachings.	The media can be one-sided and cause people to become confused.

The media have the right to express an opinion.

Knowledge check

1 What are the media?
2 Why is what the media say important?
3 Give three reasons why some people would say that the media should be allowed to criticise what religions say about matters of life and death.
4 Give three reasons why some people would say that the media should not be allowed to criticise what religions say about matters of life and death.

A01

Draw and complete a two-column table. List reasons in one column why people might argue that the media should criticise what religions say about matters of life and death. In the second column list reasons why people might argue that the media should not be allowed to criticise what religions say about matters of life and death. Use the information given to help you.

The following article reports on the activities of a religious association within a local community. It also gives quotes from both residents and members of the religious group.

School mums upset by abortion bumper stickers

An association that claims to have seen an apparition of the Virgin Mary has been criticised for displaying car bumper stickers about abortion near a primary school. The bumper stickers about abortion have upset neighbours and mothers at the school.

A local mother-of-three said: 'The first time I came up here I did not pay the women much attention.

'They are mostly old ladies, singing, and it all seemed quite sweet and innocent, but I have to say I was quite shocked by some of the bumper stickers.

'Everyone is entitled to an opinion but this kind of stuff is very right wing and fundamentalist. There is a primary school in this road and I would not want my kids exposed to such a narrow-minded view.'

One resident, who asked not to be named in case the association 'started praying' for him, said: 'Up to now they have simply been an irritant because they are always there at midday.

'If they want to go there every day and pray, fine, even if I think they are completely absurd, but to put up a notice saying "We pray for souls of aborted children" opposite a school, I think it is dreadful.'

A member from the association said: 'Abortion is the cause of the problems in the world and the Lord is helping us to provide the cure.'

When asked if she was worried about offending people, one association member said: 'Why should we be afraid when doing the work of the Lord?

'People don't like hearing the truth but the truth is the truth and it needs to be said.'

Adapted from
www.yourlocalguardian.co.uk

Why might some people think that the media should not write articles like the one above?

A02

1 In pairs, draw a consequence wheel (like the one below) around the idea of media criticising religious teaching on matters of life and death.

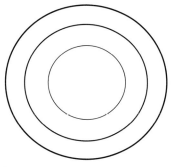

2 In the centre write: 'The media criticise what religions say about matters of life and death'.
3 In the next ring of the circle out, write down the immediate consequence of the criticism.
4 In the next ring out, write down what could be a consequence of the first consequence.
5 In the third ring, write down what could be a consequence of the consequence in the second ring.
6 Look at all the consequences of the media criticising what religions say about matters of life and death. Add any new reasons to the table you have already produced about whether the media should or should not criticise religions.

exam practice b

Do you think the media should criticise what religions say about matters of life and death? Give **two** reasons for your point of view.

Examiner's hint: Make sure you do not refer to individual people criticising religion. This is a question about the media. (A02)

exam practice c

Explain, with examples, why the media should be able to criticise what religions say about matters of life and death.

Examiner's hint: Make sure you give at least one example in your answer. It must refer to matters of life and death (these are life after death, abortion and euthanasia). (A01)

exam practice d

'The media should not criticise what religions say about matters of life and death.'
In your answer you should refer to at least one religion.
i) Do you agree? Give reasons for your answer.
ii) Give reasons why some people may disagree with you.

Examiner's hint: Develop your reasons by using examples, which come from this topic. (A02)

Examination practice

Below is guidance on how to answer the question a) from Section 2: Matters of life and death. All a) questions are worth 2 marks.

The a) questions are important as these are key words and they are used in the other questions. If you do not know what they mean then you will not be able to answer other questions on the paper.

Every section will have two a) questions and they will either ask for a definition of one of the key words or ask for two examples of the word. Look at the steps below about how to answer question 3a), then try answering question 4a).

Sample question

3a) What is euthanasia? [2]

Sample question

4a) What does quality of life mean? [2]

How to answer

The best way to get full marks on an a) question:

- ✓ Write the glossary definition supplied by the exam board – these are the ones used in this book.
- ✓ To get full marks you must provide all the information that is within the exam board's definition.
- ✓ If you leave out any information or the wording is not quite correct you may only get 1 mark out of 2.

Step 1

- ● Try to remember the key word definition.

Killing someone.

Step 2

- ● Read your answer. Could it mean something else? This could mean murder. Add words to it to make it clear that you do not mean murder.

Killing someone in a painless way, when they are dying of a painful illness.

Step 3

- ● Read your answer again. Does it include all the parts of the key word definition and is it clear? It is, but it would have been easier to learn by heart the key word definition and write it.

The painless killing of someone dying from a painful disease.

Examiner's comment

- ✓ **Learn the definitions used in this book as they are the same as those provided by the exam board.**
- ✓ **To get full marks you must provide all the information that is within the exam board's definition, even if you think there is a different definition for the same word.**

Below is guidance on how to answer the question b) from Section 2: Matters of life and death. As it is a b) question, it is worth 4 marks.

In every section there are two b) questions to choose from. Try question 3b) using the hints provided below. Then apply these steps to question 4b).

Sample question

3b) Do you think non-religious people should believe in life after death?   [4]

Sample question

4b) Do you think euthanasia should be allowed in the UK?   [4]

How to answer

To get full marks on a b) question, you must give your opinion and then support it with two reasons and develop each of the reasons.

Step 1

- Think of one reason why a non-religious person might believe in life after death. Make sure your reason is not religious.

A non-religious person might believe in life after death as it gives them comfort.

Step 2

- Think of a way to develop the reason. The easiest way to develop a reason is to give an example or a quote.

If a member of their family dies it may comfort them to know that they meet up with them in a future life.

Step 3

- Think of a second reason why a non-religious person might believe in life after death. Make sure your reason is not religious. Write the second reason as a new paragraph.

I also think a non-religious person might believe in life after death because they may have seen a ghost.

Step 4

- Develop your second reason. Ensure the development is about your reason. 'Ghosts' still answers the question of why a non-religious person may believe in life after death.

Ghosts which are shown on television programmes such as 'Most Haunted' provide a non-religious person with evidence for life after death.

Examiner's comment

- ✓ **Maximum marks will be awarded for two reasons which have been developed, as long as they answer the question.**
- ✓ **Development must link to the question set. For example: the second reason refers to ghosts; the development could not be a description of a ghost as this would not link back to why it would make a non-religious person believe in life after death.**

Religion and life

Section 3: Marriage and family life

3.1 Changing attitudes to marriage and family life

● **The main ways attitudes to family life have changed**

Over the past century attitudes to family life have changed dramatically. Statistics from the Office for National Statistics show fewer marriages and more **cohabitation**. A side-effect of this is that recent divorce statistics show there are fewer divorces (fewer marriages lead to fewer people divorcing). The Civil Partnership Act of 2004 gave same-sex couples the same rights as a married couple within a legal partnership, and this has also changed the way families are organised.

KEY WORDS

civil partnership A legal ceremony giving a homosexual couple the same legal rights as a husband and wife.

cohabitation Living together without being married.

contraception Intentionally preventing pregnancy from occurring.

homosexuality Sexual attraction to the same sex.

nuclear family Mother, father and children living as a unit

pre-marital sex Sex before marriage.

re-constituted family Where two sets of children become one family when their divorced parents marry each other.

re-marriage Marrying again after being divorced from a previous marriage.

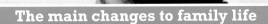

The main changes to family life

There are more single-parent families.

Some families have same-sex parents.

Many people get married more than once.

Many parents are unmarried.

Same-sex couples are able to have a **civil partnership**.

There are many **re-constituted families**.

More people get divorced.

People have sex before they are married.

● Why attitudes have changed

- Fewer people follow religious teachings about family life.
- Changes to the divorce laws mean divorce is easier and cheaper to obtain.
- More divorces lead to more single-sex parent families.
- More divorces lead to **re-marriage** and re-constituted families.
- Changes to the legal status of same-sex couples and a wider tolerance of **homosexuality** have made same-sex families acceptable.
- **Contraception** has meant that people can have **pre-marital sex** without the risk of becoming pregnant.
- More pre-marital sex leads to more single-parent families.
- The media show **nuclear families** are not the only acceptable family type.
- Adoption agencies must accept same-sex couples as possible parents.

● How attitudes have changed

British turn their back on marriage

It seems that there is a marked decline in the number of both men and women who are willing to marry. The Office for National Statistics has released figures showing that fewer people are getting married than at any other time in the past century.

In 2009, 231,490 couples were married, in 2008 this was 232,990. This is the lowest number since 1895.

The age people marry has slowly risen so that most women are almost 30 years old before they marry and men are on average 32.

The reasons suggested for these changes are many, but some people have blamed it on the cost of marrying, society's acceptance of cohabitation, women having careers, the media image of marriage as boring and even the lack of support for marriage from the government.

Knowledge check

1 What are the main changes to family life?
2 Why is divorce easier to obtain?
3 Which two changes have led to an increased number of single-parent families?
4 What factors have led to an increase in the number of same-sex couple families?

A01

Imagine you are a time traveller and have travelled from the 1920s to present day. The 1920s was a time when most families were nuclear families who lived near to their extended family (the rest of their family). People generally did not have sex before marriage as there was too great a risk of having children. Having children outside marriage was thought shameful. Male same-sex relationships were illegal. Couples did not divorce as it broke up families and went against religious teaching. The experience of the time traveller was that most people followed the normal behaviour at the time.

Write a report back to the people of the 1920s about the changes to families that have happened in the present day.

Include in your report:

✓ a description of the changes that have happened
✓ why there are more single-parent families
✓ why more people choose to live together rather than marry.

exam practice b

Do you think it is good that attitudes to family life have changed? Give **two** reasons for your point of view.

Examiner's hint: Give examples of changes that have happened that support your point of view to develop your reasons. (A02)

Two families from different eras. How has family life changed over the past 80 years?

A02

1 Look at this statement: 'Family life has changed too much in the last century'. Decide whether you agree with the statement or whether you do not agree with it.
2 Write down two reasons why you agreed or two reasons why you disagreed with the statement.

exam practice d

'Family life has changed too much.'
In your answer you should refer to at least one religion.
i) Do you agree? Give reasons for your answer.
ii) Give reasons why some people may disagree with you.

Examiner's hint: Make sure you give your opinion at the beginning of d) i) questions. (A02)

exam practice c

Explain how attitudes to family life have changed.

Examiner's hint: Write four ways that attitudes to family life have changed. This is an 'Explain how' question so does not need reasons. (A01)

3.2 Christian attitudes to sex outside marriage

Sex outside marriage means sex that does not occur with a person's marriage partner. This can be before marriage, when it is called pre-marital sex. It can also be during marriage with someone other than the person's marriage partner and this is called **adultery**. Christian attitudes towards sex outside marriage are connected to whether it is adultery or pre-marital sex.

Adultery

All Christians say that adultery is not acceptable. This is because:

- When a couple marry they promise **faithfulness**.
- Adultery goes against the Ten Commandments.
- Marriage is supposed to be an exclusive relationship.
- According to biblical teaching a married couple *become one flesh (Genesis 2:24)* and so should remain faithful.
- It causes suffering within the marital relationship.
- Jesus spoke against adultery in the Sermon on the Mount.

Pre-marital sex

Most Christians do not accept pre-marital sex because:

- They regard all sex outside marriage as fornication, which is not acceptable.
- The sexual act joins the couple as 'one flesh' and so must only occur in marriage.
- The New Testament says that a couple's relationship should not be immoral.
- Official teachings of the Catholic Church and the Church of England say that sexual relationships should be within a marital relationship as this is the proper place to raise a family.

KEY WORDS

adultery A sexual act between a married person and someone other than their marriage partner.

faithfulness Staying with your marriage partner and having sex only with them.

promiscuity Having sex with a number of partners without commitment.

Some Christians will accept sex before marriage in cases when the couple are committed to each other. In this case the sexual behaviour is not regarded as **promiscuity** as the couple are in a trusting and exclusive relationship. The reasons pre-marital sex is allowed in these kinds of relationship are as follows:

- The most important part of a relationship is love and a sexual relationship of this kind shows love.
- It can be seen as an important step towards the commitment of marriage.
- Society now accepts pre-marital sex and the Church should change with the times.
- Some Christians believe they should allow their conscience to decide what is right for them.

Knowledge check

1 What are the two different types of sex outside marriage?
2 What is adultery?
3 Why is adultery not acceptable to Christians?
4 Why do most Christians think that pre-marital sex is not acceptable?
5 Why do most Christians think that pre-marital sex is acceptable in a committed relationship?

A01

1 Carefully read the information about the different Christian attitudes on pages 58–59.
2 In pairs, looking at the information given, produce a crossword puzzle. The crossword puzzle must contain at least 12 questions in total. You should produce a blank puzzle, with questions to find the answers, which can be copied and used in class, and a completed one as an answer sheet.

Royal wedding: Archbishop backs William and Kate's decision to live together before marriage

The row came as Prince William and Kate Middleton unveiled their choices for the royal wedding service, which include classically British music and hymns, and an updated choice of marriage vows in which the bride omits the word 'obey'.

In a television interview, Dr Sentamu was asked whether it was appropriate for the Prince, who is in line to become head of the Church of England as King, to have been living with his bride before marriage.

He said he had conducted wedding services for 'many cohabiting couples' during his time as a vicar in south London.

'We are living at a time where some people, as my daughter used to say, they want to test whether the milk is good before they buy the cow,' he said. 'For some people that's where their journeys are.

'But what is important, actually, is not to simply look at the past because they are going to be standing in the Abbey taking these wonderful vows: "for better for worse; for richer for poorer; in sickness and in health; till death us do part".'

However, the Rev David Phillips, general secretary of the Church Society, a conservative evangelical group, said the Archbishop had 'missed an opportunity to set out Christian teaching'.

'What he said wasn't appropriate.' Mr Phillips said. 'He gave the impression it doesn't matter whether people live together before marriage. I thought he would have tried to get across Christian teaching on marriage that says it is not appropriate to have sex outside marriage.'

In another sign of their modern approach, the Prince and Miss Middleton published their order of service online for millions of people to join in at home.

The 28-page booklet confirms that Kate Middleton will follow the example of Diana, Princess of Wales by omitting the word 'obey' from her vows.

The Archbishop of York backed Prince William and Kate Middleton's decision to live together before marriage, saying that many modern couples want to 'test the milk before they buy the cow'.

Dr John Sentamu argued that the royal couple's public commitment to live their lives together today would be more important than their past.

But Anglican traditionalists criticised the Archbishop, the second most senior cleric in the Church of England, for failing to reinforce Christian teaching which prohibits sex outside marriage.

www.telegraph.co.uk

A02

1 In pairs discuss the different attitudes shown by the Archbishop of York and the organisation, the Silver Ring Thing. Which view do you agree with and why?
2 The Office for National Statistics shows that 75 per cent of people cohabit before they marry. Are you surprised by how high this statistic is? Do you think this statistic would be as high for Christians? Give reasons for your answer.
3 Produce a poster that could be used as part of an advertising campaign by Christians to encourage people to only have sex after marriage.

The Silver Ring Thing is an organisation that encourages Christians to wait until they are married before having sex. Their website says that 172,600 people have joined the organisation and committed not to have sex until they are married.

The people who have taken part in the Silver Ring Thing programme have committed to wait and wear a ring as a symbol and reminder of the promise they made to God to remain pure.

exam practice b

Do you think all Christians should disagree with sex outside marriage? Give **two** reasons for your point of view.

Examiner's hint: It is possible to give opposing opinions in your answer, for example:
I think Christians could agree with pre-marital sex because …
However I think they should not accept adultery because …
When you give opposing opinions in the same b) question it is important you make it clear that both opinions are your own. (A02)

exam practice c

Explain why most Christians do not accept sex outside marriage.

Examiner's hint: Start the answer by explaining what the key term in the question (sex outside marriage) means: it will not gain marks but will lead to a more coherent answer. (A01)

exam practice d

'No one should have sex outside marriage.'
In your answer you should refer to Christianity.
i) Do you agree? Give reasons for your answer.
ii) Give reasons why some people may disagree with you.

Examiner's hint: The instruction following the stimulus makes it clear that you must refer to Christianity in your answer. (A02)

3.3 Muslim attitudes to sex outside marriage

The Muslim attitude to sex outside marriage is that it is not acceptable. Sex with someone other than your marriage partner (zina) is considered to be haram – completely forbidden. It does not make any difference whether sex outside marriage refers to adultery or to pre-marital sex, Muslim teaching is the same.

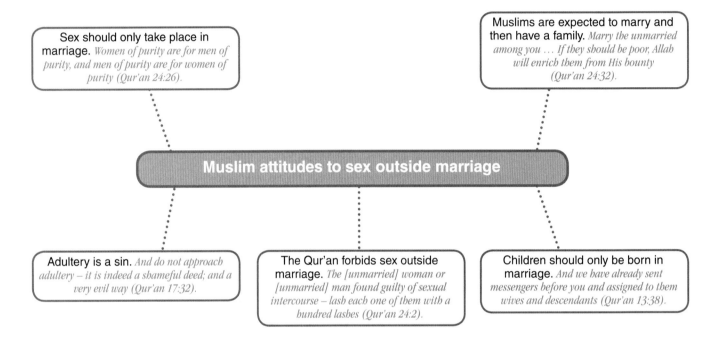

Muslims are expected to marry and then have a family. *Marry the unmarried among you … If they should be poor, Allah will enrich them from His bounty (Qur'an 24:32).*

Sex should only take place in marriage. *Women of purity are for men of purity, and men of purity are for women of purity (Qur'an 24:26).*

Muslim attitudes to sex outside marriage

Adultery is a sin. *And do not approach adultery – it is indeed a shameful deed; and a very evil way (Qur'an 17:32).*

The Qur'an forbids sex outside marriage. *The [unmarried] woman or [unmarried] man found guilty of sexual intercourse – lash each one of them with a hundred lashes (Qur'an 24:2).*

Children should only be born in marriage. *And we have already sent messengers before you and assigned to them wives and descendants (Qur'an 13:38).*

A01

Draw and complete a table to list the Muslim attitudes to sex outside marriage and the reasons for them. Use the information above to help you.

Knowledge check

1 What is the Muslim attitude to sex outside marriage?
2 What is the name given to sex with someone other than a marriage partner?
3 What does haram mean?
4 Describe the Muslim attitude to sex outside marriage in 50 words.
5 Give four reasons why Muslims think that sex outside marriage is wrong.

● Why Muslims do not accept sex outside marriage

As a Muslim the first person I kissed and the first person I slept with was my wife. This is because it is the right thing to do and it was what Allah wants.

Muslim teachings on sex before marriage protect us from emotional harm and physical hurt, families should be stable and it would not be good for society to have children before being married.

The Qur'an teaches that sex outside marriage is wrong and it lists punishments for it. This shows that Allah does not want good Muslims to have sex before marriage as well as showing that adultery is wrong.

Aaquil

By waiting to have a physical relationship my wife and I followed the command of Allah and started our married life in the right way.

A02

1 Read carefully Aaquil's explanation of why he did not have sex before he married his wife.
2 Make a list of Aaquil's reasons for not having pre-marital sex.
3 Number them to put them in order of which you think were most important.
4 Write a 50-word letter to Aaquil. In the letter explain why you agree or disagree with his point of view.

exam practice b

Do you think the attitude of one religion other than Christianity to sex outside marriage is good for families? Give **two** reasons for your point of view.

Examiner's hint: Be clear what the Muslim attitude is before you answer the question. (A02)

exam practice c

Explain why followers of one religion other than Christianity do not accept sex outside marriage.

Examiner's hint: Whenever the questions refer to one religion other than Christianity this means you must refer to Islam as that is the religion other than Christianity that you are studying. (A01)

exam practice d

'Religious people should not have sex outside marriage.'
In your answer you should refer to at least one religion other than Christianity.
i) Do you agree? Give reasons for your answer.
ii) Give reasons why some people may disagree with you.

Examiner's hint: The question asks that you refer to one religion other than Christianity. If you do not do this you cannot get more than 3 out of 6 marks. (A02)

3.4 Christian attitudes to divorce

● Different Christian attitudes to divorce

I think divorce should never happen. A couple should never end their marriage and re-marriage is not possible.

I think divorce should never happen. However I think that in some situations it might be better if a couple end their marriage. They would then be allowed to find happiness with another person but I don't think they should re-marry in a church.

I think divorce is not an ideal situation but it might be the best thing and re-marriage in church should be allowed.

● Reasons for the different Christian attitudes to divorce

Divorce should never happen and there should be no re-marriage	In some situations divorce might be allowed but no re-marriage in church	Divorce might be the best thing and re-marriage in church allowed
Marriage is a sacrament from God, so cannot be ended	*I tell you that anyone who divorces his wife, except for sexual immorality, and marries another woman commits adultery (Matthew 19:9)*	Re-marriage is allowed as it shows that the Church is forgiving
What God has joined together, let no one separate (Matthew 19:6)	It shows forgiveness	Orthodox Church law permits some re-marriage
Re-marriage when both the husband and wife are alive is adultery	It prevents suffering	The Church of England General Synod of 2002 said re-marriage is allowed in 'exceptional circumstances'
A husband must not divorce his wife. (1 Corinthians 7:11)	The Church can only recognise one marriage	The Baptist Church will re-marry divorced people if the minister feels it is appropriate

Knowledge check

1 What are the three Christian attitudes towards divorce?
2 Why do some Christians think divorce is always wrong?
3 Why do some Christians allow divorce but not re-marriage in church?
4 Why do some Christians allow divorce and re-marriage?

When Prince Charles married Camilla Parker-Bowles in 2005, they were not allowed to marry in a church. However, the government and the Church agreed to their re-marriage, even though both had been divorced. They had a church blessing after the civil ceremony.

'... to have and to hold from this day forward; for better, for worse, for richer, for poorer, in sickness and in health, to love and to cherish, till death do us part.'

Traditional Church of England wedding vows

The vows that a couple take during the Christian wedding service show they promise to stay with each other 'till death do us part' – why do you think so many marriages end in divorce?

A01

1 In pairs, produce a PowerPoint presentation to show the different Christian attitudes towards divorce and the reasons for them.
2 Add diagrams or pictures to illustrate the reasons.
3 Present your explanation of the different attitudes to the rest of the class.

A02

1 Draw and complete a table to list reasons why people might believe that people should be able to divorce and re-marry in church and reasons why they might disagree with this opinion.
2 Use this information to participate in a 'decision alley'. This is when the class divides in two, one side thinks of reasons why divorce should be acceptable for Christians and one thinks of reasons why it should not be acceptable. Each side then lines up shoulder to shoulder with an alley between. A member of the class then walks down the alley asking for advice from members on either side. When they get to the end they make a decision. At the end, the class can see what the majority view is.

exam practice b

Do you think all Christians should agree with divorce? Give **two** reasons for your point of view.

Examiner's hint: Make sure you give reasons whether Christians should agree rather than whether you agree. (A02)

exam practice c

Explain why some Christians do not agree with divorce.

Examiner's hint: This question needs reasons why some Christians do not agree with divorce – do not give reasons why they might not agree as you will not get any marks for them. (A01)

exam practice d

'Christians should never get divorced.'
In your answer you should refer to at least one religion.
i) Do you agree? Give reasons for your answer.
ii) Give reasons why some people may disagree with you.

Examiner's hint: The reasons should be based on Christian teachings. (A02)

3.5 Muslim attitudes to divorce

● Muslim attitudes to divorce

The Muslim attitude to divorce is partly based on Islamic teaching about marriage. All Muslims are expected to marry and raise children in a happy home.

Allah's apostle, Bukari, reported the Prophet Muhammad said, *O young people! Whoever among you can marry, should marry, because it helps him lower his gaze and guard his modesty.*

Marriage however is not usually regarded as only a religious event. Marriage or Nikah is a practical and legal ceremony during which the couple read the marriage contract. The couple can specify any terms and conditions for their partnership, and a gift of money (mahr) is paid to the wife by the husband.

Marriage is a special ceremony during which the couple are reminded of the purpose of marriage from the Qur'an that they are to be joined as Allah intended.

It is He who created you from a single soul, And made its mate of like nature in order that you might dwell with her in love … (Qur'an 7:189).

Divorce is allowed because:

A Muslim Nikah.

- Marriage is a legal contract which can be ended.
- The Qur'an explains the way a divorce can be given.
- The couple should not be in a marriage that is making them unhappy.
- Certain situations mean the marriage is not working, for example adultery.

All Muslims view divorce as a bad thing because:

- It splits up the family unit.
- It weakens the Muslim community.
- Prophet Muhammad said 'it is the most hated of all lawful things' (Abu Dawud).
- A husband and wife should be able to solve any problems they have.

Knowledge check ✳

1 Explain why Muslims are expected to marry.
2 What does the word nikah mean?
3 What happens during the marriage ceremony?
4 Why is divorce allowed in Islam?
5 Why is divorce regarded as a bad thing?

A01

1 In small groups discuss the Muslim attitude to divorce. Do you think it is a good view or not?
2 Draw a table to show the Muslim attitude to divorce and why divorce is not encouraged.

exam practice b

Do you think that Muslims should allow divorce? Give **two** reasons for your point of view.

Examiner's hint: The reasons you give should refer to Muslim reasons rather than non-religious ones. (A02)

exam practice c

Explain why the followers of one religion other than Christianity may allow divorce.

Examiner's hint: Using a quote like a reference to a Hadith is a good way to develop a reason. (A01)

● Divorce and its effects on society

Divorce has been shown to cause problems in families. There are higher rates of poverty, stress, illness, problems in school and law breaking in single-parent families.

After riots in British cities in 2011, Prime Minister David Cameron said 'most of these children come from lone-mother households'.

Divorce affects society as a whole because some children from divorced families do less well educationally, and as a result need more educational resources (money spent on them). These children may not achieve their full potential in society. Less well-educated children are more likely to break the law, which also has an impact on society.

Rioters and looters caused mayhem on the streets of London in August 2011.

A02

1 Research the effects that divorce has on a family and on society in general.
2 Produce a poster to show the advantages and disadvantages of allowing divorce.
3 Present the poster to the class.

exam practice d

'Divorce is not good for society.'
In your answer you should refer to at least one religion.
i) Do you agree? Give reasons for your answer.
ii) Give reasons why some people may disagree with you.

Examiner's hint: Repeating the question at the beginning of your answer helps to remind you what the point of the question is. (A02)

3.6 The importance of family life for Christians

Family life is the life that the parents and children have as a distinct group from the rest of society. Family life includes the things that the family do to socialise and educate children. For Christians, family life includes teaching children about God and to follow the Christian faith.

Why family life is important for Christians

The family is where children are raised to believe in God.

God started the family in the book of Genesis.

All Christian Churches teach that the family is an important part of society.

The family is the most secure place to have children.

They follow the example of the life of Jesus, who was raised in a family.

The Bible shows that parents and children have specific roles to care for each other.

The family is where children learn their morals; what is right and what is wrong.

A01

Write a newspaper article to explain the reasons why family life is important to Christians. The article should include examples of how Christian families are raised. You might need to refer to Section 1.1.
  Your article must include:

✓ a brief description of how Christians raise their children
✓ reasons why family life is important for Christians
✓ quotes as evidence for these reasons
✓ at least one illustration or picture.

The family is the community in which, from childhood, one can learn moral values, begin to honour God, and make good use of freedom. (Catechism of the Catholic Church 2207).

The family remains the most important grouping human beings have ever developed. Children thrive, grow and develop within the love and safeguarding of a family (Church of England website).

… put their religion into practice by caring for their own family … (1 Timothy 5:4).

A02

Prepare to answer the d)-type question: 'Family life is not important in today's society'.

1 In pairs, one person take on the role of a Christian who believes that family life is no longer important and the other person take on the role of a Christian who believes that family life is still important.
2 Each person has two minutes to convince the other that they must accept their point of view. The other person cannot interrupt or ask questions.
3 After two minutes each person can ask the other person two questions which the other person must answer.
4 At the end decide which argument was more convincing and why.

Write an answer for the d)-type question. In your answer you should refer to at least one religion.

i) Do you agree? Give reasons for your answer.
ii) Give reasons why some people may disagree with you.

exam practice b

Do you think family life is important for Christians? Give **two** reasons for your point of view.

Examiner's hint: Development must not be vague; make it specific to the point made. (A02)

exam practice c

Explain why family life is important for Christians.

Examiner's hint: Do not describe family life – answer the question by explaining why it is important. (A01)

exam practice d

'Having a family is the most important part of a Christian's life.' In your answer you should refer to at least one religion.
i) Do you agree? Give reasons for your answer.
ii) Give reasons why some people may disagree with you.

Examiner's hint: Give evidence or quotes to develop reasons. (A02)

3.7 The importance of family life for Muslims

Muslim family life means caring for each other and raising children in the faith. This means that parents have to make sure that their children have all they need to grow as good Muslims. In turn, the children will respect older generations and look after them when they are unable to care for themselves.

Why family life is important for Muslims

The family is where children are raised as good Muslims.

Families provide care and comfort to one another. The Qur'an says that on the Last Day they will be judged so they must do this to the best of their ability.

The Qur'an teaches that children should care for parents: *And We have enjoined upon man goodness to parents ... (Quran 29:8 & 46:15).*

A Hadith teaches that Muslims should take care of their mothers if they wish to enter paradise. 'Paradise lies at the feet of the mother.'

The Qur'an teaches *be kind to parents. When one or both of them attain old age in thy life, say not to them a word of contempt, nor repel them, but address them in terms of honour (Qur'an 17:23).*

Muslims should follow the example of the Prophet – *I have never seen anyone more kind to one's family than [the Prophet Muhammad] (Sahih Muslim, Hadith 1077).*

Knowledge check

1 What is meant by Muslim family life?
2 List three scriptural reasons (from the Qur'an or Hadith) which explain why Muslim family life is important.
3 List three other reasons which explain why Muslim family life is important.

A01

Work in pairs to produce an answer to the b)-type question 'Do you think family life is important for Muslims?'.

1 Using a large piece of paper take five minutes to write an answer to the question.
2 After five minutes pass the sheet to another pair who have the next five minutes to 'improve' the answer.
3 After five minutes pass the sheet to another pair who have the next five minutes to 'improve' the answer.
4 After the second re-write pass the answer back to the original pair. They can then look over the answer and write down the perfected answer in their notes.

A02

1 Work in a small group to produce a TV advert or bulletin explaining the importance of Muslim family life (which could possibly be videoed).
2 Divide the group into actors, video recorders and interviewers as needed.
3 Ensure the advert provides information about what family life includes as well as why it is important.

exam practice b

Do you think family life is important for followers of religions other than Christianity? Give **two** reasons for your point of view.

Examiner's hint: Remember when questions include the phrase 'religions other than Christianity', you should refer to Islam. (A02)

exam practice c

Explain why family life is important for Muslims.

Examiner's hint: If you can't remember any reasons try to imagine why you might think family life is important. It is likely to get you a few marks. (A01)

exam practice d

'Family life is the most important part of a religious person's life.'
In your answer you should refer to at least one religion other than Christianity.
i) Do you agree? Give reasons for your answer.
ii) Give reasons why some people may disagree with you.

Examiner's hint: A reason can be developed by quoting from scriptures, for example a reference from the Qur'an or Hadith. (A02)

3.8 Christian attitudes to homosexuality

There are three main different Christian attitudes to homosexuality. The different attitudes are each supported by different Church and biblical teachings.

● Christian attitudes to homosexuality and the reasons for them

Homosexuality is acceptable but homosexual sexual activity is not	Homosexuality is not acceptable	Homosexuality is acceptable
Civil partnerships are not equal to marriage	Civil partnerships are not equal to marriage	Civil partnerships are equal to marriage
Everyone is made in the image of God	Homosexuality is sinful	The Bible includes some examples of close same-sex relationships, for example, David and Jonathan, Ruth and Naomi, and Daniel and Ashpenaz
Pre-marital sex is not acceptable and homosexuals cannot marry in church	The Bible says that homosexuality is wrong	Science has shown that homosexuality is natural
Humans are made to reproduce. Homosexual sexual activity is not productive	*You shall not lie with a male as one lies with a female; it is an abomination (Leviticus 18:22)*	The Church of England General Synod agreed 'that homosexual orientation in itself is no bar to a faithful Christian life'
The Catechism of the Catholic Church states, 'tradition has always declared that homosexual acts are intrinsically disordered' (2357)	God created man and woman to be together, not man and man	'An act which (for example) expresses true affection between two individuals and gives pleasure to them both does not seem to us to be sinful by reason alone of the fact that it is homosexual' (*Towards a Quaker View of Sex*, 1963)

Knowledge check ✳

1 How many different Christian attitudes are there towards homosexuality?
2 What are the different attitudes towards homosexuality?
3 List three reasons why some Christians regard homosexuality as wrong.
4 List three reasons why some Christians regard homosexuality as acceptable.
5 List three reasons why some Christians regard homosexuality as acceptable but homosexual sexual activity as wrong.

A01

In small groups, create a poster to explain the three different Christian attitudes towards homosexuality. The posters should be aimed at people who have no understanding that Christians have different attitudes and should include reasons why Christians have different attitudes.

Gay couple wins discrimination case against Christian hoteliers

Devout Christian hotel owners who refused to allow a gay couple to share a double room acted unlawfully, a judge at Bristol county court ruled.

Martyn Hall and Steven Preddy, who are civil partners, won their landmark claim for discrimination in a case funded and supported by the Equality and Human Rights Commission (EHRC).

The owners of the private hotel in Cornwall, Peter and Hazel Bull, do not allow couples who are not married to share double rooms because they do not believe in sex before marriage.

The Bulls asserted that their refusal to accommodate civil partners in a double room was not to do with sexual orientation but 'everything to do with sex'. The restriction, the owners said, applied equally to heterosexual couples who are not married.

www.guardian.co.uk

A02

1 In pairs discuss the newspaper article above and think about the argument given by the hotel owners.
2 Think about Christian reasons for viewing homosexual activity as acceptable and reasons given for saying it is unacceptable. In your pair decide which are the best reasons and which are not so good.
3 Work on your own and write a list of the reasons in order starting with the best reason and finishing with the least good.
4 Draw a line across your list at the point at which you stop agreeing with the reasons.
5 Return to pair work and discuss why you have put your list in this order.

exam practice b

'Do you think all Christians should accept homosexuality?' Give **two** reasons for your point of view.

Examiner's hint: Start with: 'I think that Christians should …'. (A02)

exam practice c

Explain why there are different Christian attitudes to homosexuality.

Examiner's hint: Remember there are three different attitudes, not two, and you need to give reasons for all three of them. (A01)

exam practice d

'All Christians should accept homosexuality.'
In your answer you should refer to at least one religion.
i) Do you agree? Give reasons for your answer.
ii) Give reasons why some people may disagree with you.

Examiner's hint: Even if you are undecided you must either agree or disagree in the d) i) and give the opposite opinion in the d) ii). (A02)

3.9 Muslim attitudes to homosexuality

Muslim attitudes towards homosexuality are straightforward. The teachings of the Qur'an and Prophet Muhammad make it clear that homosexuality is not acceptable.

Reasons why most Muslims do not accept homosexuality

Allah created man and woman to be together, not man and man.

Prophet Muhammad condemned it.

Allah made people to procreate. A homosexual couple cannot procreate.

The Qur'an has passages that show homosexuality is wrong.

The Qur'an says *you approach men with desire, instead of women. Rather, you are a transgressing people (Qur'an 7:81).*

The Qur'an says it is wrong when it says *Do you approach males among the worlds, And leave what your Lord has created for you as mates? (Qur'an 26:165–66).*

Muslim scholars outlawed homosexuality. Because of this it is a crime in most Muslim countries.

A Hadith records: *The Messenger of Allah (peace and blessings of Allah be upon him) said, 'Whoever you find doing the action of the people of Loot, execute the one who does it and the one to whom it is done' (Abu Dawud).*

Knowledge check

1 What are the two attitudes to homosexuality in Islam?
2 Why do most Muslims think homosexuality is not acceptable?
3 Which references from scripture (Qur'an and Hadith) show that homosexuality is not acceptable?
4 Why do some Muslims accept homosexuality?

There are some individual Muslim people who will accept homosexuality but this is an individual decision in which a person will use their own conscience. There are a growing number of organisations and websites which support Muslims who accept homosexuality.

They say this because:

- It is acceptable in the society they live in.
- Islam is a religion of tolerance.
- They accept recent scientific developments about homosexuality.
- Allah will be the ultimate judge.
- Allah has created everyone.

A01

1 Read through the reasons that are given why the majority of Muslims do not accept homosexuality and only a few do.
2 Draw a table to show the two attitudes. Make sure you have at least four reasons in each column.

A02

In small groups produce a presentation to explain the Muslim attitudes towards homosexuality. Include explanations for all the specialist language that you use. You could include a PowerPoint presentation or references to the Qur'an in your presentation.

exam practice b

'Do you think followers of all religions should accept homosexuality?' Give **two** reasons for your point of view.

Examiner's hint: Start each reason on a new line. (A02)

exam practice c

Explain why some followers of one religion other than Christianity accept homosexuality and some do not.

Examiner's hint: Even though very few Muslims accept homosexuality make sure you know some reasons why some might. (A01)

exam practice d

'Religious people should not accept homosexuality.'
In your answer you should refer to at least one religion.
i) Do you agree? Give reasons for your answer.
ii) Give reasons why some people may disagree with you.

Examiner's hint: 'Religious people' is a phrase used to cover all religions but in a d) question you must refer to one specific religion. (A02)

3.10 Christian attitudes to contraception

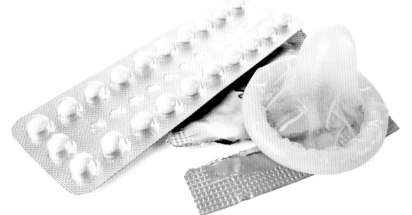

KEY WORDS

procreation Making a new life.

Contraception, which is also referred to as 'birth control', can be natural or artificial. Artificial contraception can involve chemical or barrier methods. These include the contraceptive pill, implants and condoms.

● Different Christian attitudes to contraception

Contraception is acceptable within a marriage because:

- It allows a couple to plan their family.
- It allows a couple to strengthen their marriage by having sexual love without worry.
- It protects the health of the mother.
- The Methodist Church states 'it is a welcome means towards fulfilment in marriage'.
- During the 1958 Lambeth conference of the Church of England it was said that 'the responsibility for deciding upon the number and frequency of children was laid by God upon the consciences of parents'.

However, some Christians who accept the use of contraception do not support the use of some contraceptive methods such as the morning-after pill, intrauterine devices (IUDs) and the progesterone-only pill. These methods do not prevent conception and so perhaps can be described as methods of early abortion rather than contraception.

Artificial contraception is not acceptable because:

- It interferes with God's plan for **procreation**.
- In the Bible God commanded people to *Be fruitful and multiply (Genesis 1:28)*.
- The Catholic Catechism describes artificial contraception as 'intrinsically evil' (Catechism of the Catholic Church 2370).
- It separates the unitive (joining, loving) aspects of sex from the procreative.

However, most Christians would accept the use of natural forms of contraception which involve abstinence (not having sex) and use of the woman's natural menstrual cycle. This form of contraception is natural, God provided it and it is still open to procreation.

Knowledge check

1 What are the two main Christian attitudes towards the use of contraception?
2 Why do most Christians think the use of contraception is acceptable?
3 Why do some Christians think the use of artificial contraception is not acceptable?
4 Why do some Christians who think the use of contraception is acceptable say that some forms of contraception are not acceptable?
5 Why do Christians who think the use of artificial contraception is not acceptable accept the use of natural contraception?

QuiverFull
(www.quiverfull.com)
QuiverFull is a Christian organisation which maintains that contraception is unnatural and that God should decide how many children a family has.

The Duggar family
(www.duggarfamily.com)
The Duggar family appear in a television programme about their daily lives. They do not support the use of contraception, and have (at the time of writing) nineteen children.

A01

You are a journalist and your newspaper has asked you to write an article about Christians who do not support the use of contraception, such as those involved in QuiverFull or the Duggar family.

In your article, you should include the reasons why people might support this group and the reasons why they may not. Use the two boxes of different reasons given in this section to help you.

A02

Imagine you have been employed to produce an advertising campaign to either encourage Christians to use contraception or encourage Christians not to use contraception. In groups, design either:

a) a poster campaign (a group of four posters that have a common theme); or
b) a text message campaign (a group of four texts that have a common theme); or
c) an internet pop-up campaign (a group of four pop-ups that have a common theme).

Explain your campaign to the rest of the class and decide which of the campaigns is the most effective.

exam practice b

'Do you think all Christians should object to the use of contraception?' Give **two** reasons for your point of view.

Examiner's hint: It is possible to agree and disagree with statements like this but it is easier to get marks if you stick to one point of view. (A02)

exam practice c

Explain why some Christians accept the use of contraception.

Examiner's hint: This question only wants reasons supporting the use of contraception so you will not get any marks for giving reasons saying contraception should not be used. (A01)

exam practice d

'All contraception should be acceptable to Christians.'
In your answer you should refer to at least one religion.
i) Do you agree? Give reasons for your answer.
ii) Give reasons why some people may disagree with you.

Examiner's hint: Make sure d) ii) has reasons for the opposite opinion to the one given in d) i). (A02)

3.11 Muslim attitudes to contraception

There are two main attitudes to contraception within Islam. One is that it is acceptable to married couples and the other is that it is completely unacceptable. Muslim attitudes towards pre-marital sex mean that the use of contraception is only an issue within marriage.

All Muslims are taught that raising children is an important part of Muslim life.

● Muslim attitudes to contraception and the reasons for them

Contraception is acceptable:
- Hadith show that the Prophet allowed contraception in the form of withdrawal (azl)
- Contraception may protect the health of the mother
- 'Contraception is permitted as an exception because of the likelihood of harm, so as to preserve her life, because Islam seeks to bring benefits and ward off harms' (Standing Committee for Academic Research and Issuing Fatwas)
- 'Eight out of nine of the Muslim classical legal schools permitted the practice of contraception' (*Family Planning, Contraception and Abortion in Islam*, Sa'diyya Shaikh)

Contraception is not acceptable:
- Children are a gift from Allah, it is not a person's choice to decide when they should have children
- Some methods are early abortions which is unacceptable. The Qur'an says *do not kill your children for fear of poverty. We provide for them and for you (Qur'an 17:31)*
- All Muslims should have a family as Allah intended
- Prophet Muhammad had children. Muslims should follow this example. *And indeed We sent messengers before you and made for them wives and offspring (Quran 13:38)*

Knowledge check

1 In Islam what are the two main attitudes towards contraception?
2 List four reasons why a Muslim might say that contraception is acceptable.
3 List four reasons why a Muslim might say that contraception is not acceptable.
4 Write out one quote which can be used as a reason why contraception is acceptable and explain why it is used.
5 Write out one quote which can be used as a reason why contraception is not acceptable and explain why it is used.

A01

1 Read through the reasons for the different Muslim attitudes towards the use of contraception on page 78. Note which reasons have quotes as evidence to develop the reasons.
2 In pairs, use the information given above to produce a PowerPoint presentation or poster to explain the different attitudes Muslims have towards the use of contraception.
3 Use the PowerPoint slides or poster to give a presentation to the class explaining the different Muslim attitudes towards the use of contraception.

We use contraception which is not permanent so one day we can have a family which is Allah's will; we use contraception that prevents fertilisation as I think other methods are not good as they end life.

When we married we were told that the Qur'an says that Allah will help us with a family. It says he will 'provide for them and for you'. We have chosen not to use contraception and if we have a family then that is what God's plan for us is. We know that by doing this we are following the example of Prophet Muhammad who had a family and that we will be rewarded for doing this.

When my husband and I married we decided we would like to have a large family but not yet. The Prophet (peace be upon him) allowed his followers to use contraception when he was here so followers are allowed to use it today.

A02

1 Draw two spidergrams to record the two different Muslim attitudes towards the use of contraception.
2 Use this information to participate in a 'decision alley'. This is when the class divides in two, one side thinks of reasons why contraception is acceptable for Muslims and the other side thinks of reasons why it should not be acceptable. Each side then lines up shoulder to shoulder with an alley between. A member of the class then walks down the alley asking for advice from members on either side. When they get to the end they make a decision.

exam practice b

'Do you think followers of one religion other than Christianity should accept the use of contraception?' Give **two** reasons for your point of view.

Examiner's hint: A quote is a good way to develop a reason. (A02)

exam practice c

Explain why the followers of one religion other than Christianity do not accept the use of contraception.

Examiner's hint: In questions about 'one religion other than Christianity' it is a good idea to name the religion you are referring to. (A01)

exam practice d

'Contraception should be accepted by all religious people.'
In your answer you should refer to at least one religion.
i) Do you agree? Give reasons for your answer.
ii) Give reasons why some people may disagree with you.

Examiner's hint: Even though the phrase 'all religious people' seems general you must refer to a specific religion in your answer. (A02)

Examination practice

Below is guidance on how to answer the question c) from Section 3: Marriage and family life. As it is a c) question it is worth 8 marks.

In every section there are two c) questions to choose from. Try question 5c) using the hints provided below. Then apply these steps to question 6c).

Sample question
5c) Explain why some Christians accept homosexuality.   [8]

Sample question
6c) Explain why some Christians allow divorce.   [8]

How to answer
There are several ways to get full marks on a c) question. One way is to give two separate reasons and develop each one of them.

Step 1
● Think of one reason some Christians accept homosexuality.

Some Christians think that in the Bible there are examples of close same-sex relationships.

Step 2
● Think of a way to develop the reason. This needs to expand the reason and still answer the question.

If there are same-sex relationships like David and Jonathan in the Old Testament then homosexuality should be accepted.

Step 3
● Think of another reason why some Christians accept homosexuality. Make sure you start a new line with your second reason.

Also, the General Synod of the Church of England has accepted homosexual relationships.

Step 4
● Develop the second reason. A quote is a good way to develop a reason.

It has said that being a homosexual is 'no bar to a faithful Christian life'.

Examiner's comment
✓ **Maximum marks will be awarded for two reasons which have been developed, as long as the quality of the written communication is good.**
✓ **Each reason is started on a new line. This will help examiners to identify new reasons.**
✓ **Good use of examples and quotes to develop reasons.**

Below is guidance on how to answer the question d) from Section 3: Marriage and family life. As it is a d) question, it is worth 6 marks.

In every section there are two d) questions to choose from. Each is divided into two parts d i) and d ii).

Sample question

5d) 'No religious person should be a homosexual.' In your answer you should refer to at least one religion.

   i) Do you agree? Give reasons for your opinion. [3]

   ii) Give reasons why some people may disagree with you. [3]

How to answer

There are a few things to always include in a d) question.

● Start with your opinion in d) i).

● You must read the sentence following the statement. If it says 'you should refer to at least one religion' then you must clearly refer to any one religion. If it says 'you should refer to at least one religion other than Christianity' then you must clearly refer to a religion that is not Christianity. If it says 'you should refer to Christianity' then you must clearly refer to Christianity.

The easiest way to get full marks is to give three brief reasons for d) i) and three brief reasons for d) ii).

Question 5 d) i)

Step 1

● Think whether you agree or disagree and one reason to support your opinion. Make sure you write down that it is your opinion at the beginning.

I disagree. I think all religious people are created in the image of God and he chooses for some people to be homosexual.

Step 2

● Think of a second reason; make sure it is not the same as the first reason.

Secondly, some Christian Churches like the Quakers and Church of England agree, so I think all Christians should.

Step 3

● Think of a third reason why you disagree with the statement. Write every reason as a new paragraph.

Finally, science has shown that homosexuality occurs in nature so it must be acceptable.

Question 5 d) ii)

Step 1

● This must include reasons for the opposite opinion to the one you gave as your opinion in d) i).

Some people agree with the statement. They think all religious people are created by God to 'be fruitful and multiply' and homosexuals cannot do this.

Step 2

● Think of a second reason; make sure it is not the same as the first reason.

Secondly, some Christians would say that God created a man and a woman to be together and this is what should happen.

Step 3

● Think of a third reason why a person would agree with the statement. Make it clear it is a third reason by starting with 'finally' or 'thirdly'.

Finally, some Pentecostal Churches say that homosexuality is sinful so it is wrong to be actively homosexual.

Examiner's comment

✓ **The candidate has clearly stated their own personal view; without this they cannot get full marks.**

✓ **Maximum marks will be awarded as each side of the argument has three reasons.**

Section 4: Religion and community cohesion

4.1 Changing roles of men and women in the UK

● **How the roles of men and women have changed**

The roles of men and women, or ways that they behave, have changed significantly over the past century, particularly since the 1950s. There are many reasons for these changes in roles and, as a result of these changes, family life has also altered.

A family in the 1950s.

The general picture of the 1950s' family is a family with two parents and three or more children. The mother does not work; if she does it is part time. Women's jobs were those that were seen as appropriate for women, usually domestic, teaching, nursing or secretarial. As a part-time worker a person would be paid less and have fewer employment rights. A couple would be unlikely to divorce as it was not socially acceptable, people were **prejudiced** against it. As a result there were few one-parent families or re-marriages. The role of the mother was to look after the family and the role of the father was to provide for it.

> **KEY WORDS**
>
> **discrimination** Treating people less favourably because of their ethnicity/gender/colour/sexuality/age/class.
>
> **prejudice** Believing some people are inferior or superior without even knowing them.
>
> **sexism** Discriminating against people because of their gender (being male or female).

In the 1950s ...
- A woman was likely to work until she married and then remain at home to raise a family.
- Women mostly worked part time rather than full time.
- One-third of women worked.
- Life expectancy was 65 years.
- Women were the main carers for children and elderly members of the family.
- The average age for marriage was 25.
- Divorce was difficult to obtain.
- Out of about 630 Members of Parliament (MPs) only 24 were women.

Office for National Statistics

In the 2010s …
- Women are likely to work full time.
- Women are less likely to have top jobs in firms (in 2008 only 10 per cent of the largest companies were led by women).
- Life expectancy is 80 years.
- Men often share caring for children and elderly members of the family.
- The average age for marriage is 31.
- Divorce has increased by 368 per cent since 1950.
- Re-marriage has increased by 62 per cent since 1950.
- 143 MPs were women (in 2010).
- Sexual **discrimination** (**sexism**) at work is illegal.

Office for National Statistics

The average family in the 2010s is a family with two parents and two or more children. The parents may not be in their first marriage. The mother works, possibly part time or full time. Women's jobs can be in any field but they are unlikely to earn as much as men or be in the top positions of responsibility.

A couple may divorce and children may have step-parents. The role of both the mother and the father is to provide for the family financially and to care for children and any elderly relatives, although statistics show the mother is still the main carer.

Knowledge check

1 What is meant by a person's role?
2 What was the main role of a woman in 1950?
3 What was the main role of a man in 1950?
4 What was the main role of a woman in 2010?
5 What was the main role of a man in 2010?
6 List four facts about 1950 that show what a woman's role was like.
7 List four facts about 2010 that show what a woman's role was like.

● Why the roles of men and women have changed in the UK

The Divorce Reform Act of 1969 made divorce easier to obtain.

The availability of contraception in the 1960s meant women could control when they had a family.

People are living longer so women are more likely to have to care for the elderly.

Why the roles of men and women have changed

The Equal Pay Act (1970) meant women had to be paid the same as men for the same job.

The Sex Discrimination Act (1975) meant that women have an equal right to jobs.

The feminist movement has worked to secure equal rights for women socially and politically.

The social perception that there are men's jobs and women's jobs has disappeared because of legal action against sexism.

Paid paternity leave (introduced in 2011) means that employers must allow the father two weeks' paid time off work.

A01

Imagine you are a museum historian. You need to write a leaflet for year 7 students visiting the museum who are studying the 1950s.
   The leaflet should explain:

✓ what the roles of men and women were in the 1950s
✓ how the roles of men and women have changed
✓ why the roles of men and women have changed.

A02

Prepare for a class debate on: 'The roles of men and women have not really changed'.

1 Write the debate title as a heading and then draw a table listing reasons to support the statement and reasons to argue against the statement.
2 Hold the debate. Ensure there is a chairperson and at least two people to speak on the issue. Ask questions of the speakers before taking a class vote.

exam practice b

Do you think men and women's roles have changed? Give **two** reasons for your point of view.

Examiner's hint: Make sure you start your answer with 'I think …'. (A02)

exam practice c

Explain why the roles of men and women have changed in the UK.

Examiner's hint: Write two reasons and develop each one with an example. (A01)

exam practice d

'Men have the same role as women in the UK.'
In your answer you should refer to at least one religion.
i) Do you agree? Give reasons for your answer.
ii) Give reasons why some people may disagree with you.

Examiner's hint: Start each reason on a new line. (A02)

An office in the 1950s: a female secretary serves tea to her male boss. Has working life changed in the past 50 years?

4.2 Christian attitudes to equal rights for women in religion

● Different Christian attitudes to equal rights for women in religion

There are three main Christian attitudes towards the role that women should play in religion. Different Christians have various reasons for having these attitudes.

Women should have different rights from men	Women should have equal rights in religion	Women should have equal rights but they are different from men
Some Christians teach that women should not be religious leaders. They believe that the role of a woman in religion is to raise a family in a Christian way. Women should be silent in church, which means they cannot be ministers or priests.	Other Christians teach that women can be religious leaders. They believe that the role of a woman is the same as a man. Women can teach in church and can be ministers or priests.	Some Christians, including Roman Catholics, believe that women are equal to men but have different roles. Although they cannot be priests, women can join a religious community as nuns and they have a variety of roles in the church such as reading, serving and leading children's services.

Why women should have different rights from men	Why women should have equal rights in religion	Why women should have equal religious rights but they are different from men
Jesus only chose men to be his apostles	Jesus had both male and female followers. Only men were apostles because of the culture at the time	Jesus was a man; the priest represents Jesus in the Mass
St Paul taught *women should remain silent in the churches. They are not allowed to speak, but must be in submission* (1 Corinthians 14:34)	Men and women were both created in the 'image of God'	The teaching of the Catholic Church, as explained in the Catechism of the Catholic Church, says *'the ordination of women is not possible' (1577)*
St Paul taught women should submit to their husbands: *Wives, submit yourselves to your own husbands as you do to the Lord (Ephesians 5:22)*	St Paul taught that *There is neither ... male and female. For you are all one in Christ Jesus (Galatians 3:28)*	Men and women were created to be different from each other. This is shown in the book of Genesis
In Genesis, God created man first and made woman to be a companion to him	Early Christian councils reported there being women deacons. If the early Church had women ministers so can the modern one	Jesus only chose men to be his apostles. If he had wanted women leaders he would have gone against the custom of the time as he did with other things

A01

1 In small groups discuss the different Christian attitudes to equal rights for women in religion. Which attitude do you most agree with? Why?
2 Draw a poster to describe different Christian attitudes to equal rights for women in religion. Include descriptions of the different attitudes and reasons for them, and illustrate them with quotes.

Knowledge check ✳

1 What are the three Christian attitudes towards the religious role of women?
2 Describe what Christians who think women have different rights from men believe.
3 Describe what Christians who think women have equal rights to men believe.
4 Describe what Christians who think women have equal rights but that they are different rights from men believe.

Women priests to match males by 2025

When Geraldine Granger became the female vicar of television's fictional Dibley, her congregation greeted her arrival with a combination of surprise and fury.

Within 20 years, however, most villagers in England will be more surprised if their new vicar is not a woman.

According to a report due for release this autumn, there will be as many female priests as male by 2025. The study, entitled Religious Trends, concludes that without the rapid growth in the number of women being ordained – as many women will be becoming priests as men by the end of the decade – some parishes would be forced to close.

The situation is very different from that in 1994 when *The Vicar of Dibley*, the BBC comedy starring Dawn French, first aired. Then, a tiny proportion of priests were women. Even seven years ago, just 10 per cent of the Church's 9,500 clergy were women. Some dioceses, many of them in rural locations, already report a higher number of women being ordained than men.

The report estimates that by 2016 one in every three priests will be a woman. This year, 47 per cent of new priests have been female. In the Bath and Wells diocese, 13 out of the 16 priests ordained have been women. In Wakefield, it is 10 out of 14.

The Rev. Charlie Allen, 27, a vicar in the village of Portchester, Hampshire, said that her decision to be ordained had been met with some surprise, but that being a woman priest had become much easier.

'It is not the obvious job that parents expect their daughters to do,' she said.

'The traditional stereotype of the middle-aged male priest is part of the Church's historical legacy, so when I started five years ago people would be surprised to see a young female priest. That is no longer the case. It has ceased to be a great unknown or something for people to fear or be worried about.'

www.telegraph.co.uk

A02

Read through the reasons for different Christian attitudes to women in religion on page 86 and the newspaper article above. Note the arguments given for and against women priests.

1 Prepare to answer questions about the different Christian attitudes to women's roles in religion in a hot-seat situation.
2 Decide which attitude you will support and will answer questions on.
3 Make a list of the reasons why you would have that attitude rather than the alternatives.
4 Take part in the hot-seat discussion either as the person in the hot seat being questioned or as the questioner.

exam practice c

Explain why some Christians do not accept that women should have equal rights in religion.

Examiner's hint: Only give reasons why some Christians do not accept that women should have equal rights in religion. You would get no marks for reasons why some do accept that women should have them. (A01)

exam practice b

Do you think women should have equal rights in Christianity? Give **two** reasons for your point of view.

Examiner's hint: Make sure you give answers about religion, not about general equal rights. (A02)

exam practice d

'Women should have the same rights as men in religion.'
In your answer you should refer to Christianity.
i) Do you agree? Give reasons for your answer.
ii) Give reasons why some people may disagree with you.

Examiner's hint: Make sure you include reference to Christianity in your answer. (A02)

4.3 Muslim attitudes to equal rights for women in religion

There are two main attitudes to equal rights for women in Islam. Both are based on the idea that all Muslims are equal before Allah so all people, male and female, are equal. One is not better than the other.

● Reasons for the different Muslim attitudes to equal rights for women in religion

Women are equal but different so have different roles to play	Women are equal and can have equal religious roles to men
Men and women were created differently and so should have different roles	There is evidence that the Prophet allowed women to lead prayers in a household which contained men and women
A woman should have a family and care for children as this is how she is created biologically	In early Islamic history, a few Muslim groups allowed women leaders, so why not now?
Women should be protected by men as they are physically weaker	Women are allowed to teach men about the faith so why not allow them to lead obligatory prayers?
Traditionally men, not women, have always been imams	It is written in a Hadith *All people are equal*
Scholars have written 'it is not permissible for a woman to lead a man in obligatory prayer'	There are examples of women around the world, particularly in China and Canada, who are effective imams

● Quotes supporting the different Muslim attitudes to equal rights for women in religion

Jabir ibn Abdullah: *A woman may not lead a man in Prayer, nor may a Bedouin lead a believer of the Muhajirun or a corrupt person lead a committed Muslim in Prayer (Ibn Majah).*

Abu Huraira said: *The best rows for men are the first rows, and the worst ones the last ones, and the best rows for women are the last ones and the worst ones for them are the first ones.*

O mankind, fear your Lord, who created you from one soul and created from it its mate and dispersed from both of them many men and women (Qur'an 4:1).

The Prophet said: *The seeking of knowledge is obligatory for every Muslim (Al-Tirmidhi, Hadith 74).*

Men are in charge of women by [right of] what Allah has given one over the other and what they spend [for maintenance] from their wealth (Qur'an 4:34).

The Prophet also said: *Acquire knowledge and impart it to the people (Al-Tirmidhi, Hadith 107).*

Whoever does righteousness, whether male or female, while he is a believer – We will surely cause him to live a good life, and We will surely give them their reward [in the Hereafter] according to the best of what they used to do (Qur'an 16:97).

First woman to lead Friday prayers in UK

A Canadian author will become the first Muslim-born woman to lead a mixed-gender British congregation through Friday prayers tomorrow in a highly controversial move that will attempt to spark a debate about the role of female leadership within Islam.

Raheel Raza, a rights activist and Toronto-based author, has been asked to lead prayers and deliver the khutbah at a small prayer session in Oxford.

She has been invited by Dr Taj Hargey, a self-described imam who preaches an ultra-liberal interpretation of Islam which includes, among other things, that men and women should be allowed to pray together and that female imams should lead mixed congregations in prayer.

Three of the four mainstream schools of Sunni Islam allow women to lead exclusively female congregations for prayer, but the overwhelming majority of Muslim jurists are opposed to the notion of their presiding over mixed congregations outside the home.

Raza, 60, is part of a small but growing group of Muslim feminists who have tried to challenge the mindset that has traditionally excluded women from leadership roles within the mosque. They argue that nowhere in the Qur'an are female imams expressly forbidden. Instead scholars rely on the hadiths (the words and sayings of the Prophet Muhammad) to exclude women – although Muslim feminists and some progressive scholars argue that even these are not clear enough to say with confidence that women are altogether banned.

'It was a very profound experience,' Ms Raza said yesterday in a telephone conversation from her home in Toronto. 'It's not about taking the job of an imam. It's about reminding the Muslim community that 50 per cent of its adherents are women who are equal to men. Women are equally observant, practising Muslims who deserve to be heard.'

www.independent.co.uk

A01

1 Draw a table with the following headings: 'Quotes supporting why woman are equal but have different roles to play' and 'Quotes supporting why woman can have equal religious roles to men'.
2 Complete the table.

A02

1 Read the article above carefully. Then in pairs, draw a consequence wheel (see page 52) around the idea of women leading prayers. A consequence wheel is a circle made up of a centre and three concentric rings around it.
2 In the centre, write: 'Women should not be able to lead prayers'.
3 In the next ring of the circle out, write down the immediate consequence of thinking this statement is true.
4 In the next ring out, write down what could be a consequence of the first consequence.
5 In the third ring, write down what could be a consequence of the consequence in the second ring.
6 Look at all the consequences and decide whether you agree with the original statement or not.

Knowledge check

1 What are the two Muslim attitudes to equal rights for women in religion?
2 Make a list of four reasons for Muslims believing that women have different rights from men.
3 Make a list of four reasons for Muslims believing that women have equal rights to men.

exam practice b

Do you think women should have the same religious rights as men? Give **two** reasons for your point of view.

Examiner's hint: This question is about religious rights. It asks if women should be able to do the same things in religion as men. Do not refer to things that are cultural rather than religious. (A02)

exam practice d

'Women should not have the same religious rights as men.'
In your answer you should refer to at least one religion other than Christianity.
i) Do you agree? Give reasons for your answer.
ii) Give reasons why some people may disagree with you.

Examiner's hint: Make sure you start your answer to d) i) with 'I think …'. (A02)

exam practice c

Choose one religion other than Christianity and explain why some of its followers believe in equal religious rights for men and women.

Examiner's hint: Start by stating the chosen religion is Islam. (A01)

4.4 The UK as a multi-ethnic society

The UK has historically always been a place where people of many nationalities and ethnicities have lived. As an island it has been a place that people have travelled to and moved to for many reasons.

In the past, Britain has been a place groups have conquered and started new lives in. British kings and queens have ruled over other countries and the people of those countries have travelled to the UK to live. More recently, people have come to the UK to work and for a better standard of living. Others have come to the UK to escape conflict and persecution.

The 2001 census revealed the mixture of ethnicities living in the UK (see the table below).

KEY WORDS

ethnic minority A member of an ethnic group (race) which is much smaller than the majority group.

multi-ethnic society Many different races and cultures living together in one society.

racism The belief that some races are superior to others.

Breakdown for England and Wales	
Those who say they are White:	%
White British	87.5
White Irish	1.2
White other	2.6
Those who say they are Asian:	
Indian	2.0
Pakistani	1.4
Bangladeshi	0.5
Other Asian	0.5
Those who say they are Black:	
Caribbean	1.1
African	0.9
Other Black	0.2
Those who say they are mixed race:	
White/Black Caribbean	0.5
White/Asian	0.4
Other mixed	0.3
Other ethnicities:	
Chinese	0.4
Other ethnic groups	0.4

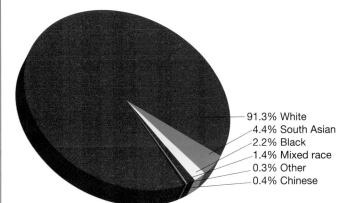

91.3% White
4.4% South Asian
2.2% Black
1.4% Mixed race
0.3% Other
0.4% Chinese

Ethnicity in England and Wales, according to the 2001 census.

Knowledge check

1 What is an **ethnic minority**?
2 Has there always been a mixture of races or ethnic groups within England and Wales?
3 Give three reasons why there is a mixture of ethnic groups within England and Wales.
4 What were the main ethnic groups within England and Wales in 2001?
5 Give three examples of ethnic minorities in England and Wales in 2001.

A01

In pairs, produce a PowerPoint or poster presentation to explain that the UK is a **multi-ethnic society**. Add diagrams or pictures to illustrate your ideas. The Office for National Statistics (www.ons.gov.uk) has more data that you can add into your presentation including statistics about your local area. Present your PowerPoint or poster to the rest of the class.

● The problems of discrimination and racism

Treating people less favourably because of their ethnicity or discriminating against someone because of their race is a problem that arises in countries that have many races living together (multi-ethnic societies). When discrimination is because of a person's race or ethnic background it is often called **racism**.

Racism happens for many reasons: some people say it is the way a person is brought up. Others think it happens because of a lack of education. Some say it is a reaction to people that are different from themselves. Whatever the reason for it, discrimination causes problems in society; it is unfair, often illegal and causes much unhappiness.

Show Racism the Red Card is a campaign that aims to end racism in football and society by educating the population and putting pressure on individuals and organisations to take action to end racism. Do you think education is able to stop racism in the UK?

exam practice b

Do you think discrimination causes problems in society? Give **two** reasons for your point of view.

Examiner's hint: Make sure you know what all the key words mean as they will be used in questions. (AO2)

exam practice c

Explain why discrimination causes problems in the UK.

Examiner's hint: You can use examples from the news or your own experience to develop reasons. (AO1)

exam practice d

'Education cannot end the problem of racism.'
In your answer you should refer to at least one religion.
i) Do you agree? Give reasons for your answer.
ii) Give reasons why some people may disagree with you.

Examiner's hint: Make sure you include a religious reason even though the question does not easily lead to a religious response. (AO2)

It leads to people being left out of society.

It means unfair judgements about a person are made.

It can lead to people not having the same chances in education as others.

Problems caused by discrimination and racism

It prevents society working as efficiently as it otherwise could.

It might lead to conflict between people.

It means that individuals are not valued for who they are.

AO2

1 Read the problems caused by discrimination and racism and pick out the three worst problems caused by racism and discrimination (or possibly find other reasons).
2 Write a list of reasons why you think these are the worst problems.
3 Write a speech, lasting three minutes, which could be presented to the class, explaining: 'The worst problems caused by racism'.

4.5 Community cohesion in the UK

In August 2011, rioting spread across UK cities. This resulted in shops being looted, buildings being set alight and violence on the streets. One such occasion in Birmingham resulted in the death of three young Asian men. In the face of this terrible tragedy, the father of one of these young men had the courage and generosity of spirit to call for calm. Below are the words of Tariq Jahan.

Riots: a father's plea

My son Haroon Jahan was 21 years old and a good lad. Everybody in the community knew him. All the street were out and basically he was looking out for the whole community.

He stood up for the community and unfortunately last night was killed with two of his friends. Basically, he was defending his community and people round here. They smashed into the petrol station and the social club.

Because he was a young chap he was inclined to join the community of all the locals round here, everyone was out on the corner and a car came out of nowhere for God knows what reason.

Something happened. I didn't see it with my own eyes. I was round the corner … I heard the car coming at high speed.

I heard the thud, ran round and I saw three people on the ground.

My instinct was to help the three people. I didn't know who they were or if they'd been injured. I was helping the first man and someone came up behind me and told me my son was lying behind me.

So I started CPR on my own son, my face was covered in blood, my hands were covered in blood. Why? Why?

The guy who killed him drove directly into the crowd and killed three innocent guys. Why? What was the point of doing that? I don't understand.

We're here defending the community from all the problems going on in this country. He was trying to help his community.

He was a good kid. He was very, very intelligent, very smart.

He was the youngest, and anything I ever wanted done, I would always ask Haroon to sort it out for me.

He was a good kid, everyone knew him and loved him. I can't describe to anyone what it feels like to lose your son. I miss him deeply but one or two days from now the whole world will forget – no one will care.

I don't blame the government, I don't blame the police, I don't blame anybody.

I'm a Muslim. I believe in divine fate and destiny, and it was his destiny and his fate, and now he's gone.

And may Allah forgive him and bless him.

Tensions are already high in the area. It's already bad enough what we are seeing on the streets without other people taking the law into their own hands.

My family wants time to grieve for my son. People should let the law deal with this.

Today we stand here to plead with all the youth to remain calm, for our communities to stand united.

This is not a race issue. The family has received messages of sympathy and support from all parts of society.

I lost my son. Blacks, Asians, whites – we all live in the same community. Why do we have to kill one another? Why are we doing this? Step forward if you want to lose your sons. Otherwise, calm down and go home – please.

Taken from a transcript of Tariq Jahan's words

● Community cohesion

As can be seen by examples of civil unrest such as Brixton in 1981 and the riots around Britain in the summer of 2011 (see the article on page 92), differences between people, whether due to ethnic type or other factors such as religion, have caused conflicts and problems within the community.

Political leaders recognise that these problems have become so serious that they must do something to ensure that all people have the right to be treated equally and to bring communities together.

The idea of everyone accepting others' differences and trying to gain from the different outlooks of other people is called **community cohesion**. One benefit of community cohesion is that it encourages people to work together for the good of everyone.

> **KEY WORDS**
>
> **community cohesion** A common vision and shared sense of belonging for all groups in society.

Government action has been taken to encourage community cohesion and also to punish those who show discrimination. Much of government action has been to pass laws that force people to treat others equally.

Schools now have a duty to promote community cohesion.

The government supports the European Convention on Human Rights against discrimination.

Government action to promote community cohesion in the UK

The Race Relations Act of 1976 made it illegal to discriminate on the grounds of race, colour, nationality, ethnic and national origin in the areas of employment, providing goods and services, education and public functions.

The Racial and Religious Hatred Act 2006 made it illegal to incite (cause) hatred against someone because of their race or religion.

The government created the Equality and Human Rights Commission in 2007 to 'promote and monitor human rights; and to protect, enforce and promote equality across "protected" grounds, including gender, race, religion and belief'.

The Equality Act 2010 replaced the previous discrimination acts. It 'sets out the different ways in which it is unlawful to treat someone, such as direct and indirect discrimination, harassment, victimisation and failing to make a reasonable adjustment for a disabled person'.

Government encourages and funds anti-racism poster campaigns.

Article 14: Discrimination
The enjoyment of the rights and freedoms set forth in this convention shall be secured without discrimination on any ground such as sex, race, colour, language, religion, political or other opinion, national or social origin, association with a national minority, property, birth or other status.
Extract from European Convention on Human Rights

Knowledge check ✳

1 What is community cohesion?
2 Why is community cohesion needed?
3 What are the benefits of having community cohesion in a country?
4 List four of the actions that governments have taken to encourage community cohesion.

Working together: equality in the work place

We live in a multicultural society, populated with a rich mix of racial groups, religions and heritage. This diversity should be embraced and celebrated but sometimes prejudice, ignorance, or just plain thoughtlessness in the workplace, as well as in society at large, can lead to misery and injustice.

The Equality Act 2010 protects all racial groups, regardless of their race, colour, national or ethnic origins. However we should be able to work together without the need for policy and legislation.

THERE ARE LOTS OF PLACES IN BRITAIN WHERE RACISM DOESN'T EXIST.

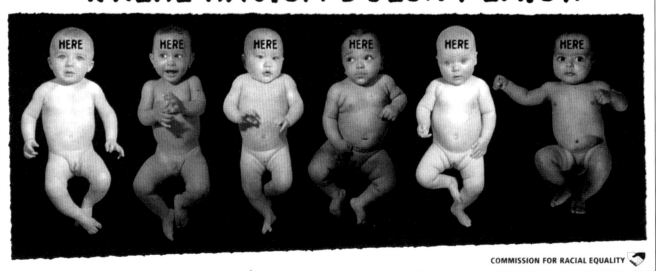

COMMISSION FOR RACIAL EQUALITY

Campaign poster from the Commission for Racial Equality.

A01

1 In small groups discuss the different ways that governments have tried to get rid of discrimination and racism.
2 There are some excellent anti-racism posters (see the example above). Some support the Equalities Act and some are aimed at local areas or schools. Try to find some examples of these.
3 Produce an anti-racism poster and ensure it contains: information about what racism is, why racism is wrong and what people can do about racism.

A02

1 In pairs, draw a consequence wheel (see page 52) about racism. In the centre, write 'Racism'.
2 In the first set of rings from the centre, write down the immediate consequence of racism.
3 In the second set of rings, write down what could be a consequence of the first consequence.
4 In the third set of rings, write down what could be a consequence of the consequence in the second ring.
5 Look at all the consequences of racism. Write a list of four of the consequences of racism in society.

exam practice b

Do you think racism is a problem in the UK? Give **two** reasons for your point of view.

Examiner's hint: The reasons you give as answers to this question do not have to be religious. (A02)

exam practice c

Explain why discrimination and racism are a problem in the UK.

Examiner's hint: Many questions are based on the key words given in the specification. Make sure you know the meaning of these words. (A01)

exam practice d

'Government action alone cannot achieve community cohesion.'
In your answer you should refer to at least one religion.
i) Do you agree? Give reasons for your answer.
ii) Give reasons why some people may disagree with you.

Examiner's hint: Make sure you know what is meant by the phrases 'government action' and 'community cohesion'. (A02)

The Citizens Advice Bureau is partly funded by the government to provide advice in cases of racism and discrimination.

4.6 Christians and racial harmony

Christians are expected to work for **racial harmony** because:

- Christian Churches have stated that Christians should work for racial harmony.
- Jesus lived in a multi-ethnic society and showed that his followers should not discriminate against others.
- Within the Christian Churches there are many people of different ethnic backgrounds, so racism would be divisive.
- There are many biblical teachings against racial discrimination.

● Christian teachings supporting racial harmony

From one man he made all the nations that they should inhabit the whole earth (Acts 17:26).

When a foreigner resides among you in your land, do not mistreat them (Leviticus 19:33).

Peter began to speak: 'I now realise how true it is that God does not show favouritism' (Acts 10:34).

So God created mankind in his own image (Genesis 1:27).

Love your neighbour as yourself (Luke 10:27).

You are all one in Christ Jesus (Galatians 3:28).

The Parable of the Good Samaritan (Luke 10:25–37) was used by Jesus to show that people should care for everyone, including those who are different races from you.

Have you not discriminated among yourselves and become judges with evil thoughts? (James 2:4).

The Church of England stated in 2011: 'As Christians we are called to seek the justice of the kingdom of God. As well as opposing the hatred of racism, we must be aware of the causes of injustice and resentment in all communities.'

The Methodist Church has stated: 'Racism is a sin and contrary to the imperatives of the Gospel. Biblically, it is against all that we perceive of the unmotivated, spontaneous and undiscriminating love of God who in Jesus Christ gave himself for all.'

The Catechism of the Catholic Church teaches that 'because of its common origin the human race forms a unity, for "from one ancestor [God] made all nations to inhabit the whole earth" ' (360).

Knowledge check ✳

1 What is the Christian teaching on racial harmony?
2 Pick out one biblical reason. Write it out and explain what it teaches about racial harmony.
3 Pick out one Church statement and explain what it teaches about racial harmony.

A01

1 Work in groups of three or four. Each group picks one of the Bible references which support racial harmony.
2 Each group has three minutes to produce a presentation to explain how the reference supports racial harmony; this can be accompanied by a drama, a poster or a PowerPoint slide.

In the following Bible verses, Jesus helps a Roman centurion. As the Romans occupied Israel at that time, Jewish people would be upset that Jesus helped a foreign soldier, particularly one of senior rank.

There a centurion's servant, whom his master valued highly, was sick and about to die. The centurion heard of Jesus and sent some elders of the Jews to him, asking him to come and heal his servant. When they came to Jesus, they pleaded earnestly with him, 'This man deserves to have you do this, because he loves our nation and has built our synagogue.' So Jesus went with them.

He was not far from the house when the centurion sent friends to say to him: 'Lord, don't trouble yourself, for I do not deserve to have you come under my roof. That is why I did not even consider myself worthy to come to you. But say the word, and my servant will be healed. For I myself am a man under authority, with soldiers under me. I tell this one, "Go," and he goes; and that one, "Come," and he comes. I say to my servant, "Do this," and he does it.'

When Jesus heard this, he was amazed at him, and turning to the crowd following him, he said, 'I tell you, I have not found such great faith even in Israel.' Then the men who had been sent returned to the house and found the servant well. (Luke 7:2–10).

A02

Using the Bible story of Jesus and the Roman centurion to guide you, write a newspaper article to explain the Christian teachings about racial harmony. Your article must include:

● a brief description of what racial harmony is
● a brief explanation of why it is important for Christians to work for racial harmony
● Christian teachings supporting racial harmony
● at least one illustration or picture.

exam practice b

Do you think all Christians must work for racial harmony? Give **two** reasons for your point of view.

Examiner's hint: It is difficult to think of reasons to disagree with this. Remember you only need to give one point of view in a b) question. (A02)

exam practice c

Explain why Christians should support racial harmony.

Examiner's hint: You could give four different Bible quotes as reasons for your answer. (A01)

exam practice d

'If everyone were religious racism would not exist.'
In your answer you should refer to at least Christianity.
i) Do you agree? Give reasons for your answer.
ii) Give reasons why some people may disagree with you.

Examiner's hint: Read the line under the stimulus and make sure you refer to Christianity. (A02)

4.7 Muslims and racial harmony

Reasons why Muslims should support racial harmony

The Qur'an has many references to the equality of human beings in front of God which means discrimination is not acceptable.

O mankind, indeed We have created you from male and female and made you peoples and tribes that you may know one another (Qur'an 49:13).

Muslims promote racial harmony as they are all created equally by Allah.

I am the Messenger of Allah to you all (Qur'an 7:158).

O People! Your God is one; your father is one; no preference of an Arab neither over non-Arab nor of a non-Arab over an Arab or red over black or black over red except for the most righteous. Verily the most honoured of you is the most righteous (Hadith, Mosnad Ahmad).

Muslims believe that they will be judged not on their race but on how they behave and that a person who is righteous (a good Muslim) will be rewarded after this life.

All mankind is from Adam and Eve, an Arab has no superiority over a non-Arab nor a non-Arab has any superiority over an Arab; also a white has no superiority over black nor a black has any superiority over white except by piety and good action (Last Sermon of Prophet Muhammad).

All people stand equal, like the teeth of a comb; no advantage shall an Arab have over a non-Arab, except in righteousness (Hadith, Al-Bukari).

Muslims are all part of the global Muslim community (ummah) and this means there are Muslims of all races. To discriminate because of race would be wrong.

And of His signs is the creation of the heavens and the earth and the diversity of your languages and your colours. Indeed in that are signs for those of knowledge (Qur'an 30:22).

Prophet Muhammad chose Bilal, an Ethiopian, to be the first person who performed the call to prayer (Adhan).

Knowledge check

1 Why do Muslims promote racial harmony?
2 Why does being part of the ummah mean Muslims should work for racial harmony?
3 Select one of the references supporting why Muslims should work for racial harmony, write it out and explain what it teaches.

The teaching of the Qur'an does not say we should all be the same, it teaches us Allah made us all different and yet we are equal before him.

All people have the same creator, the same ancestors and so should be treated the same.

Prophet Muhammad showed that he did not discriminate against any race. Muslims should try to do the same.

Everyone should be respectful of each other. If a person discriminates this is not respecting a person's individual nature that was created by Allah and so racism is wrong.

A01

1 In pairs discuss the different reasons for promoting racial harmony above and on page 98. Which ones do you think provide the best reasons?
2 Individually make a list of five reasons and write them in order, putting the best reason first.
3 Compare your list with your partner. Which ones do you agree with? Why?

A02

In small groups prepare a drama to show how a Muslim might teach others about racial harmony.

● Decide on a situation when a person might teach others about racial harmony and how your group will act out the situation.
● Include in your drama:
  – the person needing to explain the Muslim teaching on racial harmony
  – how the rest of the group will react to the teachings
  – what happens as a result of the person explaining the Muslim teachings on racial harmony.

exam practice b

Do you think all Muslims should promote racial harmony? Give **two** reasons for your point of view.

Examiner's hint: Develop your reasons using references from the Qur'an. (A02)

exam practice c

Explain why Muslims should promote racial harmony.

Examiner's hint: You could give four different Qur'anic quotes as reasons. (A01)

exam practice d

'If everyone were religious racism would not exist.'
In your answer you should refer to at least one religion.
i) Do you agree? Give reasons for your answer.
ii) Give reasons why some people may disagree with you.

Examiner's hint: Although this question does not directly refer to Islam or Christianity, you should make reference to either Christian or Muslim reasons in your answer. (A02)

4.8 The UK as a multi-faith society

The UK has become a more multi-ethnic society and, as a consequence, it is also a more **multi-faith society**. As it has become easier to travel, people have come into contact with different religions and have adopted them or people have settled in Britain with new religions.

The UK accepts that all religions should have equal rights within the UK (**religious pluralism**). All religious people have **religious freedom** where they are allowed to practise their faith. It is illegal within the UK for anyone to discriminate against someone on the grounds of their faith (the Racial and Religious Hatred Act 2006 and Equality Act 2010). This means that all faiths are welcomed and are able to grow in the UK.

The 2001 census showed that nearly 72 per cent of the population regarded themselves as Christian. The Office for National Statistics has surveyed people in 2010 and this also showed that out of the sample group, 71 per cent were Christian, 4 per cent were Muslim and 21 per cent said they were not religious.

> **KEY WORDS**
>
> **multi-faith society** Many different religions living together in one society.
> **religious freedom** The right to practise your religion and change your religion.
> **religious pluralism** Accepting all religions as having an equal right to coexist.

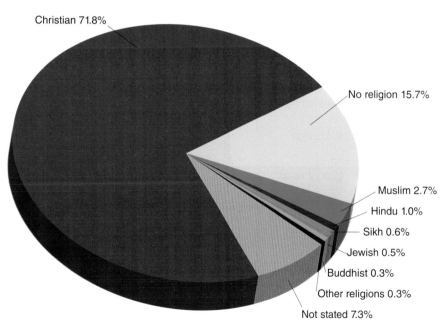

Christian 71.8%
No religion 15.7%
Muslim 2.7%
Hindu 1.0%
Sikh 0.6%
Jewish 0.5%
Buddhist 0.3%
Other religions 0.3%
Not stated 7.3%

The pie chart shows the religions of the UK, according to the 2001 census.

Knowledge check

1 What is a multi-faith society?
2 Is the UK a multi-faith society?
3 Name five faiths that are found within the UK.
4 Explain why the UK became a multi-faith society.

Benefits of living in a multi-faith society

Experience of others' methods of worship might give inspiration to a person's faith.

People can freely worship how they want.

Increased understanding of others' faiths reduces conflict.

No one faith becomes able to 'control' the views of the population.

In a multi-faith society people can experience other religions first hand rather than receiving what could be prejudiced reports about them.

People might be challenged about their own faith, helping them think more deeply about why they hold certain beliefs.

The media reflect the multi-faith society we live in and can be part of how people find out about other faiths, reducing problems of prejudice. TV soap operas have always attempted to represent everyday life and everyday society. Multi-ethnic Britain is shown in both *EastEnders* and *Coronation Street*. The latest Asian family, the Muslim Masood family, joined *EastEnders* in 2007 and have featured in many of the prominent storylines.

exam practice b

Do you think there are benefits to living in a multi-faith society? Give **two** reasons for your point of view.

Examiner's hint: Make sure you only give two reasons. (AO2)

exam practice c

Explain the benefits of living in a multi-faith society.

Examiner's hint: This question does not include the word 'why' but still needs reasons. Read questions very carefully. (AO1)

exam practice d

'Multi-faith societies are good for people.'
In your answer you should refer to at least one religion.
i) Do you agree? Give reasons for your answer.
ii) Give reasons why some people may disagree with you.

Examiner's hint: This question refers to multi-faith societies. Make sure that the reasons you give are about faith, not race or culture. (AO2)

A01

1 In small groups, create a TV advert to explain to people the advantages of living in a multi-faith society.
2 The advert should involve everyone in the group in some way.
3 The advert should include explanations of the key words multi-faith society, religious freedom and religious pluralism.
4 It must explain at least four of the reasons why it is good to live in a multi-faith society.
5 Either perform your advert for the group or video it to show the group at a later point.

A02

1 In pairs discuss the reasons given as benefits for living in a multi-faith society and decide which are the best reasons and which you feel are not so good.
2 Work on your own and write a list of the reasons in order starting with the best reason and finishing with the least good.
3 Draw a line across your list at the point at which you stop agreeing with the reasons.
4 Return to pair work and discuss why you have put your list in this order.

4.9 Issues for religions in a multi-faith society

As we have seen there are many benefits to living in a multi-faith society. However, this can also cause problems, especially for people who are followers of a religion, because religions other than their own are by definition different and have different beliefs and ways of living. Differences between faiths may cause problems when it comes to three areas: conversion, bringing up children and **interfaith marriages**.

KEY WORDS

interfaith marriages Marriage where the husband and wife are from different religions.

● Why conversion may cause problems for religious people

A religious conversion is when a person starts to believe in a new religion. This can start from having no religion or changing from one religion to another. Most religious people are very happy when a person who has no faith converts to having a faith. Problems may occur when conversion is from one faith to another. The problems happen because:

- People may then follow a religion that teaches the opposite to the religion they have left.
- All religions teach that they are the 'correct' religion in some way. This means that the followers of the convert's original faith can think the person who converts is now following the 'wrong' faith.
- It can lead to arguments between the two faiths involved.
- It might leave the followers of the original religion feeling rejected.

When people try to convert others it might cause people to feel offended. Why do you think this is?

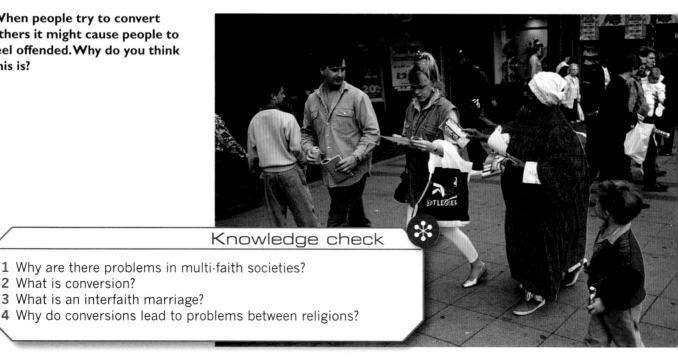

Knowledge check

1 Why are there problems in multi-faith societies?
2 What is conversion?
3 What is an interfaith marriage?
4 Why do conversions lead to problems between religions?

● Why bringing up children in a multi-faith society may cause problems for religious people

Bringing up children in a multi-faith society may cause problems for religious people. It means that children will come into contact with people of other faiths who will believe different things from the family they have been born into.

The problems happen because:

- Children may find another religion more attractive and want to convert.
- Children may mix with other children who have conflicting beliefs to their own. This might make them want to stop doing certain things in their faith, for example wanting to attend church services.
- It can lead to arguments between children and their friends.
- It might mean that parents feel that they cannot follow their religion strictly because their children might have picked up other ideas against the religion from friends or the media.
- The child may become confused about what they should believe.

A01

Imagine you are a parent and you are trying to raise your child to be the same religion as you within a multi-faith society. Write down how you might explain to another parent the difficulties you face because your child comes across so many different religions.

● Why interfaith marriages may cause problems for religious people

Marrying someone who is of a different faith may cause problems for religious people. It may affect how they are able to get married as some faiths discourage interfaith marriages. It may affect the way they are allowed to worship or the way they bring up children. Different faiths will affect the lives of the couple in different ways.

Chelsea Clinton, the daughter of former US president Bill Clinton, had an interfaith marriage in 2010. The officials at the marriage were a Reform rabbi and a Methodist minister and the couple stood under a chuppah.

My name is Mumtaz. When I fell in love with my wife things were not very easy for us, as Emma is a Christian and I am a Muslim. My family and the imam tried to explain to us how difficult life might be for us bringing up a family because of the differences in our faiths.

We chose to marry in a register office. Although we could have married in either the mosque or the church, it would have been difficult for one of our families during the service.

Muslim men can't marry women from faiths other than Christianity or Judaism, so at least I was able to marry Emma. I feel sad that she does not go to masjid (mosque) with me but I understand that our beliefs are different.

We don't have any children yet, but it will be difficult to decide what we are going to teach them, and what faith they will be.

A02

In small groups produce a presentation to explain the problems that might occur in a multi-faith society. Include explanations for all the specialist language that you use.

You could include in your presentation:

- examples of conversion, bringing up children in a multi-faith society or interfaith marriages that might cause problems
- a PowerPoint presentation
- a short drama to illustrate the problems of conversion, bringing up children in a multi-faith society or interfaith marriages.

exam practice b

'Do you think living in a multi-faith society causes problems for religious people?' Give **two** reasons for your point of view.

Examiner's hint: Remember this must link to religious people rather than general problems. (A02)

exam practice c

Explain why living in a multi-faith society may cause problems for religious people.

Examiner's hint: Start each reason with a new paragraph. (A01)

exam practice d

'Living in a multi-faith society always causes problems for religious people.'

In your answer you should refer to at least one religion.

i) Do you agree? Give reasons for your answer.

ii) Give reasons why some people may disagree with you.

Examiner's hint: Read the stimulus carefully before you decide what your opinion is going to be. (A02)

4.10 Religions and community cohesion in the UK

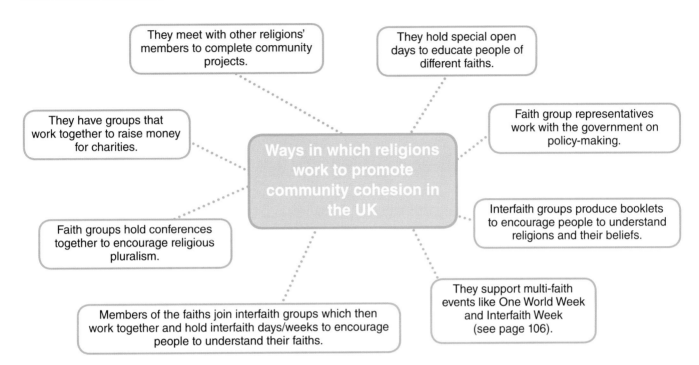

They meet with other religions' members to complete community projects.

They hold special open days to educate people of different faiths.

They have groups that work together to raise money for charities.

Ways in which religions work to promote community cohesion in the UK

Faith group representatives work with the government on policy-making.

Interfaith groups produce booklets to encourage people to understand religions and their beliefs.

Faith groups hold conferences together to encourage religious pluralism.

They support multi-faith events like One World Week and Interfaith Week (see page 106).

Members of the faiths join interfaith groups which then work together and hold interfaith days/weeks to encourage people to understand their faiths.

I love you when you bow in your mosque, kneel in your temple, pray in your church. For you and I are sons of one religion, and it is the spirit.

Khalil Gibran, 1883–1931, a philosophical writer

Knowledge check

1 Look at the different ways in which religions work to promote community cohesion among people. Read through them carefully.
2 Which ways do you think are the best at promoting community cohesion and which ones do you think are not so good?
3 Write the reasons briefly in order from the one you think is the best downwards.
4 What do you think Khalil Gibran is saying about different religions in the quote?
5 What do you think Khalil Gibran would say about interfaith groups? Why?

Interfaith in action

One way that religions try to promote community cohesion is by participating in events like Interfaith Week. During this week members of different faiths spend time running events to inform people in their local area about their faith. Many open their places of worship and organise information days where people can visit and learn about what happens in them.

Interfaith Week takes place in November. The aim of the week is to:

- strengthen good interfaith relations at all levels
- increase awareness of the different and distinct faith communities in the UK
- celebrate and build on the contribution which members make to their neighbourhoods and to wider society
- increase understanding between people of religious and non-religious beliefs.

Working together and multi-faith communities

Dr Sheikh Hojjat Ramzy.
Dr Ramzy has dedicated his life to the propagation of knowledge and the provision of accurate and accessible information concerning Islam to the communities of Oxfordshire, in which he is currently based, and far beyond, in order to further understanding and peaceful coexistence amongst different faith and non-faith groups in this ever developing, multicultural country.

How do religions work together in your local community?

The local community in which I live enjoys a diverse mix of religions and cultures, and a high level of harmony between them. One of the prominent features of this is the interfaith events which are regularly organised. These events offer the community a chance to come together and learn about the faiths of others in a friendly and welcoming environment.

Given the ties that have been made between members of different religions as a result of these events, organisations and individuals have since come together in support of many different causes. For example, members of all faiths came together to demonstrate against the war in Iraq, have come together to support local projects such as the building of local religious facilities, and also to raise money for both local and international charities in the wake of disasters and crises.

Every year for the past decade, the community organise a faith walk in which hundreds of members of all faiths walk from the local synagogue, to the church and the mosque.

Individual members of different faiths often participate in each other's celebrations by offering good tidings to their neighbours on their days of joy. During Eid celebrations for example, members of the local Christian and other faith communities are always invited to come and join in the festivities, and I myself have been invited in the days before Christmas to offer a speech during carol services about the Qur'anic story of Jesus.

A01

1 You are a journalist and your newspaper has asked you to write an article about the way that religions support community cohesion.
2 Write about the ways religions try to encourage community cohesion and why they do this.
3 Use the spidergram on page 105, the information on Interfaith Week, the article by Dr Ramzy and the information on the Faiths Forum for London website to help you.

Faiths Forum for London (FFL) is an organisation which brings together the rich diversity of faiths in London and helps to foster development and engagement with social policies and networks. www.faithsforum4london.org

A02

Imagine you have been employed to explain why religious people should encourage community cohesion. In pairs, design either:

a) a poster campaign (a group of four posters that have a common theme); or
b) a text message campaign (a group of four texts that have a common theme); or
c) an internet pop-up campaign (a group of four pop-ups that have a common theme).

Explain your campaign to the rest of the class and decide which of the campaigns is the most effective.

exam practice b

Do you think religions should encourage community cohesion? Give **two** reasons for your point of view.

Examiner's hint: Reasons can be what individuals do or what religions do as a whole. (A02)

exam practice c

Explain how religions work for community cohesion.

Examiner's hint: This c) question starts with the words 'Explain how …'. Write descriptions of the ways rather than reasons why. (A01)

exam practice d

'Religions should not work for community cohesion.'
In your answer you should refer to at least one religion.
i) Do you agree? Give reasons for your answer.
ii) Give reasons why some people may disagree with you.

Examiner's hint: If you can't think of opposite reasons try to imagine what a person would say if they were arguing with you. (A02)

4.11 The media and community cohesion

● How an issue from this section has been presented in the media

There are many different TV programmes, films and newspaper articles that refer to the issues covered in this section and can be used to answer questions about them. Issues that are likely to be covered are:

- changes in the roles of women
- racism
- prejudice
- conversion
- bringing up children in a multi-faith society
- interfaith marriages.

You will need to watch the programme or film or read the article and work out how the issue was presented and whether the treatment was fair to religious people. It does not need to show religious people in the film, but you need to consider whether the views expressed in the film would offend people from any religion.

You will not need to describe the whole of the film, programme or article in answers but you will need to give examples. Some films which are suitable are:

- *Invictus*
- *Shrek 2*
- *Bend it like Beckham*
- *Hairspray*
- *Made in Dagenham*
- *White Girl (BBC documentary)*.

When you study these films, programmes or articles you should try to find some quotes about the issue from this section that you are going to use in your answer. You should also be able to link to religious teaching about the issues.

A scene from *Bend it like Beckham*.

A scene from *Made in Dagenham*.

Films can be fair because:	Films can be unfair because:
they support the beliefs of a religion	they criticise the beliefs of a religion
they do not show things that are against the teaching of a religion	they show things that are against the teaching of a religion
they show that often decisions are difficult to make	they show that people do not consider religion in decisions that are made
they show a particular religious character in a good light	they do not show a particular religious character in a good light

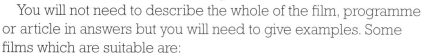

1 What issues do you need to study in this section?
2 Do you need to be able to describe the whole programme or film?
3 What will you need to be able to do to show you have watched the whole film or programme?
4 List reasons why the media might be seen as fair to religious people or beliefs.
5 List reasons why the media might be seen as unfair to religious people or beliefs.

● *My Big Fat Greek Wedding*

My Big Fat Greek Wedding is a film which shows Toula Portokalos (Nia Vardalos), a Greek Orthodox girl, falling in love with Ian Miller (John Corbett), an American who is raised in a vaguely Christian way. The film shows the prejudices the couple have to overcome and the complexities of an interfaith marriage.

How the film *My Big Fat Greek Wedding* might be regarded as fair or unfair to religious people

Gus (Toula's father) says 'There are two kinds of people – Greeks, and everyone else who wish they was Greek'. It shows prejudiced ideas.

The film makes many references to things that are very Greek ethnically which could be seen to be being mocked. This could be seen as offensive to some religious people.

Toulas says 'Nice Greek girls who don't find a husband, work in the family restaurant'. It shows the role of a woman is to get married.

Toula and her family do not ask Ian to convert to their religion; they accept him (reluctantly). It shows why God will not say yes to all prayers.

At the end, Ian Miller becomes a Greek Orthodox to marry Toula. This shows that this can be the easiest way to marry when you are from different faith backgrounds.

Toula Portokalos is a Greek Orthodox woman who works for the family business and is expected to marry a 'nice Greek boy'.

A01

1 Watch the film *My Big Fat Greek Wedding* or a film of your choice that shows multi-ethnic/interfaith conflicts.
2 Note down the parts of the film that might be regarded as fair or unfair to religion and religious beliefs.
3 In pairs, use your notes and the information given above to produce a PowerPoint presentation to show the parts of the film that might be regarded as fair or unfair to religion and religious beliefs.
4 Use your PowerPoint to explain to the class how the film might be regarded as fair or unfair to religion and religious beliefs.

A02

Draw two spidergrams.

1 One should record information as to why some programmes/films would be seen as fair to religion and religious beliefs.
2 The other should record information as to why some programmes/films would be seen as unfair to religion and religious beliefs.

exam practice b

Do you think the media are fair to religion and religious beliefs? Give **two** reasons for your point of view.

Examiner's hint: An example from a film is a good way to develop a reason. (A02)

exam practice c

Explain how the media show an issue from religion and community cohesion.

Examiner's hint: In media questions make sure you identify the form of media and the issue you are referring to. (A01)

exam practice d

'The media are not fair to religion and religious beliefs.'
In your answer you should refer to at least one religion.
i) Do you agree? Give reasons for your answer.
ii) Give reasons why some people may disagree with you.

Examiner's hint: Make sure any examples you use are from this section of the course – Religion and community cohesion. (A02)

Examination practice

Below is guidance on how to answer the question a) from Section 4: Religion and community cohesion. All a) questions are worth 2 marks.

The a) questions test the key words which are provided by Edexcel and are used in this book. It is important to make sure that you learn them.

Every section will have two a) questions and they will either ask for a definition of one of the keywords or ask for two examples of the word. Look at the steps below about how to answer question 7a), then try to answer question 8a).

Sample question
7a) What is meant by ethnic minority?   [2]

Sample question
8a) What is meant by discrimination?   [2]

How to answer
The best way to get full marks on an a) question:
✓ Write the glossary definition supplied by the exam board – these are the ones used in this book.
✓ To get full marks you must provide all the information that is within the exam board's definition.
✓ If you leave out any information or the wording is not quite correct you may only get 1 mark out of 2.

Step 1
● Try to remember the key word definition.

Greek people living in England.

Step 2
● This is an example, not a definition. Try to explain what the word means.

A member of an ethnic group.

Step 3
● This is an incomplete definition. You should learn the key word definition and write all of it as your answer.

A member of an ethnic group which is much smaller than the majority group.

Examiner's comment
✓ **Learn the definitions used in this book as they are the same as those provided by the exam board.**
✓ **To get full marks you should try to provide all the information that is within the exam board's definition, even if you think there is a different definition for the same word.**

Below is guidance on how to answer the question d) from Section 4: Religion and community cohesion. As it is a d) question, it is worth 6 marks.

In every section there are two d) questions to choose from. Each is divided into two parts d) i) and d) ii).

Sample question

7d) 'Women should have the same rights as men in religion.' In your answer you should refer to at least one religion other than Christianity.

  i) Do you agree? Give reasons for your opinion. [3]

  ii) Give reasons why some people may disagree with you. [3]

How to answer

There are a few things to always include in a d) question.

- Start with your opinion in d) i).
- You must read the sentence following the statement. If it says 'you should refer to at least one religion' then you must clearly refer to any one religion. If it says 'you should refer to at least one religion other than Christianity' then you must clearly refer to a religion that is not Christianity. If it says 'you should refer to Christianity' then you must clearly refer to Christianity.

The easiest way to get full marks is to give three brief reasons for d) i) and three brief reasons for d) ii).

Question 7 d) i)

Step 1

- Think whether you agree or disagree and one reason to support your opinion. Make sure you write down that it is your opinion at the beginning.

I disagree. I think women are different to men so should not be treated exactly the same as men.

Step 2

- Think of a second reason; point out that it is your second reason by writing 'secondly'.

Secondly, some Muslims believe that a woman is biologically made to care for the family and I agree with this.

Step 3

- Think of a third reason why you disagree with the statement. Write the new reason on a new line. Write more than 'because I am a Christian' or 'because it is in the Bible', as there are conflicting views in both and it might not get credited.

Finally, I am Christian and the Bible clearly shows that Eve was made as a companion to Adam and not his equal.

Question 7 d) ii)

Step 1

- This must include reasons for the opposite opinion to the one you gave as your opinion in d) i).

Some people agree with the statement. They think all religious people are created in the image of God, and this makes them equal.

Step 2

- Think of a second reason; make sure it starts on a new line.

Also, some Christians would say that Jesus treated women equally, so we should.

Step 3

- Think of a third reason why a person would agree with the statement. Make it clear it is a third reason by starting with 'finally' or 'thirdly'.

Finally, some Churches have women priests and it seems wrong if some Christians accept women priests and others do not. If they all follow the teaching of Jesus then they should all do the same.

Examiner's comment

✓ **The candidate has clearly stated their own personal view. Without this they cannot get full marks.**

✓ **Maximum marks will be awarded as each side of the argument has three reasons.**

✓ **It is important to make sure the reasons have enough detail. Brief answers such as 'because I was brought up to think it', 'because it is in the Bible/Qur'an' are not good answers and might not be enough to get marks.**

Religion and society

Section 5: Religion: rights and responsibilities

5.1 Making moral decisions: the authority of the Bible

● **The authority of the Bible**

The **Bible** is used by Christians as a source of advice when they have to make moral decisions. A moral decision is when a person has to make a choice between right and wrong. They are decisions which may not be easy to make, and may have different right answers in different situations.

The Bible is used by all Christians, although some use it more than others. Some will use only the Bible and some will use other things such as their conscience, the Church or **Situation Ethics**, as well as the Bible, to make their decision.

● **How the Bible was written**

Some Christians think that the Bible is the direct revelation of God. They believe that the writers of the Bible were writing exactly what God told them to write.

Christians who think this will believe everything that is written in the Bible and will follow exactly what the Bible teaches. These Christians will only use the Bible when making decisions.

The serpent handlers in the southern states of the USA read the passage in the Bible which says: *They will pick up snakes with their hands; and when they drink deadly poison, it will not hurt them at all; they will place their hands on sick people, and they will get well (Mark 16:17–18).*

KEY WORDS

Bible The holy book of Christians.
the Decalogue The Ten Commandments.
Situation Ethics The idea that Christians should base moral decisions on what is the most loving thing to do.

Religious snake handlers handle poisonous snakes to demonstrate their faith in God.

Some Christians think that God inspired the writers of the Bible to write about God. So the Bible reveals information about God, but because the writers are human, the Bible might include mistakes.

Christians who think this will believe what is written in the Bible, but will also recognise other sources of authority that might be different from the Bible.

Some Christians think that the Bible was written by human beings to tell other people about their faith and God. They do not think that God inspired them and they think that the writers would be heavily influenced by the society and culture of the time.

Christians who think this will read the Bible for advice, but will also recognise other sources of authority such as the Church or their own conscience.

Knowledge check

1 What is a moral decision?
2 What are the three different ways Christians think the Bible was written?
3 Why do some Christians think that the Bible must be correct?
4 Why do some Christians think that the Bible might contain human errors?
5 Why do some Christians think that the Bible reflects the society and culture of the people in the time it was written?

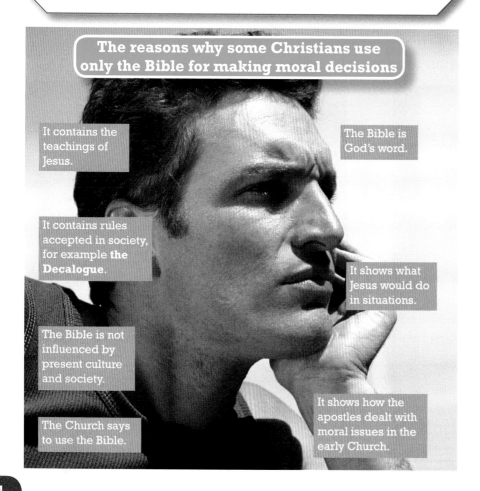

The reasons why some Christians use only the Bible for making moral decisions

It contains the teachings of Jesus.

The Bible is God's word.

It contains rules accepted in society, for example **the Decalogue**.

It shows what Jesus would do in situations.

The Bible is not influenced by present culture and society.

The Church says to use the Bible.

It shows how the apostles dealt with moral issues in the early Church.

The Bible was affected by the society and culture the writers lived in.

The Bible was written by people who had a particular message to spread.

The Bible does not contain information about all moral issues.

Why some Christians might not use only the Bible for making moral decisions

The Bible was written by people who are only human and may make mistakes.

The Bible has been translated from the original language it was written in, so it might not be accurate.

A01

Copy and complete the following table:

Reasons why some Christians use only the Bible for making moral decisions	Reasons why some Christians might not use only the Bible for making moral decisions

A02

1 Look at this statement: 'The Bible must always be used when a person has to make a moral decision'.
2 Draw a line across the page in your notes. At one end of the line write agree and at the other end write disagree.
3 Write at the agree end a reason why someone might agree with the statement.
4 Write at the disagree end a reason why someone might disagree with the statement.
5 Decide what your opinion is. Do you totally agree, totally disagree or are you somewhere in the middle? Mark on the line where your opinion might be.
6 Write down two reasons for your opinion.

exam practice b

Do you think all Christians should use the Bible when making moral decisions? Give **two** reasons for your point of view.

Examiner's hint: This question is about whether Christians should use the Bible. Do not write about whether all Christians should do the same thing – this does not answer the question. (A02)

exam practice c

Explain why some Christians use the Bible for making moral decisions.

Examiner's hint: If you can't think of four reasons then develop one of your reasons using an example. (A01)

exam practice d

'The Bible provides all the advice a person needs.'
In your answer you should refer to Christianity.
i) Do you agree? Give reasons for your answer.
ii) Give reasons why some people may disagree with you.

Examiner's hint: In this section of Unit 8 the only religion you can study is Christianity so do not refer to any other religion. (A02)

5.2 Making moral decisions: the authority of the Church

The **Church** is used as a source of advice by some Christians as they regard it as an important source of authority. These Christians believe that this authority means that the Church is able to give the best advice when making moral decisions. Many Christians will use other things as well as the Church to make their decisions.

> **KEY WORDS**
>
> **Church** The community of Christians (with a small c it means a Christian place of worship).

Why the Church has authority for some Christians
- The Church is the Body of Christ on earth and so it is able to teach as Jesus would.
- Authority to teach was given to the apostles by Jesus, and this authority has been passed down through the leaders of the Church.
- God is able to speak through the leaders of the Church.
- Christ is called the Head of the Church in the New Testament so Church teaching comes from Jesus.
- The Holy Spirit is present in the Church today.

A01

1 Read carefully the information given about Church authority and why it is used as a basis for making moral decisions.
2 In pairs, looking at the information given, produce a quiz to be used in class. The quiz must contain at least five questions.
3 You must produce a quiz sheet, which can be copied for class use, and an answer sheet, to mark the completed quiz.

Knowledge check

1 What is meant by Church with a capital C?
2 What is meant by church with a small c?
3 Give three reasons why the Church has authority for some Christians.
4 Give three reasons why some Christians use only the Church as a basis for making moral decisions.

They believe Church leaders have been appointed by God.

They respect the tradition of the Church.

They believe that Christ is head of the Church.

Reasons why some Christians use only the Church as a basis for making moral decisions

The Bible says *So Christ himself gave the apostles, the prophets, the evangelists, the pastors and teachers, to equip his people for works of service, so that the body of Christ may be built up (Ephesians 4:11–12).*

The Bible teaches *And he is the head of the body, the church (Colossians 1:18).*

Let everyone be subject to the governing authorities, for there is no authority except that which God has established. The authorities that exist have been established by God (Romans 13:1–2).

Then Jesus came to them and said, 'All authority in heaven and on earth has been given to me. Therefore go and make disciples of all nations, baptising them in the name of the Father and of the Son and of the Holy Spirit, and teaching them to obey everything I have commanded you. And surely I am with you always, to the very end of the age' (Matthew 28:18–20).

Many Christians feel that when Jesus commissioned the disciples to baptise and teach, he was giving them authority. He then said 'I am with you always'. This can be interpreted as also giving the Church authority. Do you think all Christians should ask the Church for advice before making moral decisions?

A02

1 In pairs discuss the reasons why some Christians use only the Church as a basis for making moral decisions. Which reasons do you think are good and why?
2 Produce a poster that could be used as part of an advertising campaign by Christians to encourage people to use the Church as a basis for making moral decisions.

exam practice b

Do you think all Christians should use the Church as the basis for making moral decisions? Give **two** reasons for your point of view.

Examiner's hint: It is important you start with your own opinion. (A02)

exam practice c

Explain why some Christians think the Church has authority.

Examiner's hint: Check your spelling and punctuation because you will be assessed on quality of written communication on c) questions. (A01)

exam practice d

'Christians should always follow the teaching of the Church on moral issues.'
In your answer you should refer to Christianity.
i) Do you agree? Give reasons for your answer.
ii) Give reasons why some people may disagree with you.

Examiner's hint: d) ii) must give reasons for a different opinion from the opinion you gave in d) i). (A02)

5.3 Making moral decisions: the role of conscience

A person's **conscience** is an inner feeling of right or wrong. It is thought to be imprinted on a person during their upbringing. A conscience is formed in a similar way to the way language is learned.

KEY WORDS

conscience An inner feeling of the rightness or wrongness of an action.

This is God speaking

Conscience has been described and illustrated in many ways. Which do you think is best and why?

'Conscience is a man's compass.' (Vincent van Gogh, 1853–90)

'Your conscience is the measure of the honesty of your selfishness. Listen to it carefully.' (Richard Bach, 1936–)

Thomas Aquinas (1225–74) described conscience as 'the application of knowledge to activity'. He indicated that when using a conscience the person would have to use their natural knowledge to make decisions about behaviour.

John Henry Newman (1801–90) said that conscience is 'a principle planted within us, before we have had any training'. As the creator, the planter of the conscience was God, thought Newman.

The Catholic Catechism says that conscience is 'present at the heart of the person, enjoins him at the appropriate moment to do good and to avoid evil' (1777).

Knowledge check

1 What is a conscience?
2 How is a conscience thought to be created?
3 How did Thomas Aquinas describe a conscience?
4 How does the Catholic Catechism describe a conscience?
5 List four roles of conscience.

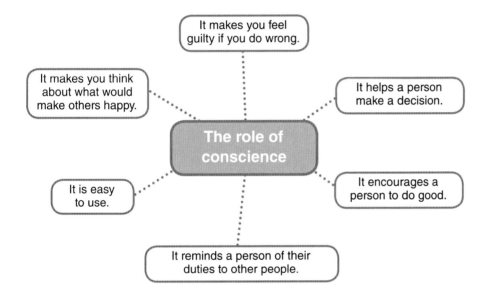

AO1

1 Discuss with a partner what you think the role of conscience is.
2 Draw and complete a poster or web page to show what the role of conscience is.

● How some Christians use conscience in making moral decisions

Mel

As a Christian, I consider that my conscience is the most important guide when I make moral decisions. My conscience has been formed by the teaching I have received from my Christian parents, my minister and at my Christian school.

My conscience is also the way I can think about what God would want me to do. I can listen to my conscience, it is an inner voice, which guides me to decide what decision I would feel comfortable with.

My conscience can be used when other sources of advice cannot, like for example, if my decision was very personal and I would not be able to find the answer in the Bible and would not feel comfortable asking my minister for help.

I use my conscience because I also think about the possible consequences of my decisions and how my conscience would make me feel in the different outcomes. My conscience would make me feel bad if I made the wrong decision.

Chris

As a Christian I would not use just my conscience as a guide when I make moral decisions. My conscience has been formed by the teaching I have received, but I might not have understood it correctly. Or someone might have given me the wrong advice.

My conscience is my inner voice, but it might be biased towards doing what I want, selfish things, so I prefer to use rules given by other authorities, like the Bible or the Church.

I also think about the possible consequences of my decisions. I do not always think about how my conscience would make me feel because I know that if I follow Christian rules then I am doing the right thing; my conscience could be wrong.

My conscience can be used when other sources of advice cannot. It is useful to ask others for advice as they might have some knowledge that I don't, and sometimes listening to advice from others makes things easier to understand.

A02

1 Read carefully Mel's explanation of why she uses her conscience to make moral decisions.
2 Make a list of at least four of Mel's reasons for using her conscience.
3 Number them to put them in order of which you think are most important.
4 Write a 50-word letter to Chris. In the letter explain why you agree or disagree with her reasons that conscience is not the most important guide.

exam practice b

Do you think it is important to use conscience when making moral decisions? Give **two** reasons for your point of view.

Examiner's hint: Make sure you only write two reasons. More than two will not be credited and will use up valuable time answering the rest of the exam paper. (A02)

exam practice c

Explain the role of conscience.

Examiner's hint: Add examples of how conscience could be used to develop your answer. (A01)

exam practice d

'Christians should always follow their conscience when making decisions.'
In your answer you should refer to Christianity.
i) Do you agree? Give reasons for your answer.
ii) Give reasons why some people may disagree with you.

Examiner's hint: You must give a personal opinion to get more than 3 out of the possible 6 marks for this type of question. (A02)

5.4 Making moral decisions: Situation Ethics

● Situation Ethics

Joseph Fletcher (1905–91)

In 1966, Joseph Fletcher published a book, *Situation Ethics: The New Morality*, where he discussed a way of making decisions not based on rules or scriptures.

Situation Ethics is based on thinking about each situation as unique and working out the best decision to make. Fletcher said that when making a decision, a person has general principles based on rules and teachings about the issue. But the person should be able to make a decision to go against their principles if the situation demands. For example, lying is usually regarded as wrong, but if it is to protect someone then it might be right.

Fletcher then went further and said that in each situation a person should decide what achieves the greatest amount of good. He said that the absolute goodness is love. A person using Situation Ethics should make a decision based on what causes the greatest amount of love. Love in this case is 'agape', love for all mankind.

Joseph Fletcher also believed that the teaching of Jesus to 'love your neighbour' means Christians should apply Situation Ethics to their decision-making.

The situationist enters into every decision-making situation fully armed with the ethical maxims of his community and its heritage, and he treats them with respect as illuminators of his problems. Just the same he is prepared in any situation to compromise them or set them aside *in the situation* if love seems better served by doing so.

Joseph Fletcher, *Situation Ethics: The New Morality*

In times of war it might be the most loving thing to go against the teaching of 'do not murder' in order to protect whole countries. Is it right to torture a person to get information that may save the lives of others?

Knowledge check

1 What is Situation Ethics?
2 Who wrote a book explaining Situation Ethics and what was it called?
3 What does Joseph Fletcher say about rules and teachings when making decisions?
4 Give an example of when a person must go against their basic principles.
5 What does Joseph Fletcher say a Christian should base their decision making on? Why?

● Reasons for different Christian attitudes to making decisions using Situation Ethics

Christians should use Situation Ethics when making moral decisions	Christians should not use Situation Ethics when making moral decisions
It is based on Jesus' teaching to *love one another (John 13:34)*	All religions have religious rules that are put in place for the well-being of their followers
It is personal, so can take into account culture and the particular time in history the decision is being made	St Paul points out that the law was put in place because humans are likely to be selfish and sinful if they try to decide themselves
It is based on the well-being of other people; it is not selfish	It might lead to evil acts being regarded as acceptable
If *God is love (1 John 4:8)* then doing the loving thing is doing what God wants	The idea of love could be difficult to apply if a person is personally involved

A01

1 In pairs, produce a PowerPoint presentation to show the different Christian attitudes towards using Situation Ethics and the reasons for them.
2 Add diagrams or pictures to illustrate the reasons.
3 Present your explanation of the different attitudes to the rest of the class.

A02

1 Use the information on pages 122–123 to participate in a decision alley.
2 The class divides in two, one side thinks of reasons why Christians should use Situation Ethics and the other side thinks of reasons why Christians should not use Situation Ethics.
3 Each side lines up shoulder to shoulder with an alley between. A member of the class then walks down the alley asking for advice from members on either side.
4 Based on the information given in the decision alley they vote to agree with Situation Ethics or disagree.
5 This can be repeated with several class members.
6 At the end, the class can count votes to find out the majority view.

exam practice b

Do you think all Christians should agree with Situation Ethics? Give **two** reasons for your point of view.

Examiner's hint: Make sure you give reasons whether Christians should agree rather than whether you agree. (A02)

exam practice c

Explain why some Christians do not agree with Situation Ethics.

Examiner's hint: Do not give reasons why Christians might agree with Situation Ethics – you will not get any marks for them. (A01)

exam practice d

'Christians should always use Situation Ethics.'
In your answer you should refer to Christianity.
i) Do you agree? Give reasons for your answer.
ii) Give reasons why some people may disagree with you.

Examiner's hint: Give your opinion about whether Christians should use Situation Ethics at the beginning of d) i). (A02)

5.5 Making moral decisions: using a variety of authorities

● The variety of authorities used for making decisions

The Bible is used because it is inspired by God, it shows what Jesus would do in situations, it contains the teachings of Jesus and it shows how the apostles dealt with moral issues in the early Church.

But Bible teaching is not flexible, it is not up to date, it is not always easy to understand and it sometimes contradicts itself.

The Church is used because:
● the Church is the Body of Christ
● the authority of Jesus has been passed down to the leaders of the Church
● Christ is the head of the Church
● the Holy Spirit is present in the Church today.

But Church teaching is not personal, it is not always easy to understand, people might not have access to it and it does not always keep up with changes in society.

Conscience is used because it is easy to use. It makes you feel guilty if you do wrong, it reminds a person of their duties to other people and it encourages a person to do good.

But conscience can be selfish. It might go against what it is acceptable in society, it might not be well formed and you might need to listen to someone else rather than deciding on your own.

Situation Ethics is used because it is based on Jesus' teaching to 'love one another'. It is personal, it is based on the well-being of other people and it is doing what God wants.

But Situation Ethics might not be a good way to make decisions because religious rules are put in place for the well-being of religious followers. Humans are likely to be selfish if they try to decide themselves. Evil acts might be regarded as acceptable and the idea of love could be difficult to apply.

Knowledge check

1 What are the four different sources of authority Christians use when making moral decisions?
2 Give four reasons why a Christian might choose to use more than one source of authority.

● Why some Christians use a variety of authorities for making moral decisions

- Some of the information from authorities may be out of date and cannot help with modern situations.
- Some sources of authority are dependent on the person having sufficient knowledge to make the decision, which they may not have.
- Some sources of authority might give solutions that are not acceptable in today's society.
- They may think that a mixture of sources of authority will give a more informed choice.
- Different authorities can be used in different situations.
- Some sources of authority might not give advice on a particular moral issue.

A01

1 Copy and complete the following table.

	Source of authority				
	Bible	Church	Conscience	Situation Ethics	Variety of authorities
Four reasons for using					
Four reasons for not using					

2 Produce a poster to show either the reasons why Christians should use a variety of sources of authority or why they should rely on one source.
3 Present the poster to the class.

exam practice c

Explain how Christians make moral decisions.

Examiner's hint: Giving a reason is a good way to develop a description. (A01)

A02

1 A Christian has to choose whether to attend a friend's birthday party when it is at the same time as they normally go to church. Explain what kind of advice they might get from each of the sources of authority (Bible, Church, conscience, Situation Ethics and other authorities).
2 Which source of authority do you think gives the best advice? Give three reasons for your opinion.

exam practice b

Do you think that Christians should use a variety of authorities when they make moral decisions? Give **two** reasons for your point of view.

Examiner's hint: The reasons you give should refer to why Christians do something rather than why you might do something. (A02)

exam practice d

'Christians should always use a variety of authorities when they make moral decisions.'
In your answer you should refer to Christianity.
i) Do you agree? Give reasons for your answer.
ii) Give reasons why some people may disagree with you.

Examiner's hint: Repeating the question at the beginning of your answer helps to remind you what the point of the question is. (A02)

5.6 Human rights in the UK

Human rights are rights which everyone should have because, as human beings, each person is equal to another person. No one person has more human rights than another person.

The United Nations (UN) produced a declaration of human rights that was adopted in 1948 by 50 countries. Further countries have adopted it since. The declaration, which can be found on the UN's website, lists 30 articles covering a number of different rights.

The legal systems of most countries have added laws to ensure that these rights are protected. In the UK, the Human Rights Act 1998 was passed to ensure that people's rights are protected as long as they do not affect anyone else's rights.

KEY WORDS

human rights The rights and freedoms to which everyone is entitled.

More on the Human Rights Act can be found on the government website: www.direct.gov.uk/en/governmentcitizensandrights/yourrightsandresponsibilities/dg_4002951

The UN's declaration of human rights: www.un.org/en/documents/udhr

Human rights include:

1 Humans are all **born free**. They should all be treated in the same way.

2 Human rights **belong to everybody**; whatever they think or believe.

3 Human beings have the **right to life**, and to **live in freedom** and **safety**.

4 Nobody has any right to make another person their slave.

5 Nobody has any right to hurt or to torture another person.

6 The law is the **same** for everyone.

7 Nobody has the right to put someone in prison without good reason.

8 If a person is frightened of being badly treated in their own country, they have the **right to go to another country to be safe**.

9 Every adult has the **right to marry and have a family** if they want to.

10 Everyone has the **right to own things**.

11 Everyone has the **right to believe in what they want**.

12 Everyone has the **right to free speech, to think and say what they like**.

13 Everyone has the right not to be subjected to the death penalty.

● Why human rights are important

- They ensure everyone is treated the same.
- They make sure that one group is not discriminated against.
- They mean everyone can be protected from harm.
- They make sure everyone is treated with dignity.
- They ensure people are treated fairly.

Knowledge check

1 What is meant by human rights?
2 Who is entitled to human rights? Why?
3 List four human rights.
4 Explain in 50 words why human rights are important. Give examples in your answer.

Slavery still taking place in UK

Police raided a farm in Bedfordshire last Sunday and later arrested four Irish men with offences against the Coroners and Justice Act 2009. If they are found to be guilty of forcing a person to work, they may go to prison for up to seven years and if they are found guilty of holding a person in servitude they may have to go to prison for fourteen years.

The 24 people, who have been described as slaves, were kept at a travellers' park and were living in cramped, broken and dirty housing. The police found that some had had to sleep in kennels and horseboxes.

The men had been made to work laying tarmac and clearing land. The four arrested men argued that they were not using them as slaves and they had been paid £30 a day and given accommodation for their work.

Many of the men described as slaves were unwell and suffered from addictions to alcohol and drugs. The Red Cross were asked to help the men, some of whom were clearly unwell.

If the police can prove that the men were ill-treated and that they were not allowed freedom to go where they wanted, then they will be able to prosecute the four men they arrested.

A spokesman for Anti-Slavery International when asked to comment on the case said: 'I was shocked, but I was not surprised.' Anti-Slavery International is running a slavery-free London campaign to ensure nothing involved with the 2012 London Olympics involves slavery.

A01

Write a letter to a newspaper to explain the reasons why protecting human rights is important. The letter should include examples of how human rights can be abused like in the example above.

Your letter must include:

✓ a brief description of what human rights are
✓ reasons why human rights are important
✓ examples of what happens when human rights are not protected.

Today people are more likely to become victims of abuse because of who they are, rather than for what they think, say or do.'

Amnesty International

'It is essential, if man is not to be compelled to have recourse, as a last resort, to rebellion against tyranny and oppression, that human rights should be protected by the rule of law.'

Universal Declaration of Human Rights

'First they came for the Jews and I did not speak out – because I was not a Jew. Then they came for the communists and I did not speak out – because I was not a communist. Then they came for the trade unionists and I did not speak out – because I was not a trade unionist. Then they came for me – and there was no one left to speak out for me.'

Martin Niemöller (1892–1984)

A02

1 In pairs, read the quotes on human rights above.
2 Decide which you think is the best quote.
3 Write it out and try to give four reasons why you think it says why human rights are important.

exam practice b

Do you think human rights need more protection? Give **two** reasons for your point of view.

Examiner's hint: Although you can describe what protection human rights have at present, you will only get marks for giving reasons why you think they need more protection, or why they do not need more protection. (A02)

exam practice c

Explain why human rights are important.

Examiner's hint: Do not explain what human rights are; the question asks why they are important. (A01)

exam practice d

'Not everyone deserves human rights.'
In your answer you should refer to Christianity.
i) Do you agree? Give reasons for your answer.
ii) Give reasons why some people may disagree with you.

Examiner's hint: Although the chapter does not refer to Christianity, all d) questions must include a religious reason. (A02)

5.7 Christians and human rights

Christians support human rights, not only because they are part of the law but also because they are part of Christian teaching. Human rights are supported in the Old and New Testaments and by the statements made by Churches today. Many different Christian organisations work to protect human rights because they see it as part of being a Christian.

KEY WORDS

the Golden Rule The teaching of Jesus that you should treat others as you would like them to treat you.

Christian Solidarity Worldwide (CSW) is a Christian organisation working for religious freedom through advocacy and human rights, in the pursuit of justice.

Everyone is entitled to human rights as everyone is loved by God.

The Bible teaches that people should 'love their neighbour'.

Christians believe in the sanctity of life. All life is holy and should be protected.

Why human rights are important for Christians

The Bible teaches that everyone was created in the image of God (Genesis).

Jesus treated those who had fewer human rights as equals: children, women, Samaritans and foreigners.

The law does not always protect human rights. Christianity should, because although the death of Jesus was lawful, it went against human rights.

The Golden Rule supports protection of human rights. No one would want to be treated as if they had no rights.

Learn to do right; seek justice. Defend the oppressed. Take up the cause of the fatherless; plead the case of the widow (Isaiah 1:17).

Knowledge check

1 How do Christians support human rights?
2 List three biblical reasons why human rights are important.
3 List three other reasons why human rights are important.

A01

1 Work in small groups to produce a TV advert or bulletin explaining the importance of human rights for Christians (which could possibly be filmed).
2 Divide the group into actors, camera operators and interviewers as required.
3 Ensure the advert provides information about what human rights are as well as why they are important for Christians.

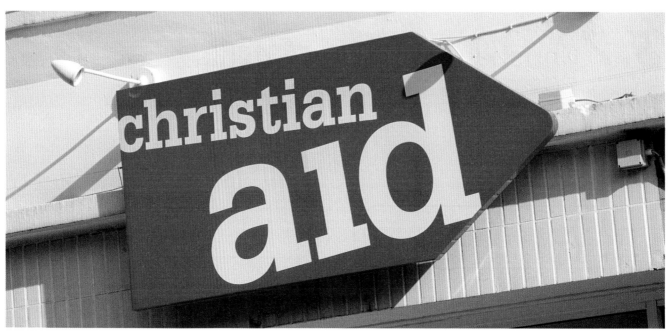

Christian Aid is a charity that seeks to end poverty. The charity recognises that many of the rights that other people have, to be able to work and to own property, are missing from people living in poverty. The charity therefore works to restore these people's rights and to end poverty.

AO2

Work in pairs to produce an answer to the following b)-type question: 'Do you think human rights are important for Christians?'

1 Using a large piece of paper take two minutes to write a reason which could be used to answer the question.
2 After two minutes, pass the sheet to another pair who have the next two minutes to develop the reason given.
3 After two minutes, pass the sheet to another pair who have the next two minutes to add a different reason to the answer.
4 Repeat step 2 with another pair.
5 After the answer to the b) question has two developed reasons, everyone should look over the answer and write the perfected version in their notes.

exam practice b

Do you think human rights are important for Christians? Give **two** reasons for your point of view.

Examiner's hint: Try to use biblical quotes to develop your reasons. (AO2)

exam practice c

Explain why human rights are important for Christians.

Examiner's hint: If you can't remember any Christian reasons think about why you might think human rights are important. (AO1)

exam practice d

'Christians should work to protect human rights.'
In your answer you should refer to Christianity.
i) Do you agree? Give reasons for your answer.
ii) Give reasons why some people may disagree with you.

Examiner's hint: A reason can be developed by quoting from scriptures, for example a reference to Isaiah 1:17. (AO2)

5.8 Living in a democracy

● Democratic and electoral processes in the UK

The UK is a democracy. People aged 18 and over can vote in elections and decide which **political party** will be elected to form a government.

Democratic processes in the UK allow all adults to have a say in what policies will become law, which in turn may lead to **social change**. This means that adults have to find out about the policies of each of the political parties. Voters are then free to join and support parties that agree or mostly agree with their ideas about running the country.

People are free to try and influence the policies that governments have by forming **pressure groups**. These groups draw attention to issues and the way that they want to change government policy. For example, student unions have formed a pressure group to protest against the government's policy of tuition fees.

- The **electoral process** for the UK national parliament is described as a first-past-the-post system. The person who gets the most votes gets elected.
- Elections to the European parliament use proportional representation. The UK is divided into nine areas and political parties will have members in the European parliament in line with the proportion of votes they receive.

> **KEY WORDS**
>
> **democratic processes** The ways in which all citizens can take part in government (usually through elections).
>
> **electoral processes** The ways in which voting is organised.
>
> **political party** A group which tries to be elected into power on the basis of its policies (e.g. Labour, Conservative).
>
> **pressure group** A group formed to influence government policy on a particular issue.
>
> **social change** The way in which society has changed and is changing (and also the possibilities for future change).

Knowledge check

1 Why is the UK described as a democracy?
2 What do democratic processes allow adults to do?
3 What does a pressure group do? Give an example.
4 What is the electoral system for the UK national government called? How does this work?
5 What is the electoral system for the European parliament called? How does this work?

Students in 2011 protesting against the government's policy on university tuition fees. Do you think pressure groups marching and striking will make a government change its policies?

A01

In small groups, create a poster to explain either what democratic processes are or what electoral processes are. The posters should be aimed at people who have no understanding of the two processes and should include the key word definitions.

It means your opinions are taken into account.

Some people in the world do not have the right to vote – you should use yours to show that it matters.

It makes sure that the people who are chosen to run the country are the right people for the job.

Why it is important to take part in democratic and electoral processes

It is essential for democracy. Otherwise the same people would remain in power all the time.

The government make decisions about the way you will be able to live your life. You should make sure you are happy with them.

It stops extremists taking over.

A02

1 In pairs discuss the reasons on the spider diagram above and think whether you could add any more.
2 In pairs, decide which are the best reasons and which are not so good.
3 Work on your own and write a list of the reasons in order starting with the best reason and finishing with the least good.
4 Draw a line across your list at the point at which you stop agreeing with the reasons.
5 Return to pair work and discuss why you have put your list in this order.

exam practice b

'Do you think everyone should vote?' Give **two** reasons for your point of view.

Examiner's hint: Start with your personal opinion. (A02)

exam practice c

Explain why it is important to take part in electoral processes.

Examiner's hint: Electoral processes is another way of saying voting. (A01)

exam practice d

'It does not matter whether a person votes.'
In your answer you should refer to Christianity.
i) Do you agree? Give reasons for your answer.
ii) Give reasons why some people may disagree with you.

Examiner's hint: Make sure you include a Christian reason in your answer. (A02)

5.9 Christian teachings on moral duties and responsibilities

There are many Christian teachings that show what is morally right. They show that it is a Christian's duty to care for others and that people should especially help those who are in need.

● The Golden Rule (Matthew 7:12)

If you would like to be loved then love others.

If you want to be cared for when you are sick then care for the sick.

Do to others what you would have them do to you (Matthew 7:12).

If you would like someone to feed you when you are hungry then feed the starving, give to charity.

If you would like someone to talk to when you are lonely then welcome the people who are not included in groups.

Knowledge check

1 What do Christian teachings about moral responsibilities teach?
2 What is the Golden Rule?
3 How does the Golden Rule tell people to act towards other people?
4 Give two examples of how the Golden Rule could be used in everyday life.
5 In the Parable of the Sheep and the Goats (opposite), who were the good people and who were the bad people?
6 What did the good people do? How were they rewarded?
7 What did the bad people do? How were they punished?

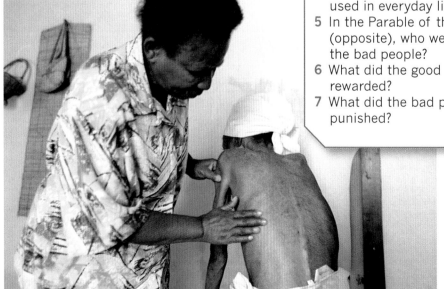

A nurse caring for her dying patient at the patient's home.

● The Parable of the Sheep and the Goats (Matthew 25:31–46)

'When the Son of Man comes in his glory, and all the angels with him, he will sit on his glorious throne. All the nations will be gathered before him, and he will separate the people one from another as a shepherd separates the sheep from the goats. He will put the sheep on his right and the goats on his left.

'Then the King will say to those on his right, "Come, you who are blessed by my Father; take your inheritance, the kingdom prepared for you since the creation of the world. For I was hungry and you gave me something to eat, I was thirsty and you gave me something to drink, I was a stranger and you invited me in, I needed clothes and you clothed me, I was sick and you looked after me, I was in prison and you came to visit me."

'Then the righteous will answer him, "Lord, when did we see you hungry and feed you, or thirsty and give you something to drink? When did we see you a stranger and invite you in, or needing clothes and clothe you? When did we see you sick or in prison and go to visit you?"

'The King will reply, "Truly I tell you, whatever you did for one of the least of these brothers and sisters of mine, you did for me."

'Then he will say to those on his left, "Depart from me, you who are cursed, into the eternal fire prepared for the devil and his angels. For I was hungry and you gave me nothing to eat, I was thirsty and you gave me nothing to drink, I was a stranger and you did not invite me in, I needed clothes and you did not clothe me, I was sick and in prison and you did not look after me."

'They also will answer, "Lord, when did we see you hungry or thirsty or a stranger or needing clothes or sick or in prison, and did not help you?"

'He will reply, "Truly I tell you, whatever you did not do for one of the least of these, you did not do for me."

'Then they will go away to eternal punishment, but the righteous to eternal life' (*Matthew 25:31–46*).

This parable shows the following to Christians:

- they will be judged at the end of time
- they must show care for those in need: the hungry, thirsty, lonely, naked, sick and prisoners
- that when they help others they are serving Jesus
- they will be rewarded for helping others
- they will be punished if they do nothing to help others.

An early depiction of the Parable of the Sheep and the Goats.

● Am I my brother's keeper? (Genesis 4:1–10)

Adam made love to his wife Eve, and she became pregnant and gave birth to Cain. She said, 'With the help of the LORD I have brought forth a man.' Later she gave birth to his brother Abel.

Now Abel kept flocks, and Cain worked the soil. In the course of time Cain brought some of the fruits of the soil as an offering to the LORD. But Abel also brought an offering – fat portions from some of the firstborn of his flock. The LORD looked with favour on Abel and his offering, but on Cain and his offering he did not look with favour. So Cain was very angry, and his face was downcast.

Then the LORD said to Cain, 'Why are you angry? Why is your face downcast? If you do what is right, will you not be accepted? But if you do not do what is right, sin is crouching at your door; it desires to have you, but you must rule over it.'

Now Cain said to his brother Abel, 'Let's go out to the field.' While they were in the field, Cain attacked his brother Abel and killed him.

Then the LORD said to Cain, 'Where is your brother Abel?'

'I don't know,' he replied. 'Am I my brother's keeper?'

The LORD said, 'What have you done? Listen! Your brother's blood cries out to me from the ground' (Genesis 4:1–10).

Cain murdering Abel.

● We should love one another (1 John 3:11–18)

For this is the message you heard from the beginning: we should love one another. Do not be like Cain, who belonged to the evil one and murdered his brother. And why did he murder him? Because his own actions were evil and his brother's were righteous. Do not be surprised, my brothers and sisters, if the world hates you. We know that we have passed from death to life, because we love each other. Anyone who does not love remains in death. Anyone who hates a brother or sister is a murderer, and you know that no murderer has eternal life residing in him (1 John 3:11–18).

These stories are important because they show:

- you should do what is right
- if you do bad things you will be punished
- God will reward the people who do what he wants
- people should care for one another
- hating someone is as bad as murdering them.

A01

1 Read through the Bible stories on pages 135–136.
2 Draw three spider diagrams or comic strips to record what each of the stories says.

A02

In small groups produce a presentation on one of the Bible stories on pages 135–136. Include in your presentation:

- either a PowerPoint presentation or a role play
- an account of the story
- an explanation of what the story teaches about how Christians should behave.

exam practice b

Do you think the Golden Rule is a good guideline? Give **two** reasons for your point of view.

Examiner's hint: Start each reason on a new line. (A02)

exam practice c

Explain why Christians should treat others the way they would like to be treated.

Examiner's hint: This refers to the Golden Rule so make sure you know all the references. (A01)

exam practice d

'Religious people should care for other people.'
In your answer you should refer to at least one religion.
i) Do you agree? Give reasons for your answer.
ii) Give reasons why some people may disagree with you.

Examiner's hint: 'Religious people' is a phrase used to cover all religions but in a d) question you must refer to one specific religion. (A02)

5.10 Genetic engineering

● The nature of genetic engineering

Genetic engineering (or genetic modification) changes the genes within a living organism by either adding DNA (deoxyribonucleic acid) from another living organism or removing DNA. This is done by using enzymes which can 'cut and paste' DNA. DNA is found within cells and contains the genetic information that tells cells how to behave. The result of changing the genes in a cell is that it can change the characteristics of an organism.

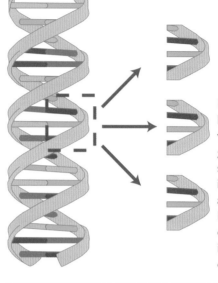

Biological science has worked out a way to cut useful genes from one sort of DNA and insert them into another type of DNA. Changing organisms this way is called genetic engineering.

Advantages of genetic engineering
- Genetic diseases can be found and removed, for example Huntington's disease and cystic fibrosis.
- Plants can be grown to yield more crops.
- Animals can be grown to be heavier and have leaner meat.
- Disease-resistant plants and animals can be grown.
- Organisms can be made to produce chemicals that are needed in medicine, for example bacteria that produce human insulin.
- Plants can be grown to improve on the characteristics they already have, for example trees grown to absorb more carbon dioxide than usual.

A side-effect of changing genetic information is that it can reduce the life expectancy of organisms.

Disadvantages of genetic engineering
- Other diseases may be caused by genetic modification.
- Science might go too far and produce unnatural organisms.
- Changes may affect the balance of biological systems.
- The long-term effects are not known.
- It could reduce the variety of animals or plants grown.

It is possible to manipulate DNA so that crops such as tomatoes are disease resistant.

Knowledge check

1 What is genetic engineering?
2 How are genes modified?
3 Why do some people think genetic engineering is good?
4 Why do some people think genetic engineering is not good?

A01

You are a journalist and your newspaper has asked you to write an article about genetic engineering

In your article, you should include the reasons why people might support genetic engineering and the reasons why they may not. Use the different reasons given in this section to help you.

● Cloning

Cloning is using techniques developed in genetic engineering to produce exact copies of entire cells or organisms. In cloning, a normal cell is removed from an organism. It then has its DNA removed and the DNA is placed into a reproductive cell. This then reproduces and forms a copy of the original cell and then the organism. This is used in stem cell research where human cells are cloned which can then be used to find out more about human disease and development.

Advantages of cloning	Disadvantages of cloning
Animals can easily be produced for eating	It can be very expensive as many clones do not survive
The genetic causes of diseases can be researched	Cloned animals often have birth defects
Diseases may be cured	Cloned organisms often have a shorter life span
Possibility of growing organs to use in organ transplants	Cloned organisms seem to be more likely to develop infections

A02

Imagine you have been employed to produce an advertising campaign to either encourage people to accept cloning or encourage people to reject cloning. In groups, design either:

a) a poster campaign (a group of four posters that have a common theme); or

b) a text message campaign (a group of four texts that have a common theme); or

c) a computer pop-up campaign (a group of four pop-ups that have a common theme).

Explain your campaign to the rest of the class and decide which of the campaigns is the most effective.

exam practice b

'Do you think humans should be cloned?' Give **two** reasons for your point of view.

Examiner's hint: It is possible to agree and disagree with statements like this but it is easier to get marks if you stick to one point of view. (A02)

exam practice c

Explain why some people accept the use of genetic engineering.

Examiner's hint: This question only wants reasons supporting the use of genetic engineering so you will not get any marks for giving reasons saying genetic engineering is wrong. (A01)

exam practice d

'Everyone should agree with cloning.' In your answer you should refer to at least one religion.
i) Do you agree? Give reasons for your answer.
ii) Give reasons why some people may disagree with you.

Examiner's hint: Make sure d ii) are reasons for the opposite opinion to the one given in d) i). (A02)

5.11 Christian attitudes to genetic engineering

There are two main Christian attitudes to genetic engineering. One attitude is that it is completely unacceptable and the other is that it is acceptable within limits. The reasons why Christians have different attitudes towards genetic engineering are based on Christian teachings such as the Golden Rule (see page 134) and the Creation (see pages 12–13).

Genetic engineering is acceptable ...	Genetic engineering is not acceptable ...
It can heal others following the example of Jesus	People are made in the image of God, not how a scientist wants them
It shows good stewardship (care) of living things	St Paul said the body is the 'Temple of the Holy Spirit' so we should not interfere with it
It can be used to feed many people especially in parts of the world where food is scarce	God created the world and everything within it. Humans should not change how God created it. *God created mankind in his own image (Genesis 1:27)*
James 2:16 says that Christians should attend to people's physical needs, 'if one of you ... does nothing about their physical needs, what good is it?'	Stem cell research involves making a human blastocyst (embryo) and then using it to experiment on, throwing it away after use. This could be regarded as ending a possible life. *You shall not murder (Exodus 20:13)*

Are the problems with genetic engineering too great to allow it to be used?

A01

1 Read through the Christian reasons for the different attitudes towards the use of genetic engineering in the table above. Note which reasons have quotes as evidence to develop the reasons.
2 In pairs, use the information given above to produce a PowerPoint slide or a poster to explain the different attitudes Christians have towards the use of genetic engineering.
3 Use your PowerPoint to give a presentation to the class of the different attitudes Christians have towards the use of genetic engineering.

Knowledge check ✱

1 What are the two main attitudes towards genetic engineering in Christianity?
2 List four reasons why a Christian might say that genetic engineering is acceptable.
3 List four reasons why a Christian might say that genetic engineering is not acceptable.

Brian

I think the use of genetic engineering goes against God's plan for the world. In Genesis it says that when he created the world, 'God saw all that he had made, and it was very good'. I think this means that we should not change what God has created and genetic engineering does this.

Although Jesus did teach us to love our neighbour, it might be more loving to allow God's plans for a person to take place, rather than try to interfere with someone's genes. To use genetic engineering or gene therapy (changing the genes in adults rather than before birth) would make a person different to how God wanted that person to be. I think genetic engineering is sinful; the body is the temple of the Holy Spirit and should not be played with.

Vicki

I think that God has enabled scientists to have the knowledge to carry out genetic engineering and that God would want people to use this knowledge to make life better.

Jesus cared for those who were ill, he healed the blind man and even raised Jairus' daughter. I think when humans use genetic engineering they are doing what Jesus wants Christians to do, to be his hands in the world today.

God created humans in his image and gave humans dominion (power) over the world. I think that we should use the creative part of being in God's image to care for the world, by increasing the amount of crops that plants give so we can ensure no one starves.

Read Brian and Vicki's views on genetic engineering.

A02

1 Draw two spider diagrams to record the two different attitudes Christians have towards the use of genetic engineering.
2 Use this information to participate in a decision alley. This is when the class divides in two, one side thinks of reasons why Christians accept the use of genetic engineering and the other side thinks of reasons why it should not be acceptable.
3 Each side then lines up shoulder to shoulder with an alley between. A member of the class then walks down the alley asking for advice from members on either side. When they get to the end they make a decision.

exam practice c

Explain why some Christians do not accept the use of genetic engineering.

Examiner's hint: Make sure your reasons are specifically Christian. (A01)

exam practice b

'Do you think Christians should accept the use of genetic engineering?' Give **two** reasons for your point of view.

Examiner's hint: A quote is a good way to develop a reason. (A02)

exam practice d

'Genetic engineering should be accepted by all Christians.' In your answer you should refer to at least one religion.
i) Do you agree? Give reasons for your answer.
ii) Give reasons why some people may disagree with you.

Examiner's hint: the answer to d) ii) must be the opposite point of view to the one given in d) i). (A02)

Examination practice

In the first section on the paper for each Unit you will be assessed on your spelling, punctuation and grammar (SPaG). There are 4 marks available for this, so write clearly, check your spelling and try to use specialist words. Below is guidance on how to answer the question a) from Section 5: Religion: rights and responsibilities. All a) questions are worth 2 marks.

The a) questions test the key words which are provided by Edexcel and are used in this book. It is important to make sure that you learn them.

Every section will have two a) questions and they will either ask for a definition of one of the key words or ask for two examples of the word. Look at the steps below about how to answer question 1a), then try to answer question 2a).

Sample question

1a) What is a pressure group? [2]

Sample question

2a) What does political party mean? [2]

How to answer
The best way to get full marks on an a) question:
- Write the glossary definition supplied by the exam board – these are the ones used in this book.
- To get full marks you must provide all the information that is within the exam board's definition.
- If you leave out any information or the wording is not quite correct you may only get 1 mark out of 2.

Step 1
- Try to remember the key word definition.

A group who want to pressure someone.

Step 2
- Read your answer. Could it mean something else? This answer could mean hurting someone. Add words to it to make it clear that you do not mean hurting someone.

A group who want to pressure the government about something they feel is important.

Step 3
- Read your answer again. Does it include all the parts of the key word definition and is it clear? It is, but it would have been easier to learn by heart the key word definition and write it.

A group formed to influence the government on a particular issue.

Examiner's comment
Learn the definitions used in this book as they are the same as those provided by the exam board.
To get full marks you must provide all the information that is within the exam board's definition, even if you think there is a different definition for the same word.

Below is guidance on how to answer the question b) from Section 5: Religion: rights and responsibilities. As it is a b) question, it is worth 4 marks.

In every section there are two b) questions to choose from. Try question 1b) using the hints provided below. Then apply these steps to question 2b).

Sample question
1b) Do you think humans should be cloned? [4]

Sample question
2b) Do you think it is important for people to vote? [4]

How to answer
To get full marks on a b) question, you must give your opinion and then support it with two reasons and develop each of the reasons.

Step 1
- Start with your opinion, think of one reason why a human should be cloned. It does not matter what your opinion is.

I think a human should be cloned because it might help sick members of the family.

Step 2
- Think of a way to develop the reason. The easiest way to develop a reason is to give an example or a quote.

For example, a clone could be grown with healthy kidneys which could be transplanted.

Step 3
- Think of a second reason why a human should be cloned. It does not matter whether your reason is religious or not. Write the second reason as a new paragraph.

I also think because I am a Christian that Jesus was a healer and cloning continues his work and should be done.

Step 4
- Develop your second reason. Ensure the development is about your reason and still answers the question.

Christians are the Body of Christ on earth and we must use our knowledge to do his healing work.

Examiner's comment
✓ **Maximum marks will be awarded for two reasons which have been developed as long as they answer the question.**
✓ **Development must link to the question set. For example: the second reason refers to Jesus as a healer; the development could not be why Christians follow the example of Jesus as this would not link back to why humans should be cloned.**

Religion and society

Section 6: Religion: environmental and medical issues

6.1 Global warming

Global warming is the phrase that is used to describe the overall increase in the earth's surface temperature. The last century has been the warmest since records began, in 1888. The nine hottest years on record have happened since 1980: the two warmest years since then were in 2005 and 2010. This was confirmed by the UN Inter-governmental Panel on Climate Change in November 2011, who also indicated that global warming was going to cause a range of extreme weather conditions.

Some people prefer to use the phrase 'climate change' as it is more accurate. Many parts of the world will not necessarily get warmer.

It is thought that global warming is caused by the greenhouse effect. Global warming is a natural process where some of the sun's rays (as radiation) pass through the earth's atmosphere to warm the earth. Without this warmth much of life on earth would not be able to survive. Some of the radiation escapes from the earth through the atmosphere as infrared radiation. This means that the earth does not warm up too much.

The greenhouse effect becomes a problem when there are extra gases released into the atmosphere such as carbon dioxide, methane, nitrous oxide and ozone. These extra gases cause the infrared radiation to be reflected back on to the earth rather than escaping through the atmosphere. This makes the earth hotter than it would have been, affecting the weather and life.

Some gases such as chlorofluorocarbons (CFCs) also cause an enhanced greenhouse effect because they break down the protective ozone layer in the upper atmosphere. This allows more harmful rays from the sun to reach the earth.

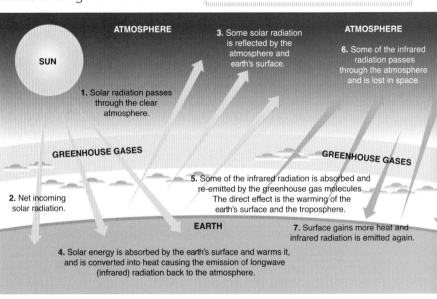

ATMOSPHERE

SUN

3. Some solar radiation is reflected by the atmosphere and earth's surface.

ATMOSPHERE

6. Some of the infrared radiation passes through the atmosphere and is lost in space.

1. Solar radiation passes through the clear atmosphere.

GREENHOUSE GASES

GREENHOUSE GASES

2. Net incoming solar radiation.

5. Some of the infrared radiation is absorbed and re-emitted by the greenhouse gas molecules. The direct effect is the warming of the earth's surface and the troposphere.

EARTH

7. Surface gains more heat and infrared radiation is emitted again.

4. Solar energy is absorbed by the earth's surface and warms it, and is converted into heat causing the emission of longwave (infrared) radiation back to the atmosphere.

The greenhouse effect.

Deforestation has meant there are fewer trees to remove carbon dioxide from the atmosphere.

The earth's population is increasing greatly. This means there are more people to burn fuel, clear land and farm food, all of which means more gases are released.

Many fertilisers, used to grow crops, release nitrous oxide.

Causes of enhanced global warming

Burning fossil fuels, such as oil and coal, releases large amounts of carbon dioxide.

CFCs are used in refrigerators and insulation materials.

Animals naturally produce methane. However, because more and more animals are farmed for meat there is more methane produced.

● Problems caused by enhanced global warming

Melting ice caps will cause sea levels to rise.

Rising sea levels will cause flooding in low-lying areas.

As low-lying land becomes flooded, people will move to higher ground, causing populations to become crowded, which could lead to increased disease.

Temperatures will increase at the poles rather than at the equator, causing the ice caps to melt.

Increasing land temperature will cause soil to dry out, leading to drought.

With less land to farm (because of flooding) and drought there might be insufficient food to feed the population.

Water will evaporate from the oceans faster, leading to violent storms, torrential rain and flooding.

A01

Write a leaflet about global warming for pupils in year 9. The leaflet should be informative, interesting to look at and factual. Include the following in your leaflet:

✓ what global warming is and how it is caused
✓ the main things humans do to make the greenhouse effect a problem
✓ what might happen as a result of enhanced global warming.

Governments meet at global conferences and agree to restrict carbon dioxide production.

People should use less energy, by using low-energy lightbulbs, for example, and turning off electrical devices rather than leaving them on standby.

Energy companies can try to produce power in environmentally friendly ways.

Possible solutions to enhanced global warming

Power can be produced in ways that do not produce harmful chemicals.

Methods of transport that do not need fossil fuels must be developed.

Use alternative ways to travel: walking, cycling and public transport are all better for the environment than cars and aeroplanes.

Increased recycling to make better use of resources.

A02

Prepare for a class debate on 'Global warming means people should change the way they live'.

1 Write the debate title as a heading and then draw a table listing reasons to support the statement and reasons to argue against the statement.
2 Hold the debate. Ensure there is a chairperson and at least two people to speak on the issue. Ask questions of the speakers before taking a class vote.

exam practice b

Do you think it is important to find solutions to global warming? Give **two** reasons for your point of view.

Examiner's hint: Make sure you start your answer with your opinion. (A02)

exam practice c

Explain why global warming may cause problems in the future.

Examiner's hint: You could write two reasons and develop each reason with an example. (A01)

exam practice d

'It is not possible to stop global warming.'
In your answer you should refer to at least one religion.
i) Do you agree? Give reasons for your answer.
ii) Give reasons why some people may disagree with you.

Examiner's hint: Make sure all reasons in d) i) are your opinion and all the reasons in d) ii) are the opposite to your opinion. Do not muddle up the opinions. (A02)

6.2 Pollution

Pollution is when something is added to an environment which causes it to be contaminated (made impure). This can be anything chemical, biological or physical, which will mean that the **environment** cannot function as it should. Often pollution will lead to problems that affect humans.

KEY WORDS

environment The surroundings in which plants and animals live and on which they depend to live.

● Forms of pollution

Air pollution
- Air pollution is when gases are added to the air, changing the balance of the gases within the air.
- Enhanced global warming (see Section 6.1) is a result of air pollution and as such it is one of the most dangerous forms of pollution.
- Gases such as carbon dioxide, sulphur oxides and nitrogen oxides are all produced in industrial processes and these cause enhanced global warming. They may also produce poisons that affect breathing and can cause problems such as asthma. They are also produced by cars and especially by aeroplanes.
- Gases such as sulphur dioxide may react in the air to produce sulphuric acid. When this mixes with rain clouds, the rain becomes acidic. Rain usually has a pH of 5.7; however, acid rain has been recorded as having a pH of 2.3. This kills trees and poisons lakes. Acid rain can also erode the stone surfaces of buildings.

A coal-fired power station produces gases. Why might these gases be harmful?

Knowledge check

Look at pages 147–149.
1 What is pollution?
2 List three types of pollution.
3 Describe two ways air can become polluted.
4 Describe two ways water can become polluted.
5 Describe two ways land can become polluted.

Water pollution

Water pollution is usually chemical or biological, and can be natural or caused by humans. Water is usually described as polluted when it cannot be used by humans. UNICEF (and the World Health Organisation) have recorded that people in all developed countries have access to unpolluted water but approximately 884 million people in other parts of the world do not.

Water is chemically polluted when chemicals enter the water system in a variety of ways:

- From air pollution when they are then washed into rivers by rain.
- From rained off surfaces, for example from fields or roads. Chemicals from 'run off' may go into the water system or directly into streams.
- Directly through accidental spillage, possibly from ships.
- From industry, although doing this purposely is against the law.

Water is biologically polluted when living things contaminate the water, such as:

- Bacteria enter the water system from sewage.
- Household rubbish that may enter the water system through drains.
- Poor care of farm animals (or pets) may result in bacteria entering the water system though their waste.

http://water.org is an excellent source of information on water.

A01

1 In small groups discuss the different kinds of pollution.
2 'Pollution is produced mainly by developed countries but has the biggest effect on developing countries, especially in the form of global warming.' Do you think this fair? Why? Give at least four reasons for your opinion.
3 Draw a poster to describe pollution. Include the different types and examples of the different problems caused by it.

Dead fish on a beach. What might be the cause of all these dead fish?

Land pollution

Land pollution is when materials are left on the land that affect the way the land can be used. Land can be polluted by:

- Chemicals: such as poisons or from air pollution deposited by the rain.
- Physical items: such as litter and rubbish, which does not break down very easily. Landfill sites are often used to store rubbish and these can cause land to be unusable for many years.

A rubbish tip. What problems might this cause?

Land pollution can make land impossible to use for growing crops or for building.

Pollution can lead to bacterial diseases being spread in water. Many can cause sickness and diarrhoea.

Some chemical pollutants can lead to increased risks of cancer and other diseases.

Problems caused by pollution

It can make air difficult to breathe, increasing problems such as asthma.

It can disrupt ecosystems. For example, acid rain has resulted in the ecosystems of whole lakes being killed.

Mercury, a chemical pollutant, can cause genetic changes leading to birth defects.

● Possible solutions to pollution

Type of pollution	Possible solution to the pollution
All types of air, land and water pollution	Governments have decided on safe limits and introduced laws. They can punish polluters
Water pollution by sewage	Sewage plants can be built to ensure no unsafe waste enters the water supply
Rubbish pollution of the land	Materials can be recycled, reducing the need to throw materials away
Air pollution	Industrial pollution can be reduced by introducing new methods of production and extra processes to capture waste gases

Each year there are more cars on the roads. What are the possible effects of this?

A02

Prepare to answer questions about pollution. Use a hot-seat situation to discuss why it is a problem and what solutions can be found.

1 Study the information in this section about pollution. Think about what questions you could be asked and what you will ask.
2 Take part in the hot-seat discussion either as the person in the hot seat being questioned or as the questioner.
3 At the end of the activity, draw two spider diagrams to summarise: a) all the ways pollution is caused and b) how pollution can be reduced.

exam practice b

Do you think there is a solution to pollution? Give **two** reasons for your point of view.

Examiner's hint: Make sure you give two reasons in your answer. (A02)

exam practice c

Explain why pollution causes problems.

Examiner's hint: If you can't think of four reasons why then write two reasons and develop each one with an example. (A01)

exam practice d

'People should not drive cars.'
In your answer you should refer to at least one religion.
i) Do you agree? Give reasons for your answer.
ii) Give reasons why some people may disagree with you.

Examiner's hint: Make sure you include reference to a religion in your answer. (A02)

6.3 Natural resources

Natural resources are found all over the world in different amounts and they are used by humans in many different ways. There are two main kinds of natural resources: renewable resources and non-renewable resources.

- Renewable resources are those that naturally replace themselves. For example, plants and animals can provide bioenergy, hot springs can produce geothermal energy and the oceans and seas can provide wave energy. Sunlight can produce solar energy and wind farms can capture the energy from the winds.
- Non-renewable resources are those that do not replace themselves or replace themselves very slowly. Metals in the earth and fossil fuels are examples.

> **KEY WORDS**
>
> **natural resources** Naturally occurring materials, such as oil and fertile land, which can be used by humans.
>
> **conservation** Protecting and preserving natural resources and the environment.

Do you think animals can be used without worrying about their future? Why?

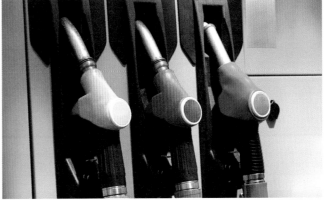

Do you agree with people who say 'As non-renewable materials will run out one day, we might as well use them'?

We may have to use natural resources to produce power in the future.

Some resources are only found in certain parts of the world, causing some countries to have much more money than others.

Why the scarcity of natural resources is a problem

When resources are used up, people will have to find alternatives which may be much more difficult to produce and less efficient.

The prices of resources that are hard to get will get higher and higher.

Some resources are only found in certain parts of the world, causing conflict between countries who have no resources and those who have resources.

Once they are used up, whole ecosystems may disappear.

Knowledge check

1 What is a natural resource?
2 What are the two main kinds of natural resources?
3 What are renewable resources?
4 What are non-renewable resources?
5 Give two examples of renewable resources.
6 Give two examples of non-renewable resources.

● Possible solutions to the problems of using up scarce natural resources

The solution to the problems of using up scarce natural resources is to take part in **conservation**. This can be done by carrying out the environmental 3Rs. These are reuse, recycle and reduce.

Reuse

- People should pass unwanted clothes and things such as gadgets and toys to other people who can reuse them. This means fewer new items are made, saving resources.
- Many supermarkets now encourage their customers to reuse plastic bags.
- The internet also has many websites where people can advertise larger items for others to reuse.

Recycle

- People and industry must start to recycle materials. All used materials that can be broken down and used again should be recycled.
- Industry must produce goods that can easily be recycled.
- People should be encouraged to recycle by the government. Poster campaigns or possibly incentives or punishments can all help.

Reduce

- Everyone must reduce the amount of materials they use. For example, packaging can be reduced.
- Renewable energy, such as wind energy, should be used in place of fossil fuels.
- Everyone must reduce the amount of gases, which contribute to global warming, being released into the atmosphere.
- Reduction can be on an industrial level or a household/individual level. For example, turning off lights is a step to reducing resources whether it is in an empty office, an unused room in a house or a classroom after hours.

A01

1 In pairs, draw a poster to show what the different kinds of resources are, including examples and the problems that are caused by using up natural resources.
2 Join up with another pair and use your poster to explain the problems caused by using up the earth's natural resources.

A02

Copy and complete a table like the one below to list ways that the scarcity of natural resources can be a problem and how the problem of scarcity of natural resources might be solved.

Problems caused by a lack of natural resources	Solutions to the problems caused by a lack of natural resources

exam practice b

Do you think a lack of natural resources causes problems in the world? Give **two** reasons for your point of view.

Examiner's hint: The easiest way to develop a reason is to give an example. (A02)

exam practice c

Explain how a scarcity of natural resources causes problems for the future.

Examiner's hint: Make sure you know the words used in the exam board specification, for example, natural resources. (A01)

exam practice d

'Everyone should recycle.'
In your answer you should refer to at least one religion.
i) Do you agree? Give reasons for your answer.
ii) Give reasons why some people may disagree with you.

Examiner's hint: Make sure you start your answer to d) i) with 'I think …'. (A02)

6.4 Christian teachings on stewardship

Christians follow teachings from the Bible and from the Church which show that they should care for the environment and ensure that God's **creation** is passed on to future generations.

Christian teachings show that God made the world and that he gave humans the world as a gift, to be in charge of and to use as they wanted. However, other teachings show that God made the world and then gave it to humans to look after.

The ways that Christians can understand the teachings are very different:

- One is that humans are allowed to do whatever they want with the world. The world belongs to humans to dominate.
- The other is that humans are looking after the earth for God. They are temporary keepers and so must ensure they return it in the condition God would want.

This second understanding of the teachings is the one that most Christians today understand as **stewardship** and see as a very important part of Christian life.

> **KEY WORDS**
>
> **creation** The act of creating the universe or the universe which has been created.
> **stewardship** Looking after something so it can be passed on to the next generation.

Then God said, 'Let us make mankind in our image, in our likeness, so that they may rule over the fish in the sea and the birds in the sky, over the livestock and all the wild animals, and over all the creatures that move along the ground' (Genesis 1:26).

The earth is the LORD's, and everything in it, the world, and all who live in it (Psalm 24:1).

Man's dominion over inanimate and other living beings granted by the Creator is not absolute; it is limited by concern for the quality of life of his neighbour, including generations to come; it requires a religious respect for the integrity of creation (Catechism of the Catholic Church 2145).

God blessed them and said to them, 'Be fruitful and increase in number; fill the earth and subdue it. Rule over the fish in the sea and the birds in the sky and over every living creature that moves on the ground' (Genesis 1:28).

For in him all things were created: things in heaven and on earth, visible and invisible, whether thrones or powers or rulers or authorities; all things have been created through him and for him (Colossians 1:16).

The LORD God took the man and put him in the Garden of Eden to work it and take care of it (Genesis 2:15).

For the Church of the 21st century, good ecology is not an optional extra but a matter of justice. It is therefore central to what it means to be a Christian (Dr Rowan Williams, while Archbishop of Canterbury).

Knowledge check

1 What is stewardship?
2 What are the two things that the different teachings show about the world God created?
3 What are the two ways that Christian teachings can be understood?
4 a) Give an example of a teaching which shows that humans rule over the world.
   b) Give an example of a teaching which shows that humans are temporary carers of the world.

● Christian attitudes to the environment

The Christian view that God is responsible for the creation of the world and everything in it is shown in many teachings. The hymn on the right, written in the nineteenth century, is an example.

Christians who believe that God gave the earth to humans to rule over (Genesis 1:26) still believe that this brings responsibilities to ensure that the world can be used in the future. They also believe that human needs may sometimes be more important than the environment's.

Christians who believe that God gave humans the earth to care for temporarily would want to ensure that the world is as God would want it. This means that all Christians work in some way to care for the environment.

Some Christians join organisations such as Christian Ecology Link, A Rocha and Operation Noah. These organisations work to improve the environment by campaigning and in practical ways.

Some Christians will organise projects in their local areas to improve the environment. For example, Sage, a group based in Oxford, organises talks and environmental activities.

Some Christians will work on their own as stewards doing what they can to improve the environment in their daily life. This might be by conserving energy or by recycling.

All things bright and beautiful,
All creatures great and small,
All things wise and wonderful:
The LORD God made them all.

Each little flow'r that opens,
Each little bird that sings,
He made their glowing colours,
He made their tiny wings

Cecil F. Alexander (1848)

www.christian-ecology.org.uk
www.arocha.org.uk
www.operationnoah.org
www.sageoxford.org.uk

A01

In pairs, produce a PowerPoint presentation to explain the main Christian teachings on stewardship. Add diagrams or pictures to illustrate the references. Present your explanation of the causation argument to the rest of the class.

A02

Imagine you have been employed by the Church to convince people to take stewardship of the environment seriously. In groups, design either:

a) a poster campaign (a group of four posters that have a common theme); or
b) a text-message campaign (a group of four texts that have a common theme); or
c) an internet pop-up campaign (a group of four pop-ups that have a common theme).

Explain your campaign to the rest of the class and decide which of the campaigns is the most effective.

exam practice b

Do you think all Christians should work to care for the environment? Give **two** reasons for your point of view.

Examiner's hint: Each reason must be developed. (A02)

exam practice c

Explain the Christian teachings on stewardship.

Examiner's hint: Give four different teachings. (A01)

exam practice d

'Christians should not waste time caring for the environment.'
In your answer you should refer to at least one religion.
i) Do you agree? Give reasons for your answer.
ii) Give reasons why some people may disagree with you.

Examiner's hint: The easiest way to answer each part should be to write three brief reasons. (A02)

6.5 Muslim teachings on stewardship

Muslims are taught that they are all khalifah or stewards of Allah's creation and that Allah created both the earth and humans to care for it.

Islamic teachings on tawhid (oneness of God) mean that Muslims accept that God is the creator and sustainer of creation. Humans can affect creation and whatever they do to one part of creation will have an effect on other parts of creation (including humans). They believe that only God is eternal and anything that is created can have an end.

Islamic teachings on judgement mean that Muslims act as khalifah because they will be judged on whether they have been good stewards. If they have not done the will of Allah they will not go to paradise.

Islamic teachings on the ummah mean that all Muslims are part of a brotherhood who should care for one another.

It is Allah who erected the heavens without pillars that you [can] see; then He established Himself above the Throne and made subject the sun and the moon, each running [its course] for a specified term (Qur'an 13:2).

If any Muslim plants any plant and a human being or an animal eats of it, he will be rewarded as if he had given that much in charity (Al-Bukhari 8:41, Hadith).

The creation of the heavens and earth is greater than the creation of mankind (Qur'an 40:57).

And to Allah belongs whatever is in the heavens and whatever is on the earth. And ever is Allah, of all things, encompassing (Qur'an 4:126).

And when your LORD said to the angels, I am going to place in the earth a khalifah (Qur'an 2:30).

The servants of the Most Merciful are those who walk upon the earth easily (Qur'an 25:63).

Knowledge check

1 What does khalifah mean?
2 What does tawhid mean?
3 Which references teach Muslims that the earth is God's creation?
4 Which Muslim teaching shows that humans were put on the earth as khalifah (to take care of it)?
5 Why do some Muslims think that taking care of living things is another way of giving to charity?

● Muslim attitudes to the environment

Muslims believe that Allah gave the earth to humans to take care of as vicegerents. This means that all Muslims should work in some way to care for the environment.

Some Muslims will work individually, and try to improve the environment locally by small actions such as recycling or by helping charity work by donating money.

Some Muslims join organisations that work for the environment. Organisations such as Islamic Relief recognise the link between poverty and environmental care. Islamic Relief states it 'believes that we all have a responsibility to maintain the balance of the earth, especially as disruption of this balance is causing widespread suffering amongst the world's poorest people. Protection of the environment is therefore crucial to Islamic Relief.'

Islamic Relief ensures that, while providing short- and long-term relief for those who are suffering, they do so in an environmentally safe way.

www.islamic-relief.org.uk

AO1

1 In small groups discuss the Muslim teachings on the environment. Work out what each of them means.
2 Divide the class into six groups. Each group should be allocated one of the Muslim references. The groups should then produce a PowerPoint presentation to explain the reference.
3 Present the PowerPoint to the class.

AO2

In pairs, make a list of reasons why some Muslims would work to care for the environment and another list of why some might not.

exam practice b

Do you think caring for the environment is important? Give **two** reasons for your point of view.

Examiner's hint: The reasons you give in b) questions do not have to be religious, but they can be. (AO2)

exam practice c

Explain why most Muslims believe that they should look after for the environment.

Examiner's hint: Try to use some Muslim specialist terms to make your answers more coherent. (AO1)

exam practice d

'Religious people cannot solve the problems in the environment.'
In your answer you should refer to at least one religion.
i) Do you agree? Give reasons for your answer.
ii) Give reasons why some people may disagree with you.

Examiner's hint: When the question says religious people replace it with Muslims, then you will answer it correctly. (AO2)

6.6 Infertility treatments

There are many different reasons why a couple may find it difficult to conceive a child. According to the National Institute for Health and Clinical Excellence (NICE), one in seven couples will have fertility problems.

● The types of infertility treatments

There are three main ways that **infertility** can be treated.

Medicines that boost fertility
Medicines to boost fertility are usually taken by the woman. Different medicines are used in different cases. However, most of the medicines aim to do the same thing, which is to ensure that ovulation takes place and, in some cases, encourage ovulation of more than one egg. This treatment is often all a couple will need.

Assisted reproduction
This is when the natural process of fertilisation is artificially assisted.
● One method is **artificial insemination**, where sperm is artificially introduced into the womb. Fertilisation then happens in the normal way.
● Another assisted method includes **in-vitro fertilisation** (IVF). This can use either the couple's sperm and egg or donated sperm or eggs. The egg is fertilised by the sperm in a laboratory test tube and the fertilised egg or zygote is then placed in the womb where the zygote develops as usual.
● IVF using sperm from the man is also called artificial insemination by husband (AIH). IVF using donated sperm is called artificial insemination by donor (AID).
● It is also possible that both the egg and sperm could be donated, in which case it is called **embryo** donation.
● Another method is **surrogacy,** where a woman agrees to carry a baby for the couple. The woman (referred to as a surrogate or surrogate mother) can be made pregnant by implantation with an embryo produced from the couple's egg and sperm or by using donated egg and sperm.

Surgery
If the infertility problem is a physical one then surgery may be an option. This is often completed using keyhole surgery and can successfully remove blockages and scarring from earlier infections.

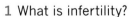
A01

Write a newspaper article to explain the different types of infertility treatments. The article should include a brief description of the problem of infertility as well as the treatments.
Your article must include:

✓ a brief description of the three types of treatment
✓ a description of the different methods of assisted reproduction
✓ at least one illustration or picture.

Knowledge check

1 What is infertility?
2 How many people does infertility affect?
3 What are the three main ways of treating infertility?
4 Why might surgery be used to treat infertility?
5 What is IVF?
6 What are the three different types of IVF?

● The importance of medical treatments for infertility

Infertility treatments allow couples, who would otherwise remain childless, to have children. In 2008 the success rate for women aged 33 or less having IVF was 33 per cent, reducing greatly in older women.

However, medical treatments for infertility have raised problems for some people. It is now possible for women past their normal child-bearing age to have children (see article). It is also possible for same-sex couples to have children. There is also the problem of the high costs and there is usually more than one embryo created. Someone has to decide what to do with these spare embryos.

Woman who became mother at 57 admits she was too old for IVF

Britain's oldest first-time mother has said an age limit should be set for women wanting IVF treatment after admitting struggling to bring up a child in her sixties.

Susan Tollefsen became a mother after receiving IVF treatment at 57 from a Russian clinic in 2008, where she conceived daughter Freya.

Many criticised her decision, saying she was too old to become a parent. At the time, Mrs Tollefsen defended her choice and pointed out that her partner Nick Mayer was 11 years her junior – and would therefore be around to care for their daughter Freya during all of her childhood. However, she says the couple have now split and concedes her critics were right as she encounters the difficulties of bringing up a three-year-old child alone at the age of 61. Mrs Tollefsen, who is deaf in one ear and

having a knee replaced, also agrees that, with hindsight, there should be an age limit of 50 for IVF treatment for women in this country.

In a newspaper interview, she said: 'Freya is without doubt the best thing I have ever done in my life, and I have no regrets. But with the benefit of hindsight I recognise that perhaps some of my critics were right.' Government guidelines recommend doctors do not offer IVF to women over 40 on the NHS, and private clinics will generally refuse to treat women older than 50. The health watchdog NICE is considering whether to scrap the age limit in favour of treating women based on tests which estimate how many eggs they have left.

www.telegraph.co.uk

exam practice b

Do you think infertility treatments are a waste of money? Give **two** reasons for your point of view.

Examiner's hint: Development must add more information to the answer to the question set. It must not be vague. (A02)

exam practice c

Explain the nature of infertility treatments.

Examiner's hint: This means explain the different types of infertility treatment. (A01)

A02

Prepare to answer the d)-type question: 'Everyone should be entitled to infertility treatment'.

1 In pairs, one person takes on the role of a person who believes there should be limits and only some infertile couples should have infertility treatment. The other person takes on the role of a person who believes that everyone should be allowed to have infertility treatment.
2 Each person has two minutes to convince the other person that they must accept their point of view. The other person cannot interrupt or ask questions.
3 After two minutes each person can ask the other person two questions which the other person must answer.
4 At the end decide which argument was more convincing and why.

exam practice d

'Everyone should support infertility treatments.'
In your answer you should refer to at least one religion.
i) Do you agree? Give reasons for your answer.
ii) Give reasons why some people may disagree with you.

Examiner's hint: Start each reason on a new line or with a new paragraph. (A02)

6.7 Christian attitudes to infertility treatments

There are two main Christian opinions about infertility treatments. One is that some infertility treatments are acceptable, but not all. The other says that all are acceptable. Most Christians recognise that raising a family is an important part of life and to many couples it is not only a desire, it is a vocation (calling from God), and because of this they recognise that treatment is helpful.

● Christian attitudes to infertility treatments

- A very few Christians would say that people should not have any form of infertility treatment because it is unnatural and that if God had wanted them to have children they would have them naturally.
- Some Christians accept the use of medicine and surgery. They do not accept assisted fertility.
- Some Christians accept any sort of infertility treatment.

● Reasons for the different Christian attitudes to infertility treatments

Assisted reproduction treatment is not usually acceptable (only medicine and surgery is acceptable)	Most infertility treatments are acceptable
Attitude of the Roman Catholic Church	**Attitude of the Church of England**
A couple should only have a child if it is the result of a natural process	Until 14 days, the cells of the embryo are not alive, so can be disposed of
Children should be born as part of the intimate relationship between the husband and wife. This does not include the actions of a laboratory	God told Adam and Eve to 'be fruitful'
During the process of IVF, several embryos are produced, some of which will be stored or disposed of. Some Christians think that as life starts at conception, these fertilised eggs should be treated as if they were alive	Jesus healed people and this continues his work on earth
Medicine and surgery are acceptable as these help the natural process rather than replace it	If God did not want the couple to have children then IVF would not work. This is a way of helping God's plans
Any process involving donors means that the child is not the product of the couple's marriage	Christians are taught that family life is important

Knowledge check ✳

1 What are the three Christian attitudes to infertility treatment?
2 Why do some people think that all infertility treatment is wrong?
3 Draw a spider diagram to show at least four reasons why some Christians think that assisted infertility treatment is not acceptable.
4 Draw a spider diagram to show at least four reasons why some Christians think that all infertility treatment is acceptable.

The origin of human life has its authentic context in marriage and in the family, where it is generated through an act which expresses the reciprocal love between a man and a woman

Dignitas Personae (Human Dignity): On Certain Bioethical Questions

Be fruitful and increase in number; fill the earth (Genesis 1:28).

The actual individual emerges with the primitive streak at about 14 days. After that twinning is no longer possible and the outer cells of the early embryo have established themselves as umbilical cord and placenta

Church of England: Board for Social Responsibility

Isaac prayed to the LORD on behalf of his wife, because she was childless. The LORD answered his prayer, and his wife Rebekah became pregnant (Genesis 25:21).

Do not conform to the pattern of this world, but be transformed by the renewing of your mind. Then you will be able to test and approve what God's will is – his good, pleasing and perfect will (Romans 12:2).

Before I formed you in the womb I knew you, and before you were born I set you apart (Jeremiah 1:5).

Hannah had [no children because] the LORD had closed her womb (1 Samuel 1: 2, 6).

A01

1 Draw and complete a Venn diagram with the following headings:
- Quotes supporting using infertility treatment.
- Quotes against using assisted reproduction treatment (including IVF).
- Quotes which can be used for both attitudes and overlap in the Venn diagram.

A02

1 In small groups discuss the different Christian attitudes towards using infertility treatment.
2 Produce a presentation using either a poster or a PowerPoint slide to explain the Christian attitudes including the reasons for them (and quotes).

exam practice b

Do you think all Christians should accept infertility treatments? Give **two** reasons for your point of view.

Examiner's hint: Read the question carefully. (AO2)

exam practice c

Explain why some Christians agree with infertility treatments and some do not.

Examiner's hint: Make sure you include reasons for both attitudes in your answer. (AO1)

exam practice d

'Christians should not accept the use of infertility treatments.'
In your answer you should refer to at least one religion.
i) Do you agree? Give reasons for your answer.
ii) Give reasons why some people may disagree with you.

Examiner's hint: It is easy to develop a reason using a quote. (AO2)

6.8 Muslim attitudes to infertility treatments

There are three main Muslim attitudes to infertility treatments. Around the world there may be small variations.

1 Some Muslims believe that if a couple are infertile they must not have infertility treatment.
2 Most Muslims believe that as long as the egg and the sperm used are from the married couple then treatment is acceptable. However, the use of donors in any way is not acceptable.
3 A few Muslims follow a recent fatwa (legal announcement) by Ayatollah Ali Hussein Khamenei in Iran. This says that donor sperm and eggs are allowed as long as the legal status of the baby is the same as a child who is not being raised by biological parents.

● Reasons for the different Muslim attitudes to infertility treatment

Knowledge check

1 What are the three Muslim attitudes to infertility treatment?
2 Why do some Muslims think that all infertility treatment is wrong?
3 List reasons why some Muslims think that assisted infertility treatment is acceptable when the egg and sperm come from the husband and wife.
4 List reasons why a few Muslims think that assisted infertility treatment is acceptable when the egg and sperm come from a donor.

IVF treatment is acceptable as long as the egg and the sperm used are from the married couple
● Marriage is a contract between the wife and husband. There should not be a third person, even in the form of cells, in the marriage.
● The use of eggs or sperm from another person is regarded as zina, or adultery.
● The couple are able to raise a Muslim family like that of the Prophet.
● Shariah law allows the extra embryos to be destroyed as they are not yet alive.

IVF with donors is allowed but the child does not have full legal rights
● Ayatollah Khamanei said egg and sperm donation is allowed, but everyone involved must keep to the religious rules about who are the parents.
● The child produced cannot inherit. They can only inherit from their biological parents.
● The infertile husband and wife are legally regarded as parents raising a child who is not their own.
● There must be special care that any donors are not related to the parents.

Muslims should not have infertility treatment
● Infertility is part of the test from Allah.
● Allah will decide who has children and who does not have children.
● Infertility is part of Allah's plan and it should not be interfered with.

He makes them [both] males and females, and He renders whom He wills barren. Indeed, He is Knowing and Competent (Qur'an 42:50).

There is no disease that Allah has sent down except that He also has sent down its treatment (Hadith, The Book of Medicine: Al-Bukhari).

To Allah belongs the dominion of the heavens and the earth; He creates what he wills. He gives to whom He wills female [children], and He gives to whom He wills males (Qur'an 42:49).

Indeed, We created man from a sperm-drop mixture (Qur'an 76:2).

And it is He who has created from water a human being and made him [a relative by] lineage and marriage. And ever is your LORD competent [concerning creation] (Qur'an 25:54).

We had three embryos that have been stored and which we might use in the future. If something happened to Faraz they would have to be destroyed as we would not be allowed to use them if you are not married. If it is Allah's wish we will now have a big family.

I was very sad when we were told that it was very unlikely we would have a baby naturally. I had always thought that like my sisters, I would have no problem having children.

My doctor suggested that we have IVF, as this would help in our case. I was unsure whether this was allowed in Islam, so I asked my imam. He told me that this was OK as long as the sperm came from my husband Faraz. This is what we did and on our second cycle of IVF I became pregnant.

A01

1 In pairs, create a poster advertising campaign (at least four posters) to explain the different Muslim attitudes towards IVF. It should be made very clear that the overwhelmingly main Muslim attitude is that IVF should be only used within a Muslim marriage and using the cells of the mother and father.
2 The posters should be aimed at people who may or may not be Muslim but who are interested in finding out more about the Muslim attitudes to IVF.
3 The posters should include explanations, reasons why and quotes.

A02

1 In pairs, discuss the Muslim reasons given for allowing IVF and decide which are the best reasons and which you feel are not so good.
2 Work on your own and write a list of the reasons in order starting with the best reason and finishing with the least good.
3 Draw a line across your list at the point at which you stop agreeing with the reasons.
4 Return to pair work and discuss why you have put your list in this order.

exam practice b

Do you think Muslims should always allow infertility treatment? Give **two** reasons for your point of view.

Examiner's hint: A quote is a good way to develop a reason. (A02)

exam practice c

Explain why some Muslims do not accept infertility treatment.

Examiner's hint: This question is one-sided and you only need reasons why infertility treatment is not acceptable. (A01)

exam practice d

'Infertility treatment should be allowed by all religious people.'
In your answer you should refer to at least one religion.
i) Do you agree? Give reasons for your answer.
ii) Give reasons why some people may disagree with you.

Examiner's hint: In this section candidates can use any religion to answer the question, so the question will not say 'Muslim' responses, it will say 'religious' responses. (A02)

6.9 Transplant surgery

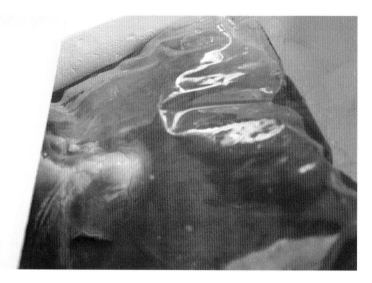

Transplant surgery is when an unhealthy organ is removed and replaced by a healthy one making a previously ill person better. Since the first successful organ transplant of a kidney in 1954, doctors have learned to transplant many different organs. Liver, heart, lungs and pancreas are just some of the organs that can be transplanted.

Organs to be transplanted can come from a deceased person whose organs have been preserved. This can be arranged more easily if a potential donor carries a donor card or has signed up to the NHS Organ Donor Register showing that they agree to **organ donation**. If the organ is something people have more than one of, for example a kidney, then the organ can come from a living donor.

In transplantation, however, at present, many donated organs are rejected by the patient's body and there are concerns about viral infections. Doctors are hoping that genetically modified animals that grow organs for transplantation will be available in the near future.

Organ transplants are important because:

- They can save the life of a seriously ill person.
- They can radically improve a sick person's quality of life.
- A transplant can prevent years of medicine being given to a person.
- They mean individuals and their families can live normal lives without lengthy hospital visits.
- The families of donors feel there has been a benefit from the death of their relative.
- They are cheaper than years of medical treatment.

KEY WORDS

organ donation Giving organs to be used in transplant surgery.

Knowledge check

1 What is transplant surgery?
2 Name four organs that can be transplanted.
3 Explain where transplant organs come from at present.
4 Explain where transplant organs may come from in the future.

A01

In small groups, produce a presentation to explain what transplant surgery is and why it is important. Include explanations for all the specialist language that you use. You could include the following in your presentation:

✓ examples of which organs can be transplanted
✓ a PowerPoint presentation
✓ a poster to show where the organs that can be transplanted are found in the body
✓ an example of a donor card.

● Responses to transplant surgery

It is not natural – it should not be done.

Although transplants are expensive, they save money in the end as the person does not have to have lengthy medical care and expensive medicines.

I don't like the idea of someone else's organs inside me, especially not an animal's.

Life expectancy after a transplant is still not normal, so it is not worth it.

Transplants save lives, otherwise people would die.

Transplants are just like any other form of medicine. They make people better. I can't see what the fuss is about.

A02

Mr A is a 35-year-old man who has heart disease. He has lost his job as a builder as he was self-employed. He is now weak and has to attend hospital regularly for treatment. He has to take lots of medicines every day, some of which are causing him to have other health problems.

Mr A has just found out that a heart donor is available and he is trying to decide whether he should go through such a serious and complicated operation. The survival rate after five years is about 70 per cent.

Write some advice to Mr A to help him make a decision. Make sure that your answer is balanced and includes advice which is specifically about his situation.

exam practice b

Do you think organ transplants are a good idea? Give **two** reasons for your point of view.

Examiner's hint: Start each reason on a new line. (A02)

exam practice c

Explain why some people agree with transplant surgery and some do not.

Examiner's hint: An example is a good way to develop a reason. (A01)

exam practice d

'Everyone should carry a donor card.'
In your answer you should refer to at least one religion.
i) Do you agree? Give reasons for your answer.
ii) Give reasons why some people may disagree with you.

Examiner's hint: Make sure you include the response of one specific religion in your answer. (A02)

6.10 Christian attitudes to transplant surgery

Some Christians believe that transplant surgery is acceptable. They have concerns that people might feel forced into selling organs but as this is illegal then transplant surgery can only be a medical benefit.

Some Christians believe that transplant surgery is not acceptable. They have many concerns based on sanctity of life and feel that although it is illegal some people who really need the money may sell their organs.

Reasons why most Christians accept transplant surgery	Reasons why some Christians do not accept transplant surgery
It is healing. Jesus healed when he was on earth so it follows his actions	The body has been created by God and should not be interfered with
It follows the command of Jesus: *Love one another (John 13:34)*	The body is the temple of the Holy Spirit and should not be changed
They believe that when you die you are transformed and do not need your physical body in heaven	Transplant surgery is taking on the role of God and may be going against his plans
It helps a person in need	Poor people may feel forced into selling their organs

Pakistani men at a police station reveal scars after their kidneys were removed in Lahore. Police raided a clandestine clinic, arresting eight people including five doctors and found ten people whose kidneys had been removed. Pakistan is known to have secret groups involved in paying poor people for their kidneys.

Knowledge check

1 What are the two main Christian attitudes to transplant surgery?
2 Draw a spider diagram to show at least four reasons why some Christians think that transplant surgery is not acceptable.
3 Draw a spider diagram to show at least four reasons why some Christians think that transplant surgery is acceptable.

A01

1 You are a journalist and your newspaper has asked you to write an article on transplant surgery to go with the picture opposite.
2 You have to write about:
- why people sell their organs
- the legality of selling organs
- the way Christians should respond to the situation.

A02

1 Look at the different Christian attitudes to transplant surgery. Read through them carefully. Which responses do you think are the best and which ones do you think are not so good?
2 Write a list of the reasons in order starting with the best reason and finishing with the least good.
3 Draw a line across your list at the point at which you stop agreeing with the reasons.
4 Does this correspond with the columns on the table? Why do you think this is the case?

exam practice b

Do you think Christians should agree with transplant surgery? Give **two** reasons for your point of view.

Examiner's hint: Reasons must relate to Christian ideas. (A02)

exam practice c

Explain why some Christians do not agree with transplant surgery.

Examiner's hint: When a c) question only asks why people 'do not agree' then you do not need to balance the answers with why some people do. (A01)

exam practice d

'Selling organs for transplantation should be allowed.'
In your answer you should refer to at least one religion.
i) Do you agree? Give reasons for your answer.
ii) Give reasons why some people may disagree with you.

Examiner's hint: Always include your opinion at the beginning of the d) i) part of the question. (A02)

6.11 Muslim attitudes to transplant surgery

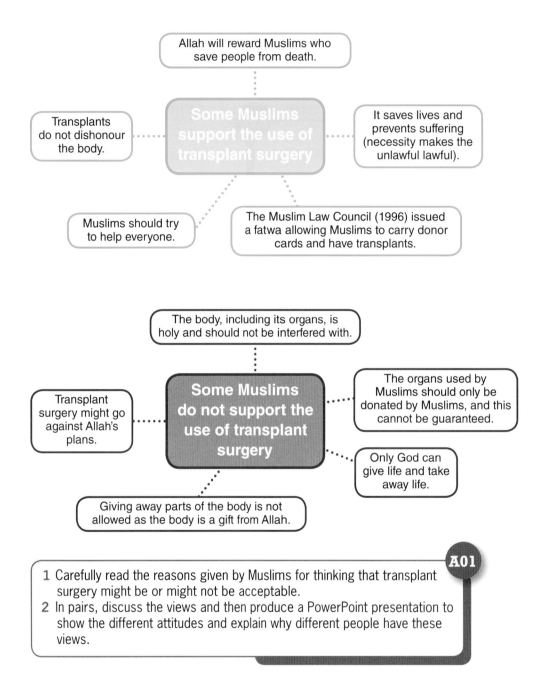

Allah will reward Muslims who save people from death.

Some Muslims support the use of transplant surgery

Transplants do not dishonour the body.

It saves lives and prevents suffering (necessity makes the unlawful lawful).

Muslims should try to help everyone.

The Muslim Law Council (1996) issued a fatwa allowing Muslims to carry donor cards and have transplants.

The body, including its organs, is holy and should not be interfered with.

Some Muslims do not support the use of transplant surgery

Transplant surgery might go against Allah's plans.

The organs used by Muslims should only be donated by Muslims, and this cannot be guaranteed.

Only God can give life and take away life.

Giving away parts of the body is not allowed as the body is a gift from Allah.

A01

1 Carefully read the reasons given by Muslims for thinking that transplant surgery might be or might not be acceptable.
2 In pairs, discuss the views and then produce a PowerPoint presentation to show the different attitudes and explain why different people have these views.

Knowledge check ✳

1 What are the two Muslim attitudes to transplant surgery?
2 List at least four reasons why some Muslims think that transplant surgery is acceptable.
3 List at least four reasons why some Muslims think that transplant surgery is not acceptable.

My sister, Khalisah, had been ill for a long time and was finally told that her only hope of getting well was to have a kidney transplant. She had been waiting for a while and had to attend hospital for dialysis. She was linked to a machine that did the work of her kidneys. She was not getting any better. Then I was told that I would be a good tissue match for her.

I offered to give her one of my kidneys. I had spoken to my Muslim teacher and he said that it was a good thing to do, and that he carried a donor card himself. He showed me lots of verses in the Qur'an that showed people helping others and he also said that as I was family, most Muslim teachers would say the same.

Tamadur

Khalisah had the operation a year ago and is now well. She does not have to have any more dialysis and, although she goes to the hospital for check-ups and has daily medicine, you would not know she had been so ill.

A02

Imagine you have been employed by an Islamic health group to explain why Muslims should carry donor cards. In groups, design either:

a) a poster campaign (a group of four posters that have a common theme); or

b) a text-message campaign (a group of four texts that have a common theme); or

c) an internet pop-up campaign (a group of four pop-ups that have a common theme).

Explain your campaign to the rest of the class and decide which of the campaigns is the most effective.

exam practice b

Do you think Muslims should carry donor cards? Give **two** reasons for your point of view.

Examiner's hint: An example is a good way to develop a reason. (A02)

exam practice c

Choose one religion other than Christianity and explain why some of its followers agree with transplant surgery and some do not.

Examiner's hint: Make sure you clearly state that you are writing about Islamic attitudes. (A01)

exam practice d

'Religious people should not carry donor cards.'
In your answer you should refer to at least one religion.
i) Do you agree? Give reasons for your answer.
ii) Give reasons why some people may disagree with you.

Examiner's hint: Do not be tempted to write a lot of detail about what happens during a transplant; it will not gain you any marks. (A02)

Examination practice

Below is guidance on how to answer the question b) from Section 6: Religion: environmental and medical issues. As it is a b) question, it is worth 4 marks.

In every section there are two b) questions to choose from. Try question 3b) using the hints provided below. Then apply these steps to question 4b).

Sample question

3b) Do you think everyone must recycle their rubbish?   [4]

Sample question

4b) Do you think all Christians should carry a donor card?   [4]

How to answer

To get full marks on a b) question you must give your opinion and then support it with two reasons and develop each of the reasons.

Step 1

○ Start by writing down your opinion on whether everyone must recycle their rubbish with one reason to support your opinion.

I think that everyone must recycle their rubbish because it would save lots of the earth's resources.

Step 2

○ Think of a way to develop the reason. The easiest way to develop a reason is to give an example or a quote.

For example, if everyone recycles their paper and cardboard we would not have to cut down as many trees.

Step 3

○ Think of a second reason to support your opinion (everyone should recycle). Write the second reason as a new paragraph.

Secondly, I think if everyone recycles it would save lots of land which could be used in better, more environmentally friendly ways.

Step 4

○ Develop your second reason. Ensure the development is about your reason and still answers the question.

For example, if people recycle, less land would be used in landfill sites for rubbish and then this land could be then used for growing plants that could make biodiesel for cars.

Examiner's comment

✓ **Maximum marks will be awarded for two reasons which have been developed as long as they answer the question.**
✓ **The best way to develop is to give an example or a quote. The examiner can then see you have added more to (developed) the answer.**

Below is guidance on how to answer the question c) from Section 6: Religion: environmental and medical issues. As it is a c) question, it is worth 8 marks.

In every section there are two c) questions to choose from. Try question 3c) using the hints provided below. Then apply these steps to question 4c).

Sample question

3c) Explain why some Christians agree with the use of infertility treatments. [8]

Sample question

4c) Choose one religion other than Christianity and explain why some of its followers do not agree with transplant surgery. [8]

How to answer

There are several ways to get full marks on a c) question. One way is to give two developed reasons.

Step 1

- Think of one reason why some Christians agree with the use of infertility treatments.

Christians are taught that family life is an important vocation.

Step 2

- Think of a way to develop this reason.

If the only way that a Christian can fulfil their calling from God to have a family is by infertility treatment then God must be providing the treatment so they can have a family.

Step 3

- Think of a second reason why some Christians agree with the use of infertility treatments. Make sure you are not repeating your first reason or your development.

In addition, Jesus was a healer and infertility treatment is healing.

Step 4

- Develop your second reason. Ensure you are still answering the question.

Christians view themselves as the Body of Christ, able to carry out the work of Jesus. They cannot work miracles, but they can use the talents given to them by God in what seems miraculous ways with infertility treatment.

Examiner's comment

✓ **Maximum marks will be awarded for two valid and developed reasons, if the quality written communication is good.**
✓ **Make sure the development is not just a repetition of the reason given. It must add some extra information.**

UNIT 8
Religion and society
Section 7: Religion: peace and conflict

7.1 The United Nations

The United Nations (UN) was formed in 1945 with 51 members. The UN now has 193 members. It was formed after the Second World War to ensure **world peace** and stability. It has expanded its peacekeeping role to include care for refugees and disaster relief.

The flag of the UN and its role

Provides mediators to talk to both sides in a conflict.

Helps organise peaceful and fair elections.

Provides a peacekeeping force of police and soldiers to ensure lawful activities are taking place.

Encourages peaceful answers to conflicts (**conflict resolution**).

The peacekeeping force works to eliminate crime; particularly drug trafficking and human **exploitation**.

Ensures people have equal rights.

The UN has a counter-terrorism programme.

The peacekeeping force helps disarm combatants, remove minefields and reintegrate soldiers.

KEY WORDS

conflict resolution Bringing a fight or a struggle to a peaceful conclusion.

exploitation Taking advantage of a weaker group.

the United Nations An international body set up to promote world peace and cooperation.

world peace The ending of war throughout the whole world (the basic aim of the United Nations).

● How the UN does its work

- The UN is divided into different councils that concentrate on different areas, for example economic and social.
- The UN publicises areas of injustice, so people are aware of their rights (and the rights of others).
- The UN gets celebrities to raise awareness of the need for justice and peace, for example, Nicole Kidman is working to end sexism and Jay-Z is campaigning for clean water for everyone. Celebrities bring the UN publicity it needs.
- The UN is responsible for the International Court of Justice (in The Hague). This settles legal problems in countries or between countries.
- The Security Council is responsible for all the peacekeeping operations. There have been 66 operations since 1948 and at present the UN has peacekeeping forces in 16 countries.

> Find out more about the UN's Messengers of Peace, currently including celebrities such as George Clooney, Charlize Theron and Edward Norton: www.un.org/sg/mop/index.shtml

Rapper Jay-Z has joined forces with the music channel MTV to educate young people on water shortages that affect billions of people around the world. The UN said that an estimated 1.1 billion people have no access to safe drinking water and another 2.6 billion do not have sanitation facilities.

Knowledge check ✳

1 What is the United Nations?
2 List at least four roles of the UN.
3 Explain, with at least four examples, how the UN does its work.
4 How many peacekeeping operations has the UN been involved in since 1948?
5 Why does the UN use celebrities to help it with its work?

A01

Imagine you are employed by the UN as a celebrity Messenger of Peace. Produce an advertisement to explain the function of the UN and how it carries out its work.

Include in your report:

✓ a description of the aims of the UN
✓ an explanation of the work of the UN
✓ a description of the UN's work in Haiti.

● **An example of the work that the UN does for peace**

Helping Haiti towards recovery and reconstruction

On 12 January 2010 a devastating earthquake shook Haiti; the earthquake killed 200,000 people and destroyed nearly 90 per cent of the buildings in Leogane near the capital Port au Prince.

The United Nations (UN) were already present in Haiti trying to ensure that the country was peaceful after an armed conflict in 2004 during which President Aristide fled the country leaving a politically insecure country behind.

The UN mission in Haiti is trying to help the recovery, reconstruction and stability of the country. It was crucial in providing medical aid during a cholera outbreak in October 2010. During the elections of 2011 the UN helped to keep peace on the streets and now it is involved in strengthening government organisations and protecting human rights.

Further information on the UN's work in Haiti can be found on the UN website: www.un.org

A02

Look at this statement: 'The UN should not get involved in conflicts around the world'.

1 Decide whether you agree with the statement or do not agree with it.
2 Write down four reasons why you have agreed or not agreed with the statement.
3 Write down four reasons why someone might have the opposite opinion to yours.

exam practice b

Do you think it is good that the UN has a peacekeeping force? Give **two** reasons for your point of view.

Examiner's hint: Give examples of what the peacekeeping force does as developments for your reasons. (A02)

exam practice c

Explain how the UN works for peace in the world.

Examiner's hint: This is an 'Explain how' question so does not need reasons, only a list of what the UN does. (A01)

exam practice d

'If the UN worked properly there would be no wars.'
In your answer you should refer to at least one religion.
i) Do you agree? Give reasons for your answer.
ii) Give reasons why some people may disagree with you.

Examiner's hint: Make sure you give your opinion at the beginning of d) i) answers. (A02)

Survivors of Haiti's earthquake wait in line for water as United Nations soldiers from Brazil distribute water in front of the National Palace in Port-au-Prince. With food, cash and medicine starting to flow, Haiti's government and aid workers are turning to the mammoth task of feeding and sheltering hundreds of thousands of earthquake survivors still living in the capital's rubble-strewn streets and filthy tent cities.

7.2 Religious organisations and world peace

Religious groups want to achieve world peace and aim to find an end to conflict in the same way that the UN does. Unlike the UN, which has member states that join the organisation, religions are found across the whole world in all different countries and share their religious ideas.

All religions believe that peace is better than war. The Golden Rule (see page 134) is found in some way in most religions and with these beliefs, religious organisations apply themselves to working for world peace.

Anglican Pacifist Fellowship (www.anglicanpeacemaker.org.uk)
The Anglican Pacifist Fellowship (APF) is a group of Anglican (Church of England) Christians who work to achieve peace using peaceful methods. The APF formed in 1937 and has 1400 members around the world. It works to achieve peace by:

- founding and taking part in the Week of Prayer for world peace
- developing and running peace education courses in the UK and around the world
- speaking at peace events
- taking part in the International Day for Peace
- campaigning against war.

Pax Christi (www.paxchristi.net)
This is an organisation founded in the Catholic Church. It began as a prayer movement and then in 1950 formally started as the 'International Catholic Movement for Peace'. It tries to achieve peace by:

- running sessions on peace and non-violence
- arranging prayer services
- lobbying the government to take peaceful action against conflict
- providing resources for prayer services
- providing teaching materials to educate about the need for peace
- being part of the National Justice and Peace Network.

Baptist Peace Fellowship (www.baptist-peace.org.uk)
This is a Baptist fellowship where Baptists who have the common aim of a non-violent way of life can join and work for peace. It especially wishes to overcome injustice by peaceful means such as prayer. The activities of the Baptist Peace Fellowship include:

- running sessions on peace and non-violence
- running and taking part in prayer services
- writing letters to the government about peace and conflict
- providing prayer materials
- educating others about the need for peace
- attending festivals such as Greenbelt to spread the message of peace.

Jesus did not fight his arrest or death, he was a pacifist.

But I tell you, love your enemies and pray for those who persecute you (Matthew 5:44).

In the Sermon on the Mount, Jesus praised the peacemakers, the merciful, and said they would be rewarded.

Why do religious organisations work for world peace?

By working for peace you are obeying the command of Jesus to 'love one another'.

Do not repay anyone evil for evil. Be careful to do what is right in the eyes of everyone. If it is possible, as far as it depends on you, live at peace with everyone (Romans 12:17–18).

A soldier prays for peace. How can an army work for world peace?

Knowledge check

1 What do religious organisations like those listed on page 175 want to achieve?
2 What does the Anglican Pacifist Fellowship do?
3 List at least four things that Pax Christi does.
4 Explain what the Baptist Peace Fellowship does.

A01

1 Carefully read the information about the different Christian organisations working for world peace on page 175.
2 In pairs, looking at the information given, produce a crossword puzzle.
   ● The crossword puzzle must contain at least 12 questions.
   ● You must produce a blank puzzle, with questions to find the answers, which can be copied and used in class, and a completed one as an answer sheet.

A02

1 In pairs discuss the different organisations that work for peace, looking at their differences and similarities.
2 Produce a poster that could be used as part of an advertising campaign by a Christian organisation to encourage people to work for peace.

exam practice b

Do you think all Christians should join organisations to work for peace? Give **two** reasons for your point of view.

Examiner's hint: It is important that you make your opinion clear at the beginning of your answer. (A02)

exam practice c

Explain how a religious organisation works for peace.

Examiner's hint: Although it is not asked for, your answer will be more coherent if you begin by saying which organisation you are referring to. (A01)

exam practice d

'All religious people should work for peace.'
In your answer you should refer to Christianity.
i) Do you agree? Give reasons for your answer.
ii) Give reasons why some people may disagree with you.

Examiner's hint: In this section the examiner can ask you to refer to 'at least one religion', 'Christianity' or 'one religion other than Christianity'. Make sure you read the question carefully. (A02)

7.3 Reasons for warfare

Wars have occurred throughout history. Although many organisations, including religious ones, work hard for peace, it seems that war is a constant feature of life. At any one time there are many conflicts around the world. Some of these have escalated to armed fighting between groups or countries and are known as wars.

Economic advantages
If one country has more resources than another then one may invade the other to gain access to the resources.

Political differences
If there are extreme differences of opinion based on political ideas then it may be impossible for agreement to be reached and conflict results.

Racial or cultural differences
Where one group of a different race or culture tries to impose superiority over another.

Why wars occur

Patriotism
Groups or individuals may get carried away with being involved in conflict for fame or to prove a point.

History
Countries that have a history of conflict with each other are more likely to come into armed conflict again over a different (or similar) issue.

Protection
Groups may need to fight back against an aggressor, or a group may attack another country in the belief that it is helping some of the members of that country.

Knowledge check ✹

1 Why do wars happen?
2 What is a war?
3 List four reasons why wars happen.

A01

Copy and complete the table below. Use the information above to help you.

Reason why wars might occur	Explanation of why this might cause war

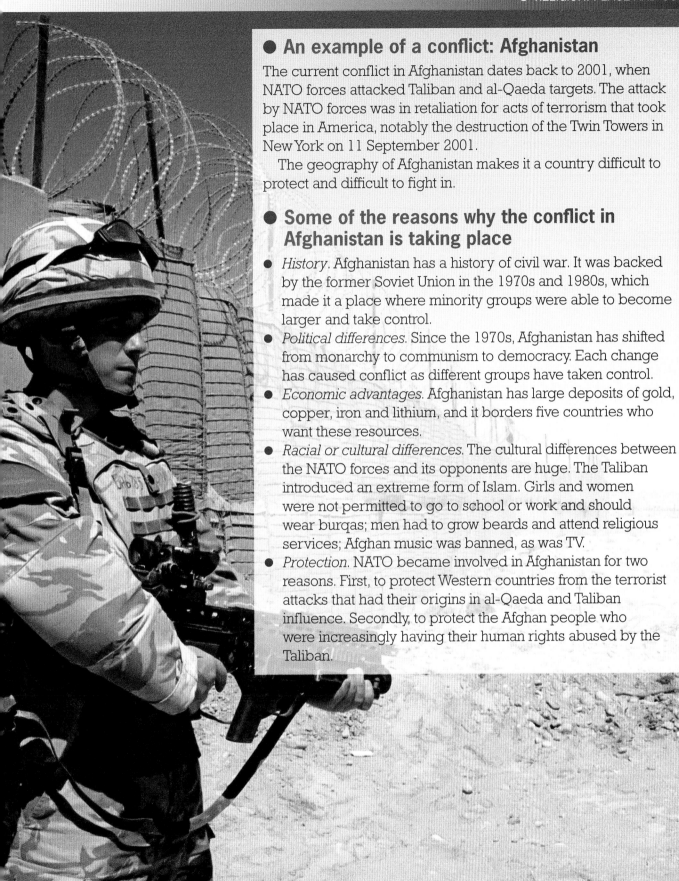

● An example of a conflict: Afghanistan

The current conflict in Afghanistan dates back to 2001, when NATO forces attacked Taliban and al-Qaeda targets. The attack by NATO forces was in retaliation for acts of terrorism that took place in America, notably the destruction of the Twin Towers in New York on 11 September 2001.

The geography of Afghanistan makes it a country difficult to protect and difficult to fight in.

● Some of the reasons why the conflict in Afghanistan is taking place

- *History*. Afghanistan has a history of civil war. It was backed by the former Soviet Union in the 1970s and 1980s, which made it a place where minority groups were able to become larger and take control.
- *Political differences*. Since the 1970s, Afghanistan has shifted from monarchy to communism to democracy. Each change has caused conflict as different groups have taken control.
- *Economic advantages*. Afghanistan has large deposits of gold, copper, iron and lithium, and it borders five countries who want these resources.
- *Racial or cultural differences*. The cultural differences between the NATO forces and its opponents are huge. The Taliban introduced an extreme form of Islam. Girls and women were not permitted to go to school or work and should wear burqas; men had to grow beards and attend religious services; Afghan music was banned, as was TV.
- *Protection*. NATO became involved in Afghanistan for two reasons. First, to protect Western countries from the terrorist attacks that had their origins in al-Qaeda and Taliban influence. Secondly, to protect the Afghan people who were increasingly having their human rights abused by the Taliban.

A02

1 Carefully read the description of the reasons for the conflict in Afghanistan.
2 Make a list of the reasons why there is conflict in Afghanistan.
3 In pairs, number them to put them in order of which you think are most important.
4 Write a 50-word explanation of why you think there is conflict in Afghanistan.

---

exam practice b

Do you think wars are always bad? Give **two** reasons for your point of view.

Examiner's hint: Look at the causes of wars. Do you think any of them are good enough reasons to fight? (A02)

---

exam practice c

Explain why one current conflict has been caused.

Examiner's hint: If you don't want to use Afghanistan as your example then enter current conflicts into a search engine to check for other conflicts that are current. (A01)

---

exam practice d

'Sometimes a war cannot be avoided.' In your answer you should refer to at least one religion other than Christianity.
i) Do you agree? Give reasons for your answer.
ii) Give reasons why some people may disagree with you.

Examiner's hint: The question asks that you refer to one religion other than Christianity; if you do not do this you cannot get more than 3 out of 6 marks. (A02)

7.4 The theory of just war

Just war theory

- The **just war** theory is used to help decide whether it is right to participate in a war (*jus ad bellum*) and how the war should be waged (*jus in bello*). The theory is based on the situation and causes of the war. It essentially works out whether it is fair or 'just' to put people's lives at risk.
- The just war concept has always existed. Any person or group going to war would work out whether it was worth the expense of lives, money and possibly land to participate. But just war theory goes further than that. The theory was developed by Thomas Aquinas (1225–74) who suggested that a war was just or morally right if three certain criteria had been met.
  (1) If it was started and controlled by the authority of a state or ruler.
  (2) If it was for the right reason.
  (3) If the aim of the war was not evil. The theory has since been added to, so that today there are six conditions (see page 182).

A depiction of a battle during the First Crusade. Would you say the Crusades were examples of just wars?

KEY WORDS

aggression Attacking without being provoked.

just war A war which is fought for the right reasons and in a right way.

weapons of mass destruction Weapons which can destroy large areas and numbers of people.

Knowledge check ✳

1 What is a just war?
2 What is the just war theory used for?
3 Who developed the just war theory and what did he teach?
4 List the six modern conditions of a just war.

A01

1 In pairs, produce a PowerPoint presentation to explain the just war theory.
2 Find and add examples and pictures to illustrate the reasons.
3 Present your explanation of the just war theory to the rest of the class.

The conditions of a just war

It must be started for a good reason (just cause).

It must be declared by the authority of the state or ruler.

It must be the last option (all other ways of solving the problem having been tried).

There must be a good chance of success.

The force used in the war must not be out of proportion to what is needed to win (not too much force).

What it intends to achieve must be good (intention).

● Why is the just war theory important?

The theory is important as it:

- provides guidelines for when a war can be said to be morally right
- gives the conflicts' participants rules they must keep to, for example not harming civilians
- makes sure that wars are waged as humanely as possible, for example not too many people are harmed
- outlines the rights that people have in conflicts.

Anne

> The existence of modern weapons including **weapons of mass destruction** means that large numbers of people are killed so war can never be fair.

> I think that the just war theory is no longer relevant. I am not sure it ever was. All wars are violent and dangerous.

> I think the just war theory is dangerous as it means that some authorities will go to war claiming the war to be a just one, when really it is **aggression** and they could have found other ways of solving their problems.

> 'Just war' seems to say that this is 'just' or fair and I don't think it is. I don't think there is ever a morally good reason for killing others, so I don't think that condition is ever met.

A02

1 Draw and complete a table to list at least four reasons why people might believe that the just war theory is important and reasons why they think that it is not important.
2 Discuss your reasons with another person and try to add more reasons to your table.
3 Use this information to participate in a decision alley. This is when the class divides in two, one side thinks of reasons why just war is important and one thinks of reasons why just war is not important. Each side then lines up shoulder to shoulder with an alley between. A member of the class then walks down the alley asking for advice from members on either side. When they get to the end they make a decision. At the end, the class can see what the majority view is.

exam practice b

Do you think the just war theory works? Give **two** reasons for your point of view.

Examiner's hint: Make sure you start by stating your opinion. (A02)

exam practice c

Explain why some people think the just war theory is important.

Examiner's hint: If you cannot think of four reasons give examples using some of the conditions. (A01)

exam practice d

'There can never be a just war.'
In your answer you should refer to at least one religion.
i) Do you agree? Give reasons for your answer.
ii) Give reasons why some people may disagree with you.

Examiner's hint: Make sure you include at least one religious reason. (A02)

7.5 Christian attitudes to war

All Christians are against the idea of war. However, some Christians accept that sometimes it is necessary and acceptable under certain conditions. Others say that war is never acceptable.

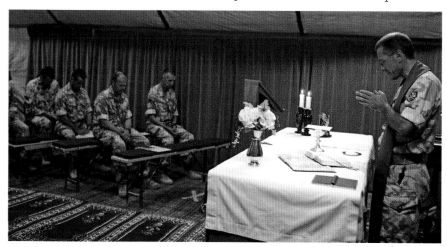

This picture shows a Christian minister helping in a war. Why do you think he does this?

Some Christians (including Anglicans and Catholics) accept war is sometimes necessary because:
- it might be needed to overcome great evil
- war can be used to achieve peace
- Jesus helped the Roman centurion (soldier), he did not condemn him
- Christians should work for justice; war may be the only way to achieve this
- the teaching 'love your neighbour' may mean fighting for them in a conflict.

Some Christians (including Quakers) believe war is never acceptable (**pacifism**) because:
- Jesus did not fight his arrest or crucifixion.
- Jesus taught love your enemies.
- Christians should follow the teaching of the Sermon on the Mount to 'turn the other cheek'.
- The teaching 'love your neighbour' can never mean killing.
- When Jesus was arrested he told Peter not to fight, saying 'put your sword back'.

Quakers declare 'the spirit of Christ which leads us into all Truth will never move us to fight and war against any man with outward weapons, neither for the kingdom of Christ, nor for the kingdoms of the world'.

Knowledge check

1 What are the two main Christian attitudes to war?
2 Draw a Venn diagram with two circles to show the reasons for the two attitudes:
   a) In one circle put reasons why war might be acceptable.
   b) In the other circle put reasons why war is never acceptable.
   c) In the overlap put reasons that can be used for both arguments.

A01

1 In small groups discuss the Christian attitudes to war.
2 Which one do you think is a good attitude?
3 In pairs, list four reasons not already given to support the attitude you prefer.

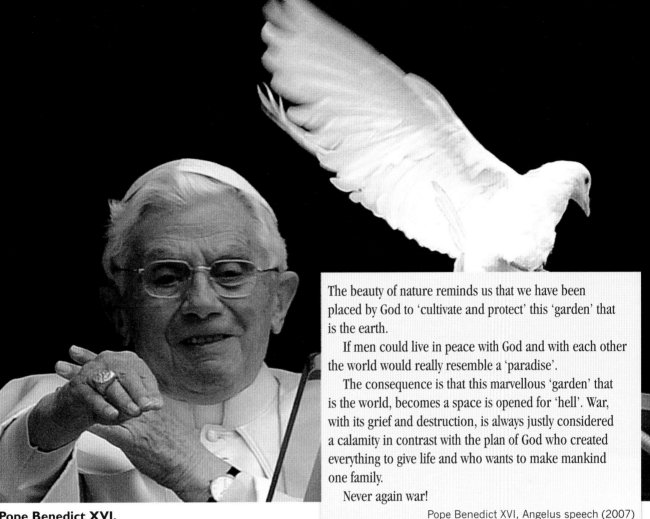

The beauty of nature reminds us that we have been placed by God to 'cultivate and protect' this 'garden' that is the earth.

If men could live in peace with God and with each other the world would really resemble a 'paradise'.

The consequence is that this marvellous 'garden' that is the world, becomes a space is opened for 'hell'. War, with its grief and destruction, is always justly considered a calamity in contrast with the plan of God who created everything to give life and who wants to make mankind one family.

Never again war!

Pope Benedict XVI, Angelus speech (2007)

Pope Benedict XVI.

A02

1 Produce a poster to show the different Christian attitudes to war, including your own view.
2 Present the poster to the class.

exam practice b

Do you think that Christians should fight in wars? Give **two** reasons for your point of view.

Examiner's hint: The reasons you give should refer to Christian reasons rather than non-religious ones. (A02)

exam practice c

Explain why some Christians might agree with war and some do not.

Examiner's hint: Make sure you give reasons for both attitudes. (A01)

exam practice d

'War is not good for the world.'
In your answer you should refer to Christianity.
i) Do you agree? Give reasons for your answer.
ii) Give reasons why some people may disagree with you.

Examiner's hint: Repeating the question at the beginning of your answer helps to remind you what the point of the question is. (A02)

7.6 Muslim attitudes to war

> O mankind, indeed We have created you from male and female and made you peoples and tribes that you may know one another (Qur'an 49:13).

The word Islam comes from Salaam, meaning peace. It also means submission. Muslims are taught that they should work or fight for justice. All Muslims will avoid war if possible.

The main Muslim attitude to war is that it is part of Muslim struggle (lesser jihad). Muslims believe that if it is necessary to go to war to achieve justice, and as long as the war is a just war, they will. The Muslim version of the just war is often called a holy war (although holy war is not the term used in the Qur'an). It has slightly different conditions from the Christian version.

Some Muslims (such as the Muslim Peace Fellowship) have a more pacifist view and will say that the references in the Qur'an to war were relevant in the past, but more should be done to avoid fighting today. However, they too will accept war if it is the last resort.

Knowledge check ✳

1 What is the basis of the word Islam?
2 What is the main Muslim attitude to war?
3 What is the minority Muslim attitude to war?

Muslim conditions for a just or holy war

It must be declared by a religious or spiritual authority.

It must be in self-defence or for the defence of Islam.

It must be the last resort.

It must stop when the enemy surrenders.

Innocent people must not suffer, land and plants should not be harmed.

A01

Write a newspaper article to explain the Muslim conditions for a just war. Your article must include:

✓ a brief description of what makes a just war
✓ explanations of the five conditions
✓ examples of the five conditions.

Fight in the way of Allah those who fight you but do not transgress. Indeed. Allah does not like transgressors (Qur'an 2:190).

Permission [to fight] has been given to those who are being fought, because they were wronged. And indeed, Allah is competent to give them victory (Qur'an 22:39).

And what is [the matter] with you that you fight not in the cause of Allah and [for] the oppressed among men, women, and children (Qur'an 4:75).

Muslim teachings on war

And if two factions among the believers should fight, then make settlement between the two … in justice and act justly. Indeed, Allah loves those who act justly (Qur'an 49:9).

If anyone killed a person not in retaliation of murder, or [and] to spread mischief in the land – it would be as if he killed all mankind, and if anyone saved a life, it would be as if he saved the life of all mankind (Qur'an 5:32).

A02

Prepare to answer the d)-type question: 'If everyone were religious there would be no wars'.

1 In pairs, one person takes on the role of a person who believes that if everyone were religious (Muslims) there would be no war, and the other person takes on the role of someone who believes that even if everyone were religious there would still be war.
2 Each person has two minutes to convince the other person that they must accept their point of view. The other person cannot interrupt or ask questions.
3 After two minutes each person can ask the other person two questions which the other person must answer.
4 At the end decide which argument was more convincing and why.

Write an answer for the d)-type question. In your answer you should refer to Islam.

i) Do you agree? Give reasons for your answer.
ii) Give reasons why some people may disagree with you.

exam practice b

Do you think it is possible to have a just or holy war? Give **two** reasons for your point of view.

Examiner's hint: Development must not be vague; make it specific to the point made. (A02)

exam practice c

Choose one religion other than Christianity and explain why most of its followers accept just war.

Examiner's hint: Do not describe just war – answer the question by explaining why it is accepted by most Muslims. (A01)

exam practice d

'War must be carried out as a last resort.'
In your answer you should refer to at least one religion.
i) Do you agree? Give reasons for your answer.
ii) Give reasons why some people may disagree with you.

Examiner's hint: Give evidence or quotes to develop reasons. (A02)

7.7 Christian attitudes to bullying

Bullying by definition is wrong. It is discrimination and can harm a person both physically and mentally. Christians, like all other people, teach that bullying is wrong. Christians believe that people who are being bullied should be helped and protected. Christians also believe that those people who are bullies also need help to find out why they bully and to stop.

Bullying causes all kinds of problems in society, but more specifically to the individual. Christianity teaches that bullying is wrong because it is discrimination and Jesus showed discrimination is wrong. Bullying can harm people and Christians should not harm others. They will be judged by the way they treat others.

KEY WORDS

bullying Intimidating/frightening people weaker than yourself.

Christian reasons why bullying is wrong

Blessed are the peacemakers, for they will be called children of God (Matthew 5:9).

Do to others as you would have them do to you (Luke 6:31).

Love one another. As I have loved you, so you must love one another (John 13:34).

In your relationships with one another, have the same mindset as Christ Jesus: Who, being in very nature God, did not consider equality with God something to be used to his own advantage (Philippians 2:5–6).

Anyone who claims to be in the light but hates a brother or sister is still in the darkness (1 John 2:9).

Cyberbullying has increased in recent years with the popularity of social networks and mobile phones.

Knowledge check

1 What is bullying?
2 What is the Christian attitude to bullying?
3 List three reasons why Christians think that bullying is wrong.
4 List three scriptural reasons (from the Bible) that explain why Christians think that bullying is wrong.

Look at the following words that come from descriptions of how people felt when they were being bullied:

scared

guilty

lonely

fear

sad

hurting

afraid

worried

stupid

invisible

silent

worthless

unhappy

weak

sick inside

humiliated

A01

1 Work in a small group to produce a TV advert or bulletin explaining why Christians should not bully others and why they should help people who are being bullied (and bullies). This could possibly be filmed.
2 Divide the group into actors, video recorders and interviewers as required.
3 Ensure the advert provides information about what bullying is, what the effects of bullying are and why Christians believe bullying is wrong.

A02

Work in pairs to produce an answer to the b)-type question: 'Do you think Christians must show love to bullies?'.

1 Using a large piece of paper take five minutes to write an answer to the question.
2 After five minutes pass the sheet to another pair who have the next five minutes to 'improve' the answer.
3 After five minutes pass the sheet to another pair who have the next five minutes to 'improve' the answer. After the second re-write, pass the answer back to the original pair. They can then look over the answer and write down the perfected answer in their notes.

7.8 Muslim attitudes to bullying

The Muslim attitude to bullying is that it is wrong. Bullies treat other people unfairly and this is not acceptable. Bullying is wrong because:

- It goes against all Muslim teaching about the care of others, especially the weak and innocent. It is against the teachings of Prophet Muhammad on brotherhood.
- It is against laws in the shariah about how to treat one another.
- Allah created everyone and no one should mistreat Allah's creation.
- It is a **sin** to use violence without a very good reason.

Bullying can be done in many ways: physically, verbally, emotionally and recently with increased use of internet cyberbullying. All of these show disrespect for the person being bullied and are harmful to a person's well-being. There are many organisations such as Kidscape and ChildLine who help people who are being bullied and members of all religious groups support these.

Knowledge check

1 What is the Muslim attitude to bullying?
2 List three reasons why Muslims think bullying is wrong.
3 List three scriptural reasons (from the Qur'an) which show why bullying is wrong.

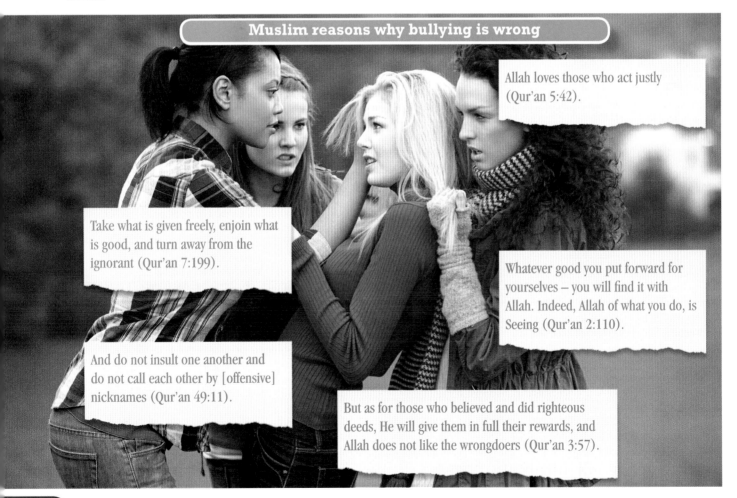

Muslim reasons why bullying is wrong

Allah loves those who act justly (Qur'an 5:42).

Take what is given freely, enjoin what is good, and turn away from the ignorant (Qur'an 7:199).

Whatever good you put forward for yourselves – you will find it with Allah. Indeed, Allah of what you do, is Seeing (Qur'an 2:110).

And do not insult one another and do not call each other by [offensive] nicknames (Qur'an 49:11).

But as for those who believed and did righteous deeds, He will give them in full their rewards, and Allah does not like the wrongdoers (Qur'an 3:57).

Take a look at this Islamic poster about Muslim attitudes to bullying:

"Allah [God] will not show mercy to a person who does not show mercy to other people"

Islam Says "No To Bullying"

What is Bullying and how does Islam view it?
Bullying is deliberate and hurtful behavior and can take place anywhere. There are many forms of bullying: Physical (hitting, kicking, snatching), Verbal (name-calling, insulting, taunting), Emotional (ignoring, spreading nasty gossip) and Cyber Bullying (using mobile phones, text messages, the internet).

Islam does not tolerate any form of bullying as it is a form of oppression. Allah [God] has mentioned many times in the Qur'aan regarding His displeasure of such actions:
"Allah does not like the oppressors." (3:140)
" O ye who believe ….. do not defame one another, nor insult one another by nicknames." (49:11)

Thus laughing at someone, defaming, being sarcastic or bullying is not acceptable.

It's not Cool to be Cruel

Ask Yourself a Question - How should we behave towards others?
The Muslim Greeting "As salamu alaikum wa rahmatullahi wa barakatuh" (May the peace, mercy, and blessings of Allah be with you)" is made up of three beautiful terms: peace, mercy, and blessings. These terms, taken together or separately, deny any association with any form of bullying. What does 'making people miserable' have to do with "peace, mercy, and blessings"?

If you see someone being bullied, do not ignore it, report it.
The Prophet Muhammad (Peace be upon Him) said: "He who amongst you sees something evil should modify it with the help of his hand; and if he has not strength enough to do it, then he should do it with his tongue, and if he has not strength enough to do it, (even) then he should (abhor it) from his heart, and that is the least of faith."
- (Sahih Muslim)

No one has the right to hurt you or make you feel bad. If you are being bullied do not tolerate it. Report it.

ISLAMIC POSTERS

© Islamic Posters Anti-Bullying Poster
Download FREE from www.IslamicPosters.co.uk

A01

In small groups, create a poster to explain the Muslim attitude towards bullying. The posters should be aimed at people who have no understanding of Islam and should include reasons why Muslims are against bullying.

A02

1 Think about the Muslim reasons for thinking bullying is wrong (all of them, not just those in the Qur'an). In your pair decide which are the best reasons and which are not so good.
2 Work on your own and write a list of the reasons in order starting with the best reason and finishing with the least good.
3 Draw a line across your list at the point at which you stop agreeing with the reasons.
4 Return to pair work and discuss why you have put your list in this order.

exam practice b

Do you think all Muslims should work to end bullying in schools? Give **two** reasons for your point of view.

Examiner's hint: Start with: 'I think that Muslims …' so that you give an opinion about Muslim actions, not what you personally would do. (A02)

exam practice c

Choose one religion other than Christianity and explain why they are against bullying.

Examiner's hint: You can develop a reason by using a quote from the Qur'an. (A01)

exam practice d

'Muslims must always speak out against bullies.'
In your answer you should refer to at least one religion.
i) Do you agree? Give reasons for your answer.
ii) Give reasons why some people may disagree with you.

Examiner's hint: Even if you are undecided you must either agree or disagree in d) i) and give the opposite opinion in d) ii). (A02)

7.9 Religious conflicts within families

Families are the place where children are raised by their parents to have the same values as themselves, and this includes their religion. Religion is a very important part of many people's lives and parents naturally want it to be as important for their children as it is for them.

As children grow up, it is natural for them to want to gain independence and to develop their own values and beliefs. These may be the same as their parents' but in some cases they are not. Many things that children may want to do or believe may go against their parents' beliefs and this may cause arguments or conflict in the family.

The main causes of religious conflict in families are:

● Choice of friends who might be of different faiths.
● Choice of partner who may have different beliefs.
● Not wanting to attend worship.
● Wanting to do things which are against the rules in their belief.
● Wanting to convert to another faith.

KEY WORDS

respect Treating a person or their feelings with consideration.

Religious conflict occurs when parents and children have different opinions.

A01

In small groups produce a presentation to explain why religion causes conflict in families. Include explanations for all the specialist language that you use. You could include a PowerPoint presentation and examples of conflict.

Knowledge check

1 Why do parents want their children to have the same religious beliefs as themselves?
2 List at least four causes of religious conflict in families.
3 Explain at least four reasons why these causes result in arguments.

Parents may fear that their children are sinning (may result in a bad afterlife).

Changes in lifestyle may lead to children excluding their family.

Children may feel forced into doing something against their will.

Parents may feel ashamed of their children's choices.

Reasons why causes of conflict may result in arguments

Children may feel their parents want them to do something that is no longer important to them.

Parents may feel their children no longer **respect** them.

Parents may feel they have failed in their role to bring their children up in the best way.

When I started at my secondary school I made friends with lots of new and different people. My closest friends are not religious and can't understand why I have to go home early on a Saturday night so I get to church on time on a Sunday. I don't see why I have to go to church. When I told my parents there was a big argument.

I met Olav and we started seeing each other about a year ago but I didn't tell my parents as he is not the same religion. I told my parents about him last weekend because Olav asked me to marry him. We had an argument. They are worried about my future.

I have just had a huge row with my family. They caught me eating food that is forbidden in my religion. I told them it is only food and everyone else eats it.

exam practice b

Do you think religion should cause conflict in families? Give **two** reasons for your point of view.

Examiner's hint: Start each reason on a new line. (A02)

exam practice c

Explain why religion may cause conflict in families.

Examiner's hint: Make sure you give reasons why conflict is caused rather than describing what causes conflict. (A01)

exam practice d

'Religious families should not argue.' In your answer you should refer to at least one religion.
i) Do you agree? Give reasons for your answer.
ii) Give reasons why some people may disagree with you.

Examiner's hint: In a d) question you must refer to one specific religion, this is most easily done with an example. (A02)

A02

1 Read the quotes above.
2 Imagine you have been asked by the family to explain why they are upset.
3 Write a reply to each of the people, try to encourage them to see both sides of the argument and try to suggest a solution to their conflict.

7.10 Christian teachings on forgiveness and reconciliation

Christians are taught that one of Jesus' most important teachings was to forgive.

Christian Churches teach that Christians should forgive one another and **forgiveness** is central to the teachings of Christianity. It shows that people should show love to others and that, if they want to be forgiven by God, they must forgive other people.

KEY WORDS

forgiveness Stopping blaming someone and/or pardoning them for what they have done wrong.

reconciliation Bringing together people who were opposed to each other.

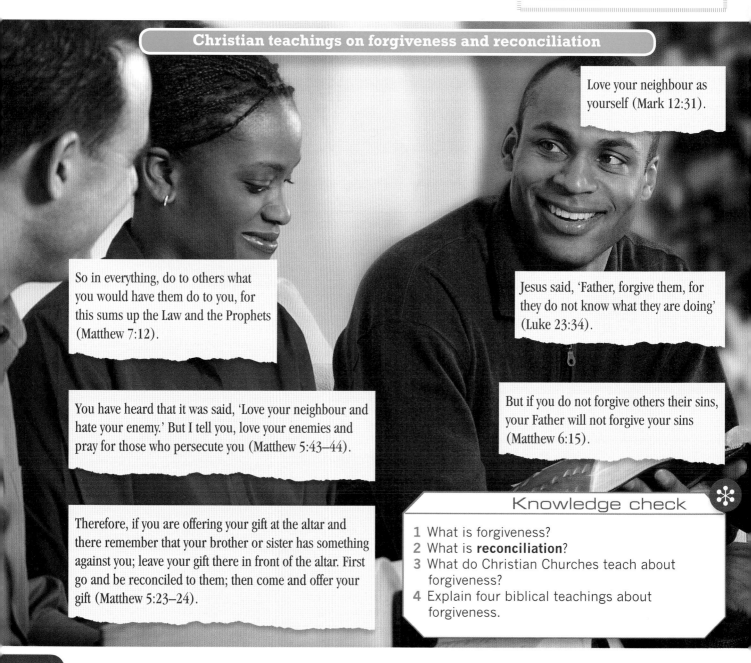

Christian teachings on forgiveness and reconciliation

Love your neighbour as yourself (Mark 12:31).

So in everything, do to others what you would have them do to you, for this sums up the Law and the Prophets (Matthew 7:12).

Jesus said, 'Father, forgive them, for they do not know what they are doing' (Luke 23:34).

You have heard that it was said, 'Love your neighbour and hate your enemy.' But I tell you, love your enemies and pray for those who persecute you (Matthew 5:43–44).

But if you do not forgive others their sins, your Father will not forgive your sins (Matthew 6:15).

Therefore, if you are offering your gift at the altar and there remember that your brother or sister has something against you; leave your gift there in front of the altar. First go and be reconciled to them; then come and offer your gift (Matthew 5:23–24).

Knowledge check

1 What is forgiveness?
2 What is **reconciliation**?
3 What do Christian Churches teach about forgiveness?
4 Explain four biblical teachings about forgiveness.

● Why Christian teachings on forgiveness and reconciliation are important

Christian teachings are important because:

- If Christians want to be forgiven, they need to forgive others first.
- Some people think a sinful person will not be able to go to heaven, they need to be forgiven first.
- Jesus taught to forgive others, even when he was on the cross.
- It means that Christians can then have a good relationship with other people (and with God).
- When a person forgives another person and restores a relationship they feel better.

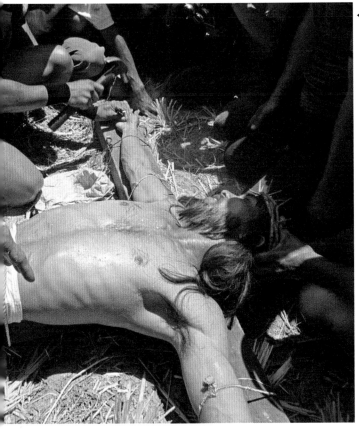

◀ **This photograph is from a re-enactment of the crucifixion of Jesus. These re-enactments help to remind some people of Jesus' teachings. Many of his teachings were about how people should treat each other. When on the cross,** *Jesus said, 'Father, forgive them, for they do not know what they are doing' (Luke 23:34).*

A01

Imagine you have been employed to produce an advertising campaign to encourage Christians to forgive one another. In groups, design either:

a) a poster campaign (a group of four posters that have a common theme); or
b) a text message campaign (a group of four texts that have a common theme); or
c) an internet pop-up campaign (a group of four pop-ups that have a common theme).

Explain your campaign to the rest of the class and decide which of the campaigns is the most effective.

A02

You are a journalist and your newspaper has asked you to write an article about Christians and forgiveness. In your article, you should include the reasons why Christians might want to forgive other people and the ways they should do this.

exam practice b

Do you think Christians should always forgive others? Give **two** reasons for your point of view.

Examiner's hint: It is possible to agree and disagree with statements like this but it is easier to get marks if you stick to one point of view. (A02)

exam practice c

Explain why Christians think forgiveness is important.

Examiner's hint: You may want to develop your reasons using Bible references. (A01)

exam practice d

'Religious people should always forgive.'
In your answer you should refer to at least one religion.
i) Do you agree? Give reasons for your answer.
ii) Give reasons why some people may disagree with you.

Examiner's hint: Make sure d) ii) are reasons for the opposite opinion to the one given in d) i). (A02)

7.11 Muslim teachings on forgiveness and reconciliation

Muslims believe that it is important to forgive each other. They base this on the actions and teachings of Prophet Muhammad and what they have been told to do in the Qur'an.

So pardon and overlook until Allah delivers His command (Qur'an 2:109).

Muslims should forgive people and it will be Allah who decides who is punished.

Whoever pardons and makes reconciliation – his reward is [due] from Allah (Qur'an 42:40).

Allah will reward those who are sorry for their wrongdoings.

But if you pardon and overlook and forgive – then indeed, Allah is Forgiving and Merciful (Qur'an 64:14).

If you forgive those who go against you (especially family members), Allah will forgive and so should they.

In the name of God, the Merciful, the Compassionate (Qur'an – Muslim teachings on forgiveness and reconciliation)

Those who, when they commit an immorality or wrong themselves [by transgression], remember Allah and seek forgiveness for their sins … their reward is forgiveness from their LORD and gardens beneath which rivers flow [in Paradise], wherein they will abide eternally (Qur'an 3:135–36).

People who ask forgiveness from Allah will be given a place in paradise.

O My servants who have transgressed against themselves [by sinning], do not despair of the mercy of Allah. Indeed, Allah forgives all sins. Indeed, it is He who is the Forgiving, the Merciful (Qur'an 39:53).

Countries which have a history of conflict with each other are more likely to come into armed conflict again over a different (or similar) issue.

And indeed, the Hour is coming; so forgive with gracious forgiveness (Qur'an 15:85).

Muslims must forgive each other so on judgement day they will be rewarded for it.

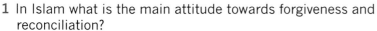

Knowledge check

1 In Islam what is the main attitude towards forgiveness and reconciliation?
2 What are the two main sources of Muslim teachings on forgiveness and reconciliation?
3 Write out an explanation of at least four Muslim teachings on forgiveness and reconciliation.

● Why Muslim teachings on forgiveness and reconciliation are important

- Muslims are taught that if they realise they have done wrong, promise not to do the same again and ask for forgiveness from Allah they will be forgiven for their own sins.
- They also recognise that they are all part of the ummah and so should have good relationships with each other.
- Muslims are taught that if they wish to go to paradise on the Day of Judgement then they must have shown mercy (forgiveness) to others.
- The Qur'an is full of passages about the forgiveness of Allah and his instruction that Muslims should also forgive. It is important that Muslims do the will of God.

exam practice b

'Do you think religious people should always forgive?' Give **two** reasons for your point of view.

Examiner's hint: A quote is a good way to develop a reason. (A02)

exam practice c

Choose one religion other than Christianity and explain its teachings on forgiveness.

Examiner's hint: In questions about one religion other than Christianity it is a good idea to name the religion you are referring to. (A01)

exam practice d

'Religious people must always forgive others.'
In your answer you should refer to at least one religion.
i) Do you agree? Give reasons for your answer.
ii) Give reasons why some people may disagree with you.

Examiner's hint: Even though the phrase 'all religious people' seems general you must refer to a specific religion in your answer. (A02)

A01

1 Read through the Muslim teachings on forgiveness and reconciliation. Note which teachings you can explain easily.
2 In pairs, use the Muslim teachings and explanations to produce a PowerPoint presentation or a poster to explain the Muslim teachings on forgiveness and reconciliation.
3 Give a presentation to the class explaining the Muslim teachings on forgiveness and reconciliation using the PowerPoint slide or poster.

A02

1 In small groups, discuss the Muslim teachings on forgiveness and reconciliation.
2 Put them in order of which you think are the best teachings (perhaps the easiest to understand or the ones that apply to everyday life).
3 In pairs, produce a poster to record one of the teachings and explain why it is important for Muslims.

Examination practice

Below is guidance on how to answer the question c) from Section 7: Religion: peace and conflict. As it is a c) question, it is worth 8 marks.

In every section there are two c) questions to choose from. Try question 5c) using the hints provided below. Then apply these steps to question 6c).

Sample question

5c) Choose one religion other than Christianity and explain why forgiveness is important in that religion. [8]

Sample question

6c) Explain why forgiveness is important to Christians. [8]

How to answer

There are several ways to get full marks on a c) question. One way is to give three separate reasons and develop one of them.

Step 1

○ Think of which religion you are using to answer your question and your first reason why forgiveness is important in that religion.

Muslims think that forgiveness is important as in the Qur'an it says that they should show mercy to others.

Step 2

○ Think of a way to develop the reason. This needs to expand the reason and still answer the question. A good way to do this is to give a quote from scripture.

For example the Qur'an says 'But if you pardon and overlook and forgive – then indeed, Allah is Forgiving and Merciful.'

Step 3

○ Think of your second reason why forgiveness is important in Islam (as that is the religion you have chosen). Make sure you start a new line with your second reason.

Secondly, Muslims are taught that they are all part of the ummah and so should have good relationships with each other which can only be done if they forgive each other.

Step 4

○ Think of a third reason why forgiveness is important in Islam. Make sure you start a new line with your third reason.

Muslims are taught that if they wish to go to paradise on the day of judgement then they must have shown mercy (forgiveness) to others.

Examiner's comment

✓ **Maximum marks will be awarded as there are three reasons with one developed reason (if the quality of written communication is good).**

✓ **Each reason is started on a new line. This will help examiners identify new reasons.**

✓ **Good use of a quote to develop the first reason.**

Below is guidance on how to answer the question d) from Section 7: Religion: peace and conflict. As it is a d) question, it is worth 6 marks.

In every section there are two d) questions to choose from. Each is divided into two parts, d) i) and d) ii). Try question 5d) using the hints provided below.

Sample question
5d) 'No religious person should take part in a war.' In your answer you should refer to at least **one** religion.
  i) Do you agree? Give reasons for your opinion.   [3]
  ii) Give reasons why some people may disagree with you.
                   [3]

How to answer
There are a few things to always include in a d) question.
- You must give your opinion in d) i).
- You must read the sentence under the statement. If it says 'you should refer to at least one religion' then you must clearly refer to any one religion. If it says 'you should refer to at least one religion other than Christianity' then you must clearly refer to a religion that is not Christianity. if it says 'you should refer to Christianity' then you must clearly refer to Christianity.

One way to get full marks on a d) question is to give three brief reasons for d) i) and three brief reasons for d) ii).

Question 5d) i)
Step 1
- Think whether you agree or disagree and one reason to support your opinion. Make sure you write down that it is your opinion at the beginning.

I agree. I think religious people might not want to go to war because they think it is killing and killing is murder.

Step 2
- Think of a second reason; make sure it is not the same as the first reason.

Secondly, some Christians like the Quakers are pacifists. They think peace cannot be achieved by fighting because Jesus did not fight.

Step 3
- Think of a third reason why you disagree with the statement. Write every reason as a new paragraph. If you include the word 'because' in your reason you can be sure you are not just describing.

Finally, Muslims would say you should not fight unless you are attacked because that is what a just or holy war states.

Question 5d) ii)
Step 1
- This must include reasons for the opposite opinion to the one you gave as your opinion in d) i).

Some people disagree with the statement. They think religious people should go to war because they should fight to protect the weak and the innocent.

Step 2
- Think of a second reason; make sure it is not the same as the first reason.

Secondly, some Christians would say that they might go to war because if it is a just war then it is morally right to fight.

Step 3
- Think of a third reason why a person would agree with the statement. Make it clear it is a third reason by starting with 'finally' or 'thirdly'.

Finally, some Muslims would say they should fight because in the Qur'an it says 'Permission to fight has been given to those who are being fought, because they were wronged'.

Examiner's comment
✓ **The candidate has clearly stated their own personal view. Without this they cannot get full marks.**
✓ **Maximum marks will be awarded as each side of the argument has three reasons.**

Religion and society

Section 8: Religion: crime and punishment

8.1 Law and justice

● Why society needs rules

Laws are simply rules that everyone must obey because they have been agreed by Parliament and the **justice** system. Laws are enforced or applied by the police and the courts to make sure that everyone follows them.

> **KEY WORDS**
>
> **crime** An act against the law.
> **justice** Due allocation of reward and punishment/the maintenance of what is right.
> **law** Rules made by Parliament and enforceable by the courts.

Laws mean everyone behaves in a predictable manner, for example everyone drives on the left-hand side of the road.

Laws mean everyone knows what is right and what is wrong, for example what age children should attend school until.

Laws mean people know they will be punished if they commit a **crime**, for example a person who steals repeatedly will be given a prison sentence.

Society needs rules because:

Laws protect the weaker members of society, for example it is easy to take advantage of the young, sick or elderly. Laws prevent this happening.

Laws prevent people being selfish, for example they keep people under control (riots show people out of control of the law).

Knowledge check

1 What is a crime?
2 What is justice?
3 What is a law?
4 Who makes laws?
5 Who makes sure that people keep to the laws?
6 List at least four reasons why a country needs laws.

It is easy to think about why society needs rules if you think about what it would be like without rules. This is a photo from the summer 2011 riots in England.

● Justice

Justice uses the law system to reward people who do right and to punish people who do wrong. It is also a wider idea of fairness and people getting what they deserve.

Why society needs justice

It ensures people are treated fairly.

It makes sure that any punishment a person gets is truly deserved.

It means that the punishments given are proportional to the crime committed, for example a person stealing food would not get a life sentence in prison.

It means that people who have worked hard for something will get rewarded rather than have it taken away from them.

Justice is seen by everyone, so people are less likely to do wrong.

The justice system guarantees human rights.

The most frequently used symbol of justice is Lady Justice. She is shown holding scales and a sword and is blindfolded. Scales show that justice weighs up each side, a blindfold symbolises justice is not biased and the sword represents that justice has the power to strike and deal punishment.

A01

Imagine you work for a court of law. You need to write a leaflet for year 7 students visiting the courts who are studying law and justice.
    The leaflet should explain:

● what law and order is
● why laws are needed
● why justice is needed.

A02

Prepare for a class debate on: 'A good society needs laws'.

1 Write the debate title as a heading and then draw a table listing reasons to support the statement and reasons to argue against the statement.
2 Hold the debate. Ensure there is a chairperson and at least two people to speak on the issue. Ask questions of the speakers before taking a class vote.

exam practice b

Do you think laws are always needed? Give **two** reasons for your point of view.

Examiner's hint: Make sure you start your answer with 'I think …' to help you give your point of view. (A02)

exam practice c

Explain why justice is important.

Examiner's hint: Write two reasons and develop each one with an example. (A01)

exam practice d

'People should always obey the law.'
In your answer you should refer to at least one religion.
i) Do you agree? Give reasons for your answer.
ii) Give reasons why some people may disagree with you.

Examiner's hint: Start each reason on a new line. (A02)

8.2 Theories of punishment

For society to maintain the laws and treat everyone with justice there must be punishment for those who break the law. There are different theories behind punishment and they are supported and opposed by different people.

● Different theories of punishment

There are four main theories of punishment:

Deterrence   Protection   Retribution   **Reform**

Deterrence

This kind of punishment tries to put people off committing crimes and convince an offender not to commit further crimes. This works because:
- the punishments are so severe that others do not want to experience them
- they may be done in public so others become scared of them
- they are publicised so people are aware of them
- people will naturally not want to be treated in a humiliating way.

Protection

This kind of punishment does not try to stop offenders before they break the law, but it does protect society by imprisoning criminals. This works because:
- the punishment removes the offender from society
- it makes the public feel safer, especially from dangerous criminals
- people are aware that the offender is no longer around
- it restricts the offender so they cannot commit further crime.

Retribution

This kind of punishment does not try to stop offenders before they break the law, but it means that the victim feels that the offender is punished properly. This works because:

- the punishments often give something to the victim, for example money
- the punishment makes the victim feel that the offender has paid for their crime
- the offender may be made to help directly, for example community work for vandalism
- retribution may be done in public so victims can see justice has been done.

Reform

This kind of punishment tries to change people so that they do not want to commit crimes in the future. This works because:

- it educates them so they realise that breaking the law is not good
- it may train them in jobs that will not lead back to crime
- the offender will not feel resentful at being punished
- it will improve society in general
- **rehabilitation** of the offender is possible.

Knowledge check

1 Why are punishments needed?
2 Name the four main theories of punishment.
3 What does deterrent punishment mean?
4 What does protection as a theory of punishment mean?
5 What does retribution as a theory of punishment mean?
6 What does reform as a theory of punishment mean?

A01

1 In small groups discuss the different theories of punishment. Which theory do you most agree with? Why?
2 Draw a poster (or produce a PowerPoint presentation) to describe theories of punishment. Include descriptions of the different theories and reasons why they work. Illustrate them with examples.

Type of punishment	Criticisms of the punishment
Deterrence	<ul><li>Punishments have to be very severe</li><li>There is no proof that it works</li><li>It may humiliate the offender</li><li>It may not respect human rights</li></ul>
Protection	<ul><li>The offender does not change when released</li><li>There is no proof that it works</li><li>It may cause the offender to become resentful</li><li>There are some crimes that are not dangerous to other people</li></ul>
Retribution	<ul><li>There is no proof that it works</li><li>It may humiliate the offender</li><li>It may not respect human rights</li><li>It may cause the offender to become resentful</li></ul>
Reform	<ul><li>It might be seen as an easy option (not a real punishment)</li><li>It might not work for dangerous criminals</li><li>Offenders may 'pretend' to be reformed</li><li>Victims may resent it</li></ul>

A02

Read through the reasons for punishments on pages 203–204 and the criticisms in the table above.

1 Prepare to answer questions about the different theories of punishment.
2 Decide which theory you will choose to support (and will answer questions on).
3 Make a list of the reasons why you would support that theory rather than the alternatives.
4 Take part in the hot-seat discussion either as the person in the hot seat being questioned or as the questioner.

exam practice b

Do you think punishment is always right? Give **two** reasons for your point of view.

Examiner's hint: Try to develop your reasons with examples. (A02)

exam practice c

Explain why some people agree with reform as a theory of punishment and some do not.

Examiner's hint: You need to give reasons for and against reform. Do not give a one-sided answer. (A01)

exam practice d

'Retribution is the best theory of punishment.'
In your answer you should refer to Christianity.
i) Do you agree? Give reasons for your answer.
ii) Give reasons why some people may disagree with you.

Examiner's hint: Make sure you include reference to Christianity in your answer. (A02)

8.3 Why justice is important for Christians

To Christians, justice is very important as it ensures that people are treated fairly. Justice means everybody everywhere receiving reward for good and punishment for bad, but making sure that everyone has their human rights. This follows the teachings and actions of Jesus.

> If you are neutral in situations of injustice, you have chosen the side of the oppressor. If an elephant has its foot on the tail of a mouse and you say that you are neutral, the mouse will not appreciate your neutrality.
>
> Archbishop Desmond Tutu

● Christian teachings on justice

He has sent me to proclaim freedom for the prisoners and recovery of sight for the blind, to set the oppressed free (Luke 4:18).

And what does the LORD require of you? To act justly and to love mercy and to walk humbly with your God (Micah 6:8).

All the believers were together and had everything in common. They sold property and possessions to give to anyone who had need (Acts 2:44–45).

So God created mankind in his own image, in the image of God he created them; male and female he created them (Genesis 1:27).

Do not pervert justice; do not show partiality to the poor or favouritisms to the great, but judge your neighbour fairly (Leviticus 19:15).

It is not good to be partial to the wicked and so deprive the innocent of justice (Proverbs 18:5).

This is what the LORD says: Maintain justice and do what is right (Isaiah 56:1).

Knowledge check

1 Why do Christians think justice is important?
2 Why does Archbishop Desmond Tutu think people must not ignore injustice?
3 Look at the biblical reasons why justice is important. Pick the one that you like the best. Write it out and explain why you think it is important.

● Christians who work for justice

Throughout history Christians have spoken up for justice. Jesus spoke up for those who were treated badly, like women, children and sick people. Martin Luther King spoke out for equal rights and Óscar Romero spoke out for the poor in El Salvador.

Today, Christians work in various organisations to make sure that the Old Testament message of Micah, 'to act justly', is carried out. Charities like Christian Aid, CAFOD and Tearfund work to ensure that people in poverty around the world are treated justly by their governments. Groups such as Housing Justice and Church Action on Poverty work in the UK to ensure that poor people have their human rights respected.

Individuals such as Archbishop Desmond Tutu, Bono from U2 and Christian pacifist Norman Kember have all worked to end injustice based on the teachings of the Bible and the natural sense of unfairness that injustice brings.

A01

1 Copy and complete the following table.

Bible reference about justice	What this means for Christians today

2 How do you think Christians can work to achieve justice today?

A02

1 In pairs, draw a consequence wheel (see page 52) around the idea that: 'Christians must work for justice'. A consequence wheel is a circle made up of a centre and three concentric rings around it.
2 In the centre, write: 'Christians must work for justice'.
3 In the next ring of the circle, write down the immediate consequence of thinking this statement is true.
4 In the next ring, write down what could be a consequence of the first consequence.
5 In the third ring, write down what could be a consequence of the consequence in the second ring.
6 Look at all the consequences and decide whether you agree with the original statement or not.

Find out more about the work of some Christian organisations:

Christian Aid: www.christianaid.org.uk

CAFOD: www.cafod.org.uk

Tearfund: www.tearfund.org

Housing Justice: www.housingjustice.org.uk

Church Action on Poverty: www.church-poverty.org.uk

Bono, frontman of U2, speaking at the release of the DATA (Debt, AIDS, Trade, Africa) report. 'You see, Africa makes a fool of our idea of justice … It doubts our concern. It questions our commitment. Because there is no way we can look at what's happening in Africa, and if we're honest, conclude that it would ever be allowed to happen anywhere else.'

exam practice b

Do you think all Christians must work for justice? Give **two** reasons for your point of view.

Examiner's hint: Give reasons which answer the question – why Christians should or should not work for justice – rather than whether Christians should or should not do anything. (A02)

exam practice c

Explain why Christians think justice is important.

Examiner's hint: Reasons can be developed by Bible references. (A01)

exam practice d

'Christians do not need to work for justice.' In your answer you should refer to at least one religion other than Christianity.
i) Do you agree? Give reasons for your answer.
ii) Give reasons why some people may disagree with you.

Examiner's hint: Make sure you start your answer to d) i) with 'I think …'. (A02)

8.4 Why justice is important for Muslims

I believe that Allah is just and he will reward those who show justice to others.

The blame is only against those who oppress men … defying right and justice: for such there will be a penalty grievous (Qur'an 42:42). I think that this means Muslims must not only avoid doing things that are not just, but must also work for justice.

On the Day of Judgement everyone will be judged by Allah. Allah is merciful. The good people who have shown justice to others will be rewarded.

One of the Five Pillars of Islam is to give zakah (charity). We do this to try and end the injustice of poverty.

The Qur'an says that even when we are with people who are enemies, Muslims should say *I have been commanded to do justice among you (Qur'an 42:15).* This means I should treat everyone with justice.

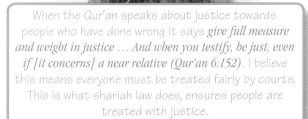

When the Qur'an speaks about justice towards people who have done wrong it says *give full measure and weight in justice … And when you testify, be just, even if [it concerns] a near relative (Qur'an 6:152).* I believe this means everyone must be treated fairly by courts. This is what shariah law does, ensures people are treated with justice.

How can I say I am part of the ummah if I do not treat my brother with justice?

The Muslims on the previous page have shown that justice is important to Muslims because:

- it is in the Five Pillars of Islam
- it will affect judgement on the Day of Judgement
- the Qur'an says that people who do not work for justice will be punished (Qur'an 42:42)
- Allah will reward those who work for justice
- all Muslims are part of the ummah and should care for one another
- shariah law or Islamic law is based on treating others with justice.

Knowledge check

1 What is an ethnic minority?
2 Write out two references from the Qur'an which show that Muslims must work for justice.
3 List at least four reasons why justice is important for Muslims.

A01

1 In pairs, produce a PowerPoint presentation (or poster) to explain why justice is important to Muslims.
2 Add quotes or examples to explain the reasons.
3 Present your PowerPoint slides (or poster) to the rest of the class.

● How Muslims work for justice

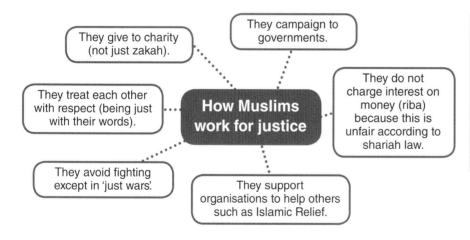

Find out more about the work of some Muslim organisations:
Islamic Relief:
www.islamic-relief.org.uk
Ummah Welfare Trust:
www.uwt.org
Muslim Hands:
www.muslimhands.org

A02

A Muslim child gives money to a beggar after a ceremony to mark the Eid-al-Fitr festival in Dongguan mosque in Xining, China. Muslims attach great importance to charity and good deeds during this day, and they will share their blessings by feeding the poor and making contributions to mosques.

1 Read the reasons why justice is important to Muslims and what they do to work for justice.
2 Write a list of the reasons why justice is important and the best ways Muslims can work to achieve justice.
3 Write a speech, lasting three minutes, which could be presented to the class, explaining: 'Why Muslims should work for justice'.

exam practice b

Do you think justice is important? Give **two** reasons for your point of view.

Examiner's hint: Although you do not have to give Muslim reasons in your answer to this question it is easily answered using Muslim reasons. (A02)

exam practice c

Explain why justice is important to Muslims.

Examiner's hint: You can use quotes to develop reasons. (A01)

exam practice d

'Muslims cannot end the problem of injustice.' In your answer you should refer to at least one religion.
i) Do you agree? Give reasons for your answer.
ii) Give reasons why some people may disagree with you.

Examiner's hint: Although this question says Muslims, in the examination it will say religious people. As you have studied Islam, wherever it says 'religious people', imagine it says Muslims. (A02)

8.5 Capital punishment

Capital punishment is punishment for crimes which are regarded as so serious that the person's life must be taken from them. **Capital punishment** is not legal in the UK, but it was used in 67 countries around the world in 2010. (It is legal in other countries; however, they have not used it recently.)

The UN has held votes several times to try and get capital punishment made illegal under the human right to life but has been unsuccessful. Countries who use capital punishment maintain the right to use it for very serious crimes. In some countries serious crimes are serial murder or drug smuggling. The methods used to execute a criminal vary from country to country and crime to crime.

Left, protesters against the death penalty hold a night vigil outside a US prison to oppose the execution of John Evans, a prolific armed robber, who murdered a shopkeeper. Below, people showing their support for the execution of Timothy McVeigh, a militia movement sympathiser. McVeigh exploded a bomb outside a US government building murdering 168 people and injuring 800 others.

● Non-religious arguments about capital punishment

Arguments in favour of capital punishment	Arguments against capital punishment
It is the only punishment severe enough to punish a person who has committed a very serious crime	No crime is serious enough to justify taking a life
It is the ultimate deterrent – it will put would-be murderers off	Most murders are 'crimes of passion', not premeditated, so it does not put people off. Statistically, countries with the death penalty do not have fewer serious crimes than those without it
It prevents a person committing the crime again; it protects society from them	It might make someone who has killed once kill even more people rather than risk getting caught. The wrong person might be executed. There have been cases where an innocent person has been killed
It makes the victims (or their families) feel better (see article below)	Killing another person will not change what has happened to the victim. Killing a person in retaliation for a killing makes the country using capital punishment as bad as the offender
The person who commits serious crimes should lose all their rights including the right to live	The UN Declaration of Human Rights states that every human has the right to life and the right not to be tortured or to suffer; capital punishment goes against these rights

Knowledge check ✳

1 What is capital punishment?
2 Where is capital punishment used?
3 Why is capital punishment used?

Bring back the death penalty

Joanna Yeates was murdered on 17 December 2010 and her body hidden. Her killing was frontpage news when her body was found on Christmas morning. A time her family will never forget.

Ms Yeates' murderer, Vincent Tabak, was found guilty in October 2011 and was sentenced to a minimum of 20 years in prison for a crime the judge said was: 'a dreadful, evil act committed against a vulnerable unsuspecting young woman'.

Joanna's parents have issued a statement saying: 'it is with regret that capital punishment is not a possible option for his sentence. The best we can hope for him is that he spends the rest of his life incarcerated'.

A01

1 In small groups discuss the different arguments for and against capital punishment.
2 In pairs, prepare two posters: one in favour of capital punishment and one against capital punishment. Ensure they contain: information about capital punishment, why capital punishment is acceptable or not acceptable and examples of why capital punishment is acceptable or not acceptable.
3 Present your posters to the class.

A02

Prepare for a class debate on: 'Some criminals deserve capital punishment'.

1 Write the debate title as a heading.
2 Draw a table. The first column should list reasons to support the statement, such as Bible references which indicate that capital punishment can protect people.
3 The second column should list reasons to disagree with the statement, such as it is against human rights to take someone's life.
4 Hold the debate. Ensure that there is a chairperson and at least two people to speak on the issue. Ask questions of the speakers before taking a class vote.

exam practice b

Do you think capital punishment should be legal in the UK? Give **two** reasons for your point of view.

Examiner's hint: The reasons you give as answers to this question do not have to be religious. (A02)

exam practice c

Explain why some people agree with capital punishment.

Examiner's hint: Many questions are based on the key words given in the specification. Make sure you know the meaning of capital punishment. (A01)

exam practice d

'Some criminals deserve capital punishment.'
In your answer you should refer to at least one religion.
i) Do you agree? Give reasons for your answer.
ii) Give reasons why some people may disagree with you.

Examiner's hint: Make sure you start d) i) answers with your own opinion. (A02)

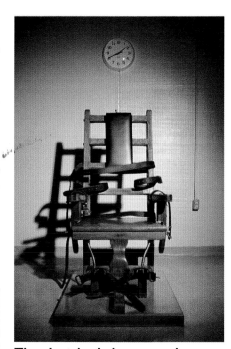

The electric chair was used as a means of execution in many US states, although it is now being replaced by lethal injection.

8.6 Christian attitudes to capital punishment

There are two main attitudes to capital punishment among Christians. Some Christians think that capital punishment should be used in serious cases where the guilt of the person is beyond doubt. Other Christians think that capital punishment is wrong as there are no situations when punishment in this way is acceptable.

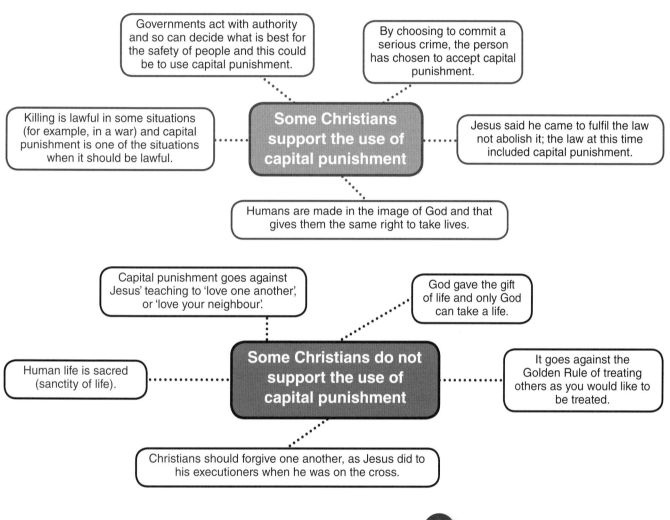

Governments act with authority and so can decide what is best for the safety of people and this could be to use capital punishment.

By choosing to commit a serious crime, the person has chosen to accept capital punishment.

Killing is lawful in some situations (for example, in a war) and capital punishment is one of the situations when it should be lawful.

Some Christians support the use of capital punishment

Jesus said he came to fulfil the law not abolish it; the law at this time included capital punishment.

Humans are made in the image of God and that gives them the same right to take lives.

Capital punishment goes against Jesus' teaching to 'love one another', or 'love your neighbour'.

God gave the gift of life and only God can take a life.

Human life is sacred (sanctity of life).

Some Christians do not support the use of capital punishment

It goes against the Golden Rule of treating others as you would like to be treated.

Christians should forgive one another, as Jesus did to his executioners when he was on the cross.

Knowledge check

1 What are the two main Christian attitudes towards capital punishment?
2 Pick one reason why Christians support the use of capital punishment and explain why it shows that the death penalty can be used.
3 Pick one reason why Christians do not support the use of capital punishment and explain why it shows that the death penalty is wrong.

● Christian teachings on capital punishment

Whoever sheds human blood, by humans shall their blood be shed (Genesis 9:6).

If you do wrong, be afraid, for rulers do not bear the sword for no reason (Romans 13:4).

But I tell you, love your enemies and pray for those who persecute you (Matthew 5:44).

This conference … urges the Church to speak out against all governments who practise capital punishment, and encourages them to find alternative ways of sentencing offenders so that the divine dignity of every human being is respected and yet justice is pursued.

Church of England – Lambeth conference 1988, resolution 33

The principle set forth in the new Catechism of the Catholic Church remains valid: 'If bloodless means are sufficient to defend human lives against an aggressor and to protect public order and the safety of persons, public authority must limit itself to such means, because they better correspond to the concrete conditions of the common good and are more in conformity to the dignity of the human person.

Pope John Paul II, *Evangelium Vitae* (*The Gospel of Life*)

You have heard that it was said, 'Eye for eye, and tooth for tooth.' But I tell you, do not resist an evil person. If anyone slaps you on the right cheek, turn to them the other cheek also (Matthew 5:38–39).

Do not judge, or you too will be judged (Matthew 7:1).

Let everyone be subject to the governing authorities, for there is no authority except that which God has established. The authorities that exist have been established by God. Consequently, whoever rebels against the authority is rebelling against what God has instituted, and those who do so will bring judgement on themselves (Romans 13:1–2).

Anyone who strikes a person with a fatal blow is to be put to death. However, if it is not done intentionally, but God lets it happen, they are to flee to a place I will designate. But if anyone schemes and kills someone deliberately, that person is to be taken from my altar and put to death (Exodus 21:12–14).

A01

1 In pairs, read through the Christian reasons for and against capital punishment.
2 Draw a table to record at least four Christian reasons against capital punishment and four Christian reasons supporting capital punishment.

A02

Write a newspaper article to explain the Christian teachings about capital punishment. Your article can refer to the Bible quotes on pages 216–217 and must include:

● a brief description of the two different attitudes to capital punishment
● Christian teachings supporting capital punishment
● Christian teachings against capital punishment
● at least one illustration or picture.

exam practice b

Do you think all Christians should support the use of capital punishment? Give **two** reasons for your point of view.

Examiner's hint: Remember you should only give one point of view in a b) answer. (A02)

exam practice c

Explain why some Christians do not support the use of capital punishment.

Examiner's hint: You could give four different Bible quotes as reasons for your answer. (A01)

exam practice d

'Capital punishment should never be used.'
In your answer you should refer to at least Christianity.
i) Do you agree? Give reasons for your answer.
ii) Give reasons why some people may disagree with you.

Examiner's hint: Read the line following the stimulus and make sure you refer to Christianity. (A02)

8.7 Muslim attitudes to capital punishment

The main Muslim attitude towards capital punishment is that it is acceptable for certain crimes. A few Muslims think that in today's society it is not needed and there are other forms of punishment that can be used, but on the whole it is acceptable and Muslim states (countries) have the death penalty.

● Reasons why most Muslims support capital punishment

Humans have free will, which means they can do evil, and may face discipline such as capital punishment.

Shariah law says that capital punishment can be used for murder and for 'spreading mischief in the land' (this means apostasy, treason, rape, piracy, terrorism, adultery or homosexuality).

Prophet Muhammad supported capital punishment.

The Qur'an has passages which outline that capital punishment can be used.

Capital punishment not only punishes the offender, but it is also a reminder to society not to break the law.

Is the threat of death a deterrent?

● Reasons why some Muslims do not support capital punishment

Humans do evil, but there are better methods of punishment than capital punishment.

It is recommended in the Qur'an, but is not compulsory (for example, payment can be taken instead).

On occasions, capital punishment has been used on innocent people and this makes execution unacceptable.

Reasons why a few Muslims do not support capital punishment

Shariah law can be used incorrectly by people and governments and this results in unfair treatment of people. It does not reflect the importance of justice in Islam.

Some Muslim scholars have said that society is different today and that capital punishment in no longer appropriate.

Knowledge check

1 What are the Muslim attitudes to capital punishment?
2 List four reasons why Muslims may support the use of capital punishment.
3 List four reasons why Muslims may not support the use of capital punishment.

A01

In pairs, prepare a PowerPoint presentation or poster to teach future GCSE classes about Muslim attitudes towards capital punishment. Include in your presentation:

● the Muslim attitudes to capital punishment
● the reasons for the Muslim attitudes towards capital punishment
● at least three Muslim teachings (see the table below) about capital punishment and what they mean.

● Muslim quotes to support the use of capital punishment

Quote	What it means
Prescribed for you is legal retribution for those murdered – the free for the free, the slave for the slave, and the female for the female. But whoever overlooks from his brother anything, then there should be a suitable follow-up and payment to him with good conduct (Qur'an 2:178)	A life can be taken for a life or a victim's family can choose payment instead
Whoever kills a soul unless for a soul or for corruption [done] in the land – it is as if he had slain mankind entirely (Qur'an 5:32)	Capital punishment is allowed for taking another soul (murder) but otherwise it is against the sanctity of life
So not kill the soul which Allah has forbidden [to be killed] except by [legal] right. This has He instructed you that you may use reason (Qur'an 6:151)	Capital punishment can be used when it is legally required
Whoever disbelieves in Allah after his belief … except for one who is forced [to renounce his religion] while his heart is secure in faith. But those who [willingly] open their breasts to disbelief, upon them is wrath from Allah, and for them is a great punishment (Qur'an 16:106)	Capital punishment is the great punishment for disbelieving (apostasy) although some think this quote means the punishment will come from God

A02

1 In pairs, discuss all of the different Muslim reasons for accepting or not accepting the use of capital punishment. Which ones do you think provide the best reasons?
2 Individually, make a list of five reasons and write them in order, putting what you think is the best reason first.
3 Compare your list with your partner. Which ones do you agree with? Why?

exam practice b

Do you think all Muslims should accept the use of capital punishment? Give **two** reasons for your point of view.

Examiner's hint: Develop your reasons using references from the Qur'an.
(A02)

exam practice c

Explain why Muslims should accept the use of capital punishment.

Examiner's hint: You could give four different Qur'anic quotes as reasons.
(A01)

exam practice d

'Real justice must mean using capital punishment.'
In your answer you should refer to at least one religion.
i) Do you agree? Give reasons for your answer.
ii) Give reasons why some people may disagree with you.

Examiner's hint: Although this question does not directly refer to Islam, you should make reference to Muslim reasons in your answer.
(A02)

8.8 Drugs and alcohol: the law

Alcohol: the law

The laws regarding alcohol in the UK are very strict. In order for a shop to be permitted to sell alcohol it has to have a licence. This licence can be taken away if the shop sells alcohol to the wrong people.

It is against the law for:

- anyone under the age of five to be given alcohol unless for medical reasons
- anyone under the age of fourteen to be in licensed premises, except in a family room
- alcohol to be sold to anyone under eighteen years of age
- anyone to buy alcohol for anyone who is under eighteen
- anyone to try to buy alcohol who is under eighteen
- anyone under eighteen to drink alcohol in a licensed place (except if they are eating a meal when they can have beer or cider)
- anyone to be drunk in public while being in charge of a child who is younger than seven years old.

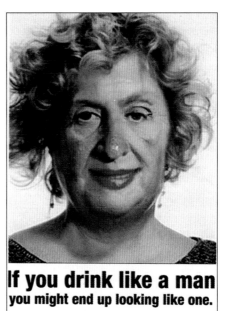

If you drink like a man you might end up looking like one.

Wine doesn't just come with cheese. For women it's also accompanied by hair loss, wrinkles, obesity, breast cancer, early menopause and memory loss.

An alcohol awareness poster aimed at young women.

Drugs: the law

Not all drugs are illegal drugs. However, all drugs are subject to certain conditions and are carefully regulated by medical authorities. This section refers to the use of drugs in a non-medical way. Drugs when used in a non-medical way are referred to as controlled drugs (substances).

The Misuse of Drugs Act 1971 explains the legality of the use and possession of controlled drugs and this depends on how harmful a drug can be (the classification of a drug):

- Class A drugs are considered to be the most harmful. These include cocaine, ecstasy, heroin and LSD.
- Class B drugs are the next most harmful and these include amphetamines, barbiturates, codeine and cannabis. (Although if these are prepared for injection they are regarded as class A.)
- Class C drugs are the lowest class of controlled drugs and these include steroids, tranquillisers and ketamine.

The Misuse of Drugs Act lists various punishments:

- Possession, production or selling Class A drugs can result in up to seven years' imprisonment for possession and up to life for producing and selling.
- Possession, production or selling Class B drugs can result in up to five years' imprisonment for possession and up to fourteen years (or unlimited fine) for producing and selling.
- Possession, production or selling Class C drugs can result in up to two years' imprisonment for possession and up to fourteen years (or unlimited fine) for producing and selling.

An anti-drugs poster.

Knowledge check ✳

1 Who is allowed to sell alcohol?
2 What limits are put on the age at which alcohol can be drunk?
3 Which drugs are called controlled drugs?
4 Why are drugs classified into different classes?

A01

1 In small groups, create a TV advert to explain to people *either* the law regarding alcohol *or* the laws regulating controlled drugs.
2 The advert should involve everyone in the group in some way.
3 The advert should include explanations of the key parts of the laws.
4 Either perform your advert for the group or video it to show the group at a later point.

A02

1 In pairs, discuss the laws about alcohol and controlled drugs.
2 Write a list of the reasons why you think these laws are good or why you think these laws are not good.
3 Look at the posters on page 220 encouraging people not to drink or take controlled drugs. Do you think these types of posters work? Give three reasons for your opinion.

exam practice b

Do you think the laws about alcohol are too strict? Give **two** reasons for your point of view.

Examiner's hint: Make sure you only give two reasons. (A02)

exam practice c

Explain the laws which control the use of drugs and alcohol.

Examiner's hint: This question does not include the word 'why' and does not need reasons. Read questions very carefully and work out whether you need to give description or reasons. (A01)

exam practice d

'It does not matter if people take controlled drugs.' In your answer you should refer to at least one religion.
i) Do you agree? Give reasons for your answer.
ii) Give reasons why some people may disagree with you.

Examiner's hint: This question refers to controlled drugs. Make sure you explain that their use is illegal at some point in your answer. (A02)

8.9 Drugs and alcohol: social and health problems

As we have seen, in the UK there are laws in place which control the way that drugs and alcohol are used. The reasons why these laws have been passed is because of the harmful effects that alcohol and drugs can have on people. These substances can cause **addiction**, which badly affects a user's health and often also causes problems for society as a whole.

KEY WORDS

addiction A recurring compulsion to engage in an activity regardless of its bad effects.

responsibility Being responsible for one's actions.

Health problems caused by drugs and alcohol

Drug abuse may lead to infections, especially those passed on by dirty needles (for example HIV and hepatitis).

Drug and alcohol abuse may cause problems in conceiving children (infertility).

The Institute of Alcohol Studies says that the risk of cancers and cirrhosis of the liver is increased significantly by alcohol abuse.

Drug and alcohol abuse may cause depression and difficulties coping with a normal life.

Drug and alcohol abuse may cause accidents. Loss of control means abusers are likely to get into fights and be hurt.

Drugs and alcohol change how a person's brain works and this can lead to mental illness.

Drugs and alcohol reduce a person's sense of responsibility. Why might this cause problems?

Knowledge check

1 What is addiction?
2 What is **responsibility**?
3 Why have laws been put into place to control who is allowed to have drugs and alcohol?

Drug and alcohol abuse may lead to people being unable to work, placing pressure on companies and possibly resulting in unemployment.

Drug and alcohol abuse leads to increased health spending on all forms of care – accident, cancer and mental care as well as on rehabilitation.

People who are addicted may steal to get money to buy drugs or alcohol. This causes problems for the victims and increased spending on policing and prisons.

Problems to society caused by drugs and alcohol

Drug and alcohol abuse may lead to addiction which can affect the ways families function and may lead to the breakdown of marriages.

Drug and alcohol abusers are likely to get into fights and this leads to an increase in spending on policing.

Drug and alcohol abuse may lead to people causing damage to public areas. This has an impact on society because it upsets people and it costs money to repair.

Drug and alcohol abuse may lead to reduced responsibility; people still drive under the influence of drugs and alcohol and cause accidents which have an impact on society.

A01

Imagine you are a parent and are trying to raise your child to avoid drugs and alcohol. Write down how you might explain to a child of twelve why they should not get involved in drugs or alcohol.

A02

In small groups, produce a presentation to explain the problems that might occur because of drugs and alcohol. Include explanations for all the specialist language that you use. You could include the following in your presentation:

● the health problems caused
● the problems caused in society by drug and alcohol abuse
● a PowerPoint presentation
● a short drama to illustrate the problems of drug and alcohol abuse.

exam practice b

Do you think drugs cause problems in society? Give **two** reasons for your point of view.

Examiner's hint: Remember reasons do not have to be religious as it is a b) question. (A02)

exam practice c

Explain how drug and alcohol may cause health problems.

Examiner's hint: Start each reason with a new paragraph. (A01)

exam practice d

'Drugs and alcohol do not cause problems in society.' In your answer you should refer to at least one religion.
i) Do you agree? Give reasons for your answer.
ii) Give reasons why some people may disagree with you.

Examiner's hint: Read the stimulus carefully before you decide what your opinion is going to be. (A02)

8.10 Christian attitudes to drugs and alcohol

The main Christian attitude is that abuse of drugs and alcohol is not acceptable. All Christians regard the illegal use of controlled drugs as wrong, and should try to help those who for any reason have found themselves addicted to controlled drugs. Some Christians regard the consumption of alcohol as acceptable as long as it is not abused. Other Christians do not accept the consumption of alcohol at all.

Christians have different views about the use of alcohol – which view do you agree with? Why?

Why most Christians accept the use of alcohol in moderation	**Why some Christians do not accept the use of alcohol (Methodists and Salvation Army)**
<ul><li>Alcohol is a gift from God and can be used.</li><li>Jesus drank and turned water into wine.</li><li>Alcohol is used as a symbol of blessing in the Old Testament.</li><li>Alcohol was used in the Last Supper where Jesus said to do this in memory of him.</li><li>Alcohol can lead to a person's happiness (in moderation).</li></ul>	<ul><li>Alcohol affects the way a person behaves towards others, which might not be appropriate.</li><li>It may lead to hangovers which could interfere with a Christian's relationship with God.</li><li>The body is a 'temple of the Holy Spirit' and should not be interfered with.</li><li>It may lead to other problems such as drunk driving, which causes great harm.</li><li>Alcohol addiction might cause a person to crave or put alcohol before other things including God or their family.</li></ul>

Why Christians do not accept the use of controlled substances
- They are illegal and Christians should accept the authority of the government.
- Drugs affect the way a person thinks; they might not treat each other as they should.
- Drugs might interfere with worship or prayer and prevent a Christian's relationship with God.
- The body is a 'temple of the Holy Spirit' and should not be interfered with.
- They may lead to other problems such as stealing.
- They can stop a person living life to the full.

Knowledge check

1 What is the Christian attitude to controlled drugs?
2 How would a Christian treat someone who became addicted to drugs?
3 What are the different Christian attitudes to alcohol?

The threshing floors will be filled with grain; the vats will overflow with new wine and oil (Joel 2:24).

Supply them liberally from your flock, your threshing floor and your winepress (Deuteronomy 15:14).

So whether you eat or drink, or whatever you do, do it all for the glory of God (1 Corinthians 10:31).

References used by Christians about drugs and alcohol

Be alert and of sober mind. Your enemy the devil prowls around like a roaring lion looking for someone to devour (1 Peter 5:8).

May God give you heaven's dew and earth's richness – an abundance of grain and new wine (Genesis 27:28).

Do you not know that your bodies are temples of the Holy Spirit, who is in you, whom you have received from God? You are not your own (1 Corinthians 6:19).

Do not get drunk on wine, which leads to debauchery. Instead, be filled with the Spirit (Ephesians 5:18).

Hope UK (www.hopeuk.org) work to educate young people about drug and alcohol misuse. They also try to provide alcohol-free meeting places for young people so they have alternatives to alcohol.

When I was about fourteen I had a group of friends who I hung out with. We started drinking after school, for a laugh at first and then because we didn't have much else to do and my family weren't in much.

This carried on all through the summer holidays and I thought I was having a great time. I realised it was a problem when I trashed my bedroom and couldn't remember anything about it the next morning.

My parents were so upset and worried they took me to a doctor and a counsellor. They helped me work out what was causing my problems.

George

I stopped hanging out with that group of friends as they would expect me to drink. I started working harder for my exams. My family spent more time with me and everyone is much closer now. I have a new group of friends and alcohol is no longer part of my life.

A01

1 You are a journalist and your newspaper has asked you to write an article about Christian attitudes to drugs and alcohol.
2 Write about the following:
  ● the Christian attitudes that are the same (about controlled drugs and misuse of alcohol)
  ● the different attitudes that Christians have
  ● the reasons for the different Christian attitudes.

A02

Imagine you have been employed to explain why Christians should not misuse drugs or alcohol. Think about George's experience described above. Design either:

a) a poster campaign (a group of four posters that have a common theme); or
b) a text message campaign (a group of four texts that have a common theme); or
c) an internet pop-up campaign (a group of four pop-ups that have a common theme).

Explain your campaign to the rest of the class and decide which of the campaigns is the most effective.

exam practice b

Do you think Christians should drink alcohol? Give **two** reasons for your point of view.

Examiner's hint: Remember to start with 'I think' although you are commenting on what Christians should do. (A02)

exam practice c

Explain why some Christians agree with drinking alcohol and some do not.

Examiner's hint: This c) question starts with the words 'Explain why', so make sure you give reasons. (A01)

exam practice d

'It does not matter if Christians drink alcohol or take drugs.' In your answer you should refer to at least one religion.
i) Do you agree? Give reasons for your answer.
ii) Give reasons why some people may disagree with you.

Examiner's hint: If you can't think of opposite reasons, try to imagine what a person would say if they were arguing with you. (A02)

8.11 Muslim attitudes to drugs and alcohol

All Muslims agree that the misuse of alcohol and drugs is not acceptable. Muslim teaching about alcohol and drugs is that they are not acceptable unless they are being used for medical purposes under supervision. The teachings of Islam forbid the use of alcohol and drugs.

Prophet Muhammad taught that alcohol was haram (forbidden).

The Qur'an teaches not to pray while intoxicated (drunk).

The Qur'an says that alcohol is used by Satan to make Muslims do wrong things.

Reasons Muslims do not accept the use of drugs and alcohol

Alcohol makes the body impure (leads to illness).

Drugs and alcohol spoil a person's relationship with Allah.

It goes against the Golden Rule of treating others as you would like to be treated yourself.

Knowledge check

1 What do Muslims teach about the misuse of drugs and alcohol?
2 What do Muslims teach about the use of drugs and alcohol for medical reasons?

Muslims in France can eat halal meals at the new fast food restaurants, like this one, that cater to the country's large Islamic population. Like many halal restaurants, it does not serve alcohol.

Muslims publicly show that selling drugs is wrong. Do you think this will stop people selling them? Why?

● References which show that Muslims should not accept the use of drugs and alcohol

Every intoxicant is khamr [alcohol], and every khamr is haram [forbidden] (Hadith).

They ask you about wine and gambling. Say, 'In them is great sin and [yet, some] benefit for people. But their sin is greater than their benefit' (Qur'an 2:219).

Intoxicants, … are but defilement from the work of Satan, so avoid it that you may be successful (Qur'an 5:90).

Satan only wants to cause between you animosity and hatred through intoxicants (Qur'an 5:91).

Do not approach prayer while you are intoxicated until you know what you are saying (Qur'an 4:43).

A01

Draw two spider diagrams.

1 One should be titled 'Why Muslims do not allow the use of drugs and alcohol'.
2 The other should be titled 'References to support why Muslims do not allow the use of drugs and alcohol'.

A02

In small groups produce a presentation to explain the Muslim attitude towards drugs and alcohol. Include explanations for all the specialist language that you use. You could include the following in your presentation:

● examples of why drugs and alcohol are wrong
● a PowerPoint presentation
● references to the Qur'an.

exam practice b

Do you think religious people should ever agree with the use of alcohol? Give **two** reasons for your point of view.

Examiner's hint: An example is a good way to develop a reason. (A02)

exam practice c

Choose one religion other than Christianity and explain why drugs and alcohol are not acceptable to followers of that religion.

Examiner's hint: Make sure you identify the religion to which you are referring. (A01)

exam practice d

'No religious person should take drugs.' In your answer you should refer to at least one religion.
i) Do you agree? Give reasons for your answer.
ii) Give reasons why some people may disagree with you.

Examiner's hint: This answer could refer to drugs that are required for medical reasons. (A02)

Examination practice

Below is guidance on how to answer the question a) from Section 8: Religion: crime and punishment. All a) questions are worth 2 marks. This is the first section on the paper and in it you will be assessed on your spelling, punctuation and grammar (SPaG). There are 4 marks available for this, so write clearly, check your spelling and try to use specialist words.

The a) questions test the key words that are provided by the exam board and are used in this book. It is important to make sure that you learn them.

Every section will have two a) questions and they will either ask for a definition of one of the key words or ask for two examples of the word. Look at the steps below about how to answer question 7a), then try to answer question 8a).

Sample question   **Sample question**
7a) What is a law?   [2]   **8a)** What is meant by
                                             rehabilitation?   [2]

How to answer
The best way to get full marks on an a) question:
✓ Write the glossary definition supplied by the exam board – these are the ones used in this book.
✓ To get full marks you must provide all the information that is within the exam board's definition.
✓ If you leave out any information or the wording is not quite correct you may only get 1 mark out of 2.

Step 1
● Try to remember the key word definition.

A driver must drive on the left in England.

Step 2
● This is an example, not a definition. Try to explain what the word means.

A rule made by Parliament.

Step 3
● This is an incomplete definition. You should learn the key word definition and write all of it as your answer.

Rules made by Parliament and enforceable by the courts.

Examiner's comment
✓ **Learn the definitions used in this book as they are the same as those provided by the exam board.**
✓ **To get full marks you must provide all the information that is within the exam board's definition, even if you think there is a different definition for the same word.**

Below is guidance on how to answer the question d) from Section 8: Religion: crime and punishment. As it is a d) question, it is worth 6 marks.

In every section there are two d) questions to choose from; each is divided into two parts, d) i) and d) ii). Try question 7d) using the hints provided below. Then apply these steps to question 8d).

Sample question

7d) 'Religious people should be allowed to drink alcohol.'
In your answer you should refer to at least one religion.
    i)   Do you agree? Give reasons for your opinion.   [3]
    ii) Give reasons why some people may disagree with you.   [3]

Sample question

8d) 'Every religious person should support capital punishment.' In your answer you should refer to at least one religion other than Christianity.
    i)   Do you agree? Give reasons for your opinion.   [3]
    ii) Give reasons why some people may disagree with you.   [3]

How to answer

There are a few things to always include in a d) question.

- Start with your opinion in d) i).
- You must read the sentence under the statement:
  - if it says 'you should refer to at least one religion' then you must clearly refer to any one religion
  - if it says 'you should refer to at least one religion other than Christianity' then you must clearly refer to a religion that is not Christianity
  - if it says 'you should refer to Christianity' then you must clearly refer to Christianity.

For example, Question 7d) states 'refer to one religion' so can refer to any religion. Question 8d) states 'refer to one religion other than Christianity' so you should refer to Islam in your answer.

One way to get full marks is to give three brief reasons for d) i) and three brief reasons for d) ii). In either d) i) or d) ii) you must ensure there is a religious answer, otherwise you cannot get more than 3 marks out of 6.

Question 7d) i)
Step 1
- Think whether you agree or disagree and give one reason to support your opinion. Make sure you write down that it is your opinion at the beginning.

I disagree. I think some religious people, for example Muslims, should not support drinking alcohol because a hadith records that Prophet Muhammad said it was haram.

Step 2
- Think of a second reason; point out that it is your second reason by writing 'secondly'.

Secondly, because Muslims are taught in the Qur'an that alcohol is used by Satan to make Muslims do sinful things.

Step 3
- Think of a third reason why you disagree with the statement. Write the new reason on a new line. Make sure it is a different reason and says more than because it is in the Qur'an – this would be too vague to be creditable.

Finally, because some Christians believe that alcohol is wrong as it interferes with a person's relationship with God.

Question 7d) ii)
Step 1
- This must include reasons for the opposite opinion to the one you gave as your opinion in d) i).

Some people agree with the statement because they think all religious people can decide what they want to do because God created wine and as long as they use it responsibly it is acceptable.

Step 2
- Think of a second reason; make sure it starts on a new line.

Also, because some Christians would say that Jesus drank wine at the Last Supper so it must be acceptable.

Step 3
- Think of a third reason why a person would agree with the statement. Make it clear it is a third reason by starting with 'finally' or 'thirdly'.

Finally, because some Churches use wine in their Sunday services so it must be acceptable.

Examiner's comment
- ✓ **The candidate has clearly stated their own personal view. Without this they cannot get full marks.**
- ✓ **Maximum marks will be awarded as each side of the argument has three reasons.**
- ✓ **It is important to make sure the reasons have enough detail to get the mark.**
- ✓ **Using the word 'because' to identify the reason is helpful; it stops a candidate thinking description is a reason.**

Glossary

abortion: the removal of a foetus from the womb before it can survive

addiction: a recurring compulsion to engage in an activity regardless of its bad effects

adultery: a sexual act between a married person and someone other than their marriage partner

aggression: attacking without being provoked

agnosticism: not being sure whether God exists

artificial insemination: injecting semen into the uterus by artificial means

assisted suicide: providing a seriously ill person with the means to commit suicide

atheism: believing that God does not exist

Bible: the holy book of Christians

bullying: intimidating/frightening people weaker than yourself

capital punishment: the death penalty for a crime or offence

Church: the community of Christians (with a small c it means a Christian place of worship)

civil partnership: a legal ceremony giving a homosexual couple the same legal rights as a husband and wife

cohabitation: living together without being married

community cohesion: a common vision and shared sense of belonging for all groups in society

conflict resolution: bringing a fight or struggle to a peaceful conclusion

conscience: an inner feeling of the rightness or wrongness of an action

conservation: protecting and preserving natural resources and the environment

contraception: intentionally preventing pregnancy from occurring

conversion: when your life is changed by giving yourself to God

creation: the act of creating the universe or the universe which has been created

crime: an act against the law

the Decalogue: the Ten Commandments

democratic processes: the ways in which all citizens can take part in government (usually through elections)

deterrence: the idea that punishments should be of such a nature that they will put people off (deter) committing crimes

discrimination: treating people less favourably because of their ethnicity/gender/colour/ sexuality/age/class

electoral processes: the ways in which voting is organised

embryo: a fertilised egg in the first eight weeks after conception

environment: the surroundings in which plants and animals live and on which they depend to live

ethnic minority: a member of an ethnic group (race) which is much smaller than the majority group

euthanasia: the painless killing of someone dying from a painful disease

exploitation: taking advantage of a weaker group

faithfulness: staying with your marriage partner and having sex only with them

forgiveness: stopping blaming someone and/or pardoning them for what they have done wrong

free will: the idea that human beings are free to make their own choices

global warming: the increase in the temperature of the earth's atmosphere (thought to be caused by the greenhouse effect)

the Golden Rule: the teaching of Jesus that you should treat others as you would like them to treat you

homosexuality: sexual attraction to the same sex

human rights: the rights and freedoms to which everyone is entitled

immortality of the soul: the idea that the soul lives on after the death of the body

infertility: not being able to have children

interfaith marriages: marriage where the husband and wife are from different religions

in-vitro fertilisation: the method of fertilising a human egg in a test tube

judgement: the act of judging people and their actions

just war: a war which is fought for the right reasons and in a right way

justice: due allocation of reward and punishment/the maintenance of what is right

law: rules made by Parliament and enforceable by the courts

miracle: something which seems to break a law of science and makes you think only God could have done it

moral evil: actions done by humans which cause suffering

multi-ethnic society: many different races and cultures living together in one society

multi-faith society: many different religions living together in one society

natural evil: things which cause suffering but have nothing to do with humans

natural resources: naturally occurring materials, such as oil and fertile land, which can be used by humans

near-death experience: when someone about to die has an out of body experience

non-voluntary euthanasia: ending someone's life painlessly when they are unable to ask, but you have good reason for thinking they would want you to do so

nuclear family: mother, father and children living as a unit

numinous: the feeling of the presence of something greater than you

omni-benevolent: the belief that God is all-good

omnipotent: the belief that God is all-powerful

omniscient: the belief that God knows everything that has happened and everything that is going to happen

organ donation: giving organs to be used in transplant surgery

pacifism: the belief that all disputes should be settled by peaceful means

paranormal: unexplained things which are thought to have spiritual causes, e.g. ghosts, mediums

political party: a group which tries to be elected into power on the basis of its policies (e.g. Labour, Conservative)

prayer: an attempt to contact God, usually through words

prejudice: believing some people are inferior or superior without even knowing them

pre-marital sex: sex before marriage

pressure group: a group formed to influence government policy on a particular issue

procreation: making a new life

promiscuity: having sex with a number of partners without commitment

quality of life: the idea that life must have some benefits for it to be worth living

racial harmony: different races/colours living together happily

racism: the belief that some races are superior to others

reconciliation: bringing together people who were opposed to each other

re-constituted family: where two sets of children (stepbrothers and stepsisters) become one family when their divorced parents marry each other

reform: the idea that punishments should try to change criminals so that they will not commit crimes again

rehabilitation: restore to normal life

reincarnation: the belief that, after death, souls are reborn in a new body

religious freedom: the right to practise your religion and change your religion

religious pluralism: accepting all religions as having an equal right to coexist

re-marriage: marrying again after being divorced from a previous marriage

respect: treating a person or their feelings with consideration

responsibility: being responsible for one's actions

resurrection: the belief that, after death, the body stays in the grave until the end of the world when it is raised

retribution: the idea that punishments should make criminals pay for what they have done wrong

sanctity of life: the belief that life is holy and belongs to God

sexism: discriminating against people because of their gender (being male or female)

sin: an act against the will of God

Situation Ethics: the idea that Christians should base moral decisions on what is the most loving thing to do

social change: the way in which society has changed and is changing (and also the possibilities for future change)

stewardship: looking after something so it can be passed on to the next generation

surrogacy: an arrangement whereby a woman bears a child on behalf of another woman *or* where an egg is donated and fertilised by the husband through IVF and then implanted into the wife's uterus

the United Nations: an international body set up to promote world peace and cooperation

voluntary euthanasia: ending life painlessly when someone in great pain asks for death

weapons of mass destruction: weapons which can destroy large areas and numbers of people

world peace: the ending of war throughout the whole world (the basic aim of the United Nations)

Index

The Publishers would like to thank the following for permission to reproduce copyright material:

Acknowledgements:
Bible extracts are from *The New International Version of the Holy Bible,* Hodder & Stoughton, 2011.
p17 InterVarsity Press for *Knowing Christianity* by J.I. Packer, 1973; **p37** CNN, a transcription of a broadcast interview with Richard Dawkins, 2010; **p44** © Guardian News & Media Ltd 2010; **p47** BBC News website, 2011; **p51** © Newsquest Media Group, www.yourlocalguardian. co.uk, 2011; **p60** © Telegraph Media Group Limited 2011; **p73** © Guardian News & Media Ltd 2011; **p87** © Telegraph Media Group Limited 2007; **p89** © Jerome Taylor, *The Independent,* Independent Print Limited, 2010; **p122** Westminster John Knox Press, for *Situation Ethics: The New Morality* by Joseph Fletcher, 1966; **p159** © Telegraph Media Group Limited 2011.

Photo credits:
p1 Lisa F. Young–Fotolia; **p3tl** Getty Images, *tr* World Religions Photo Library/Alamy, *ml* Jenny Matthews/Alamy, *mr* Theresa Martinez–Fotolia, *bl* Photodisc/Getty Images, *br* Rim Light/Photodisc/Getty Images; **p4l** Mary Evans Picture Library/Douglas McCarthy, *r* Imagestate Media (John Foxx); **p6t** itsallgood–Fotolia, *b* Imagestate Media (John Foxx); **p8** INTERFOTO/Friedrich/Mary Evans; **p9** Rainer Plendl–Fotolia; **pp10–11** NASA; **p11l** maxime SCHAAL–Fotolia, *r* zayatssv–Fotolia; **p12** INTERFOTO/A. Koch/Mary Evans; **p13** NASA; **p17** Photodisc/Getty Images; **p18** AFP/Getty Images; **p19t** Bettmann/Corbis, *m* Wendy Stone/Corbis, *b* Getty Images; **p20** Brebca–Fotolia; **p21** Barcroft Media via Getty Images; **pp22–23** Imagestate Media (John Foxx); **p23** Everett Collection/Rex Features; **p24** Colin Anderson/Blend Images/Corbis; **p25** NASA; **p28** Lilya–Fotolia; **p29** The Gallery Collection/Corbis; **p35** Diane Kolka; **p36** Justin McIntosh/Wikimedia Commons; **p37** AFP/ Getty Images; **p39l** Viviane Moos/Corbis, *r* Stephanie Maze/Corbis; **p41** Athanasia Nomikou–Fotolia; **p44** Jonathan Hordle/Rex Features; **p47** Getty Images; **p51** Cathus–Fotolia; **p55t** Imagestate Media (John Foxx), *b* Kim Kulish/Corbis; **p56** iofoto–Fotolia; **p57l** Diane Kolka, *r* iofoto–Fotolia; **p59** Artsem Martysiuk–Fotolia; **p60** AFP/Getty Images; **p65** Bob Collier/Rex Features; **p66** daniella christoforou/Alamy; **p67** Getty Images; **p68** Mary Evans Picture Library; **p70** Imagestate Media Partners Limited–Impact Photos/Alamy; **p73** Robert Gray; **p76** Lusoimages–Fotolia; **p78** Odua Images–Fotolia; **p82** Diane Kolka; **p83** Skip Nall Photography/Photodisc/Getty Images; **p84l** Retro Kitsch/Alamy, *r* Imagestate Media (John Foxx); **p85** Stockbyte; **p87** Robert Gray; **p89** maxblackphotos–Fotolia; **p91** Kirk O'Rourke/ Rangers FC/Press Association Images; **p92** Rui Vieira/PA Archive/Press Association Images; **p94t** Yuri Arcurs–Fotolia, *b* Advertising Archives; **p95** Robert Gray; **pp98–99** Getty Images; **p101** Gideon Mendel/Corbis; **p102** Homer Sykes/Corbis; **p103** Genevieve de Manio/ Handout/Corbis; **p106** With thanks to Sheikh Dr Hojjat Ramzy; **p108t** 20thC.Fox/Everett/Rex Features, *b* Sony Pics/Everett/Rex Features; **p109** AF archive/Alamy; **p113** Getty Images; **p114** Imagestate Media (John Foxx); **p117** altec5–Fotolia; **p118tl** xalanx–Fotolia, *br* James Steidl–Fotolia; **p122** Corbis; **p130** Roberto Herrett/Alamy; **p131** philhol–Fotolia; **p132** AFP/ Getty Images; **p134** Gideon Mendel/Corbis; **p135** The Art Gallery Collection/Alamy; **p136** Mary Evans Picture Library; **p138l** Zbigniew Kosmal–Fotolia, *r* PhotoAlto; **p140t** Petra Reinartz–Fotolia, *b* chrisharvey–Fotolia; **p145tl** MOKreations–Fotolia, *tr* Ronald Hudson– Fotolia, *b* Kwest–Fotolia; **p147** Ian Bracegirdle/iStockphoto.com; **p148** Brandon Seidel– Fotolia; **p149** Stockbyte/Photolibrary Group Ltd; **p150** Robert Gray; **p151l** Imagestate Media (John Foxx), *r* cerbi–Fotolia; **p152l** Robert Gray, *c* Lucian Milasan–Fotolia, *r* Robert Gray; **p153** So-Shan Au; **p154** NASA; **p155** ktsdesign–Fotolia; **p156** NASA; **p158** Monkey Business Images–Fotolia; **p161** SuperStock/Ingram Publishing Limited; **p163** arietoursino–Fotolia; **p164** mauritius images GmbH/Alamy; **p166** AFP/Getty Images; **p172** Lawrence Manning/ Corbis; **p173** Redferns; **p174** Eliana Aponte/Reuters/Corbis; **p176** Marcel Mooij–Fotolia; **p179** Patrick Chauvel/Corbis; **p181** Heritage Images/Corbis; **p182** Lali–Fotolia and Helmut Niklas–Fotloi; **p184t** Getty Images, *b* Peter Marshall/Alamy; **p185** AFP/Getty Images; **p186** Getty Images; **p188** Imagestate Media (John Foxx); **p190** Monkey Business Images–Fotolia; **p191** islamicposters.co.uk; **p192** Moviestore Collection/Rex Features; **p194** Vibe Images– Fotolia; **p195** Bettmann/Corbis; **p196** Pascal Deloche/Godong/Corbis; **p200** Getty Images; **p201** spline_x–Fotolia; **p203t** Joe Bell/AP/Press Association Images, *b* Scott T. Baxter/ Photodisc/Getty Images; **p204t** Getty Images, *b* Andy Aitchison/In Pictures/Corbis; **p206** WireImage; **p208** AFP/Getty Images; **p211** Getty Images; **p212t** Bettmann/Corbis, *b* Reuters/Corbis; **p214** SCPhotos/Alamy; **p218** Image Source/Rex Features; **p220t** Advertising Archives, *b* Dan Atkin/Alamy; **p222** Peter Dench/In Pictures/Corbis; **p224l** Patricia Hofmeester–Fotolia, *r* IngridHS–Fotolia; **p227l** Jacky Naegelen/Reuters/Corbis, *r* Eric Lafforgue/Alamy.

Every effort has been made to trace all copyright holders, but if any have been inadvertently overlooked the Publishers will be pleased to make the necessary arrangements at the first opportunity.